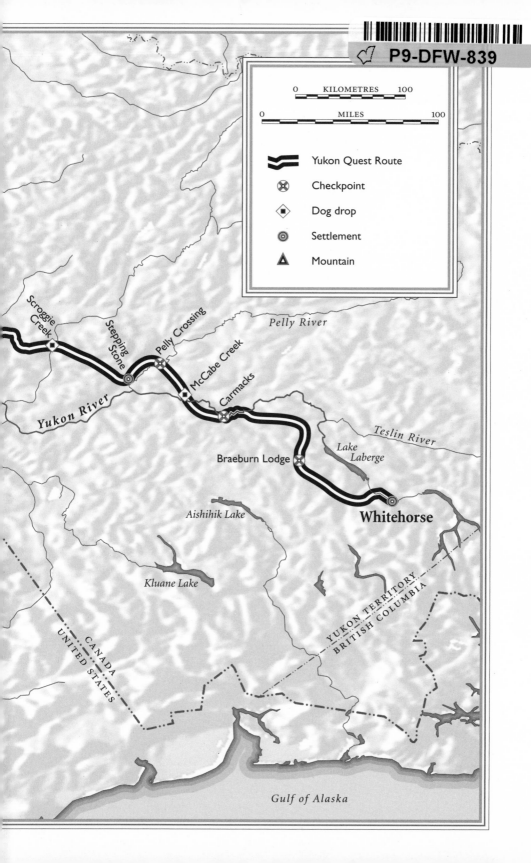

RACING THE
WHITE SILENCE

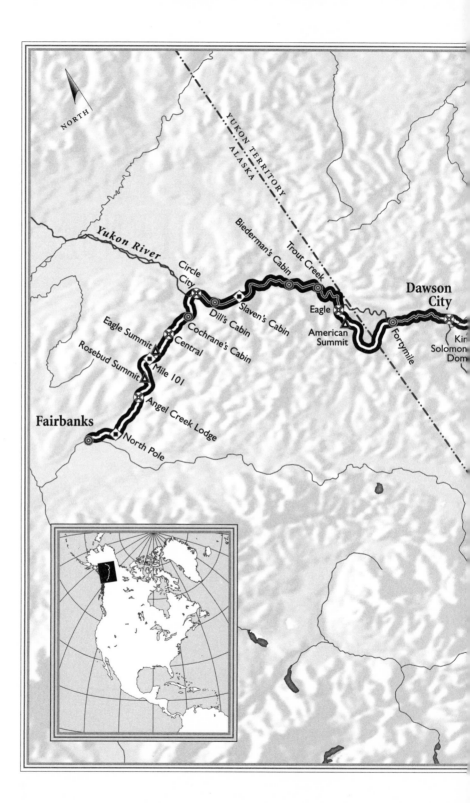

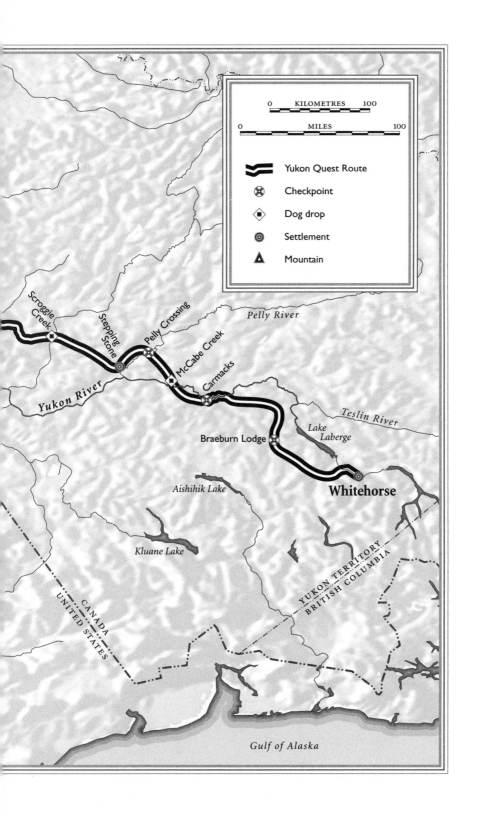

Nature has many tricks wherewith she convinces man of his finity—the ceaseless flow of the tides, the fury of the storm, the shock of the earthquake, the long roll of heaven's artillery—but the most tremendous, the most stupefying of all, is the passive phase of the White Silence. All movement ceases, the sky clears, the heavens are as brass; the slightest whisper seems sacrilege, and man becomes timid, affrighted at the sound of his own voice. Sole speck of life journeying across the ghostly wastes of a dead world, he trembles at his audacity, realizes that his is a maggot's life, nothing more. Strange thoughts arise unsummoned, and the mystery of all things strives for utterance. And the fear of death, of God, of the universe, comes over him—the hope of the Resurrection and the Life, the yearning for immortality, the vain striving of the imprisoned essence—it is then, if ever, man walks alone with God.

—Jack London, *The White Silence,* 1899

RACING THE WHITE SILENCE

On the Trail of the Yukon Quest

ADAM KILLICK

PENGUIN
CANADA

PENGUIN CANADA

Published by the Penguin Group

Penguin Books, a division of Pearson Canada, 10 Alcorn Avenue, Toronto, Ontario,
Canada M4V 3B2

Penguin Books Ltd, 80 Strand, London WC2R ORL, England

Penguin Putnam Inc., 375 Hudson Street, New York, New York 10014, U.S.A.

Penguin Books Australia Ltd, 250 Camberwell Road, Camberwell, Victoria 3124,
Australia

Penguin Books India (P) Ltd, 11, Community Centre, Panchsheel Park,
New Delhi – 110 017, India

Penguin Books (NZ) Ltd, cnr Rosedale and Airborne Roads, Albany,
Auckland 1310, New Zealand

Penguin Books (South Africa) (Pty) Ltd, 24 Sturdee Avenue, Rosebank 2196,
South Africa

Penguin Books Ltd, Registered Offices: 80 Strand, London WC2R ORL, England

First published 2002

1 3 5 7 9 10 8 6 4 2

"Yukon Quest" is a registered trademark.
www.yukonquest.org

Printed and bound in Canada on acid free paper ⊚

NATIONAL LIBRARY OF CANADA CATALOGUING IN PUBLICATION DATA

Killick, Adam, 1970–
Racing the white silence : on the trail of the Yukon Quest / Adam Killick

Includes bibliographical references.
ISBN 0-14-301352-1

1. Killick, Adam, 1970– 2. Yukon Quest International Sled Dog Race. I. Title.

SF440.15.K54   2002   798.8'3'092   C2002-903653-4

British Library Cataloguing in Publication Data Available
American Library of Congress Cataloguing in Publication Data Available

Visit Penguin Books' website at **www.penguin.ca**

*To the memory of my mother, Iona, who instilled in me
a passion for the printed word and a love for great stories*

AUTHOR'S NOTE

Except where noted, all of the measurements in this book are in metric, and temperatures are listed in degrees Celsius. Fahrenheit and Celsius meet at forty degrees below zero.

CONTENTS

Acknowledgements   x

Prologue: The Freezing Point of Fear   1

The Toughest Race on Earth   7

Grandma   23

Lights in the Sky   51

The Finest Athletes in the World   67

Soft Snow   83

Ice   105

Hup!   117

Into the White Silence   137

Klondike   147

Jack   173

Frozen Air   181

The Last Frontier   193

The Code of the Trail   217

Visions   233

Mountaineering in Mukluks   245

The End   263

Epilogue: A Perfect World   271

Selected Bibliography   275

ACKNOWLEDGEMENTS

THIS BOOK WOULD NOT HAVE BEEN POSSIBLE without the help of many friends along the way who provided love, advice, hospitality, and support.

First, my heartfelt thanks goes to the mushers who competed in the 2001 Yukon Quest International Sled Dog Race, as well as those who live along its trail. As a group, they are not reputed to be the most generous of conversationalists. However, numerous mushers, officials, and trailside residents opened their homes, and their hearts, to me. I am especially grateful to Frank Turner, Anne Tayler, their daughter Candice, and their eighty-five dogs for allowing me into their lives for several months, and for patiently instructing me in the finer points of living with—and running— dogs. There is nobody who sets a better example of how to provide and care for the true heroes of long-distance sled dog racing. I would also like to thank William Kleedehn, Joran Freeman, David and Jeanne Sawatzky, Bill Pinkham, Andrew Lesh, Hugh Neff, Jim Hendrick, and Bill Steyer, all of whom invited me into their homes to relate their stories. Bruce Lee gave me a good lecture over the telephone about the importance of the Quest to northern culture. Arleigh Reynolds, D.V.M. and sprint-musher extraordinaire, patiently explained canine physiology while I sat in the passenger seat of his truck trying to spell "rabdomyalisis." If there is an error of fact concerning that subject, it is mine. Ray and Val Mackler invited me over to show me how a dog sled was built.

Along the trail, Sebastian Jones, Shelley Brown, Mark Gilmore, Dick Hutchinson, Dan Woodruff, Carol and Jim Tredger, Steve Watson, and Peter Kamper allowed me into their homes, cabins, and lodges, gave me food, and told engaging tales.

It is impossible to be everywhere at once on a race where, by the end, several hundred kilometres separate the leader and the last-place team. Among the other media following the Quest, I would like to single out Libby Casey, who provided me with taped material garnered from places and times on the trail where she was (and I wasn't). I would also like to thank Laurent Dick, Sam Harrel, Amy Miller, Mardy Derby, Peter Carr, Kathy Ramsay, Gillian Rogers, Steve Roberston (and the rest of the wonderful staff at the *Yukon News*), Nick Wrathall, John McWhorter, Jason Small, and Roy Corral for their friendship, advice, and company.

A special thanks to John Firth, who selflessly offered me the material in his excellent book, *Yukon Quest,* a wonderful anecdotal compendium of the first fourteen years of the race.

Dick Watts, the Canadian co-chair of Yukon Quest Intern-ational, Jim Bennett, his American counterpart, race manager Leo Olesen, and Quest marketing consultant Derek Charlton were instrumental in helping me get to remote (and not-so-remote) sections of the trail. So were Gerd Mannsperger, Brian McDonald, and Gary Nance. Dave Monson, Darren Rorabaugh, Doug Harris, Dave O'Farrell, Mark Lindstrom, Margy Terhar, Al Hallman, John Overell, Darren "Woody" Woodson, and Nene Wolfe were always quick to answer questions about race rules, dog care and treatment, or what to eat at the Riverside Café in Eagle.

For their hospitality and support before and after the race, Karyn and Robin Armour, Theresa Bakker, Mike Bradley, Mario Carlucci, Kevin and Jennifer Clowes, Andrea Cohen, Renee Crain, Jason Cunning, Patricia Cunning, A. P. Hovasse, Kazuo Kojima, Jen Kolivosky, Les Perreaux, Sean Silcoff, Paul Souders, David Walmsley, and Andrea Wilson have my gratitude.

Thanks also to my long-suffering near and extended family, in particular Ruth and Harry Goldhar, Ann and Leo Shimerl, Dennis Killick and Joan and Sidney Roxan.

I owe a debt to Roy MacGregor for introducing me to Barbara Berson, the senior editor at Penguin who gently guided this book from start to finish, providing a considerable dose of psychological help along the way. Her support was buttressed by Meg Masters, whose gentle, skilful, and patient hands edited the manuscript. Catherine Marjoribanks made the copy readable.

To my dog, Django, who has no intention of ever running the Yukon Quest, I'm sorry I came home smelling adulterously of other dogs.

Finally, my greatest debt is to my wife, Kathleen Goldhar, who sacrificed a great deal during the writing of this book, which I might never have finished were it not for her love.

Adam Killick
September 2002

THE FREEZING POINT
OF FEAR

IT WAS SNOWING HEAVILY. The musher whistled to his dogs as they left the checkpoint. "C'mon, Jake," he called, and Jake and the other nine dogs shook themselves to their feet, shuddering in that typical dog way that starts with a violent oscillation of their heads, creating a wave of snow-shedding movement that moves along their backs and ends with a stiffening, then a relaxing, of their tails.

The leaders looked back, and the musher nodded to them. "Okay," he said, softly, and the team began to lurch forward with the fatigue of 1,300 kilometres weighing on their legs. Jake required special treatment: he was blind, probably the only blind dog ever to run the race. More sensitive than most dogs to the words of the musher, his ears perked up, pointed forward, and he leaned into his tugline. The sled broke free of the crust that had built up around its runners over the last eight hours. After arriving from their last run, the dogs had eaten, been massaged, had healing ointment rubbed into their feet, slept, and eaten some more. Although the musher had slept too, his rest was fitful, marred by worries about the summit ahead, the most terrifying part of the race. It was a mountain crossing, a thousand metres almost straight up, taking the team from a damp river valley up a series of switchbacks and finally ending on an exposed, slippery, thirty-degree climb. Nothing much more than rocks survived at the summit. Even the snow had difficulty clinging to the ground as the wind screamed across the saddle slung between two soaring mountaintops.

The front end of the race had long since passed through (the first teams had already crossed the finish line in Fairbanks, some 400 kilometres away), and most of the spectators, reporters, race officials, and hangers-on had moved on as well. Only one veterinarian and race marshal were still at the checkpoint, waiting for the back of the pack to arrive.

As he turned onto the trail, big, fluffy flakes of snow sparkled briefly in the glare of his headlamp before they stung his eyes. He peered down at his dogs, their tails up (a good sign), as they fell into the rhythmic pattern he had listened to for nearly two straight weeks. *Chink-chink-chink-chink,* the sound of the rings on their collars clanging against their necklines, mixed with the *huff-huff-huff-huff* of their breathing. Subtler, providing the underscore, was the uptempo *tick-tick-tick* of forty feet hitting the snow in unison, and the slow, droning *hiss* of the runners as the sled glided along.

Soon, the trail took a sharp turn to the left, leaving the road behind, and the musher and his dogs were alone in the Alaskan wilderness, which, although a long way from Glenwood Springs, Colorado, where the musher lived, seemed like home now. As the snow picked up and the temperature dropped below minus twenty Celsius, he pulled his parka tighter around his neck to slow the chill creeping down the front of his shirt. Mushing is like that, a constant clothing adjustment—either too hot or too cold—like fiddling with the heater in the car on a rainy day.

From what he could see of the terrain—and he couldn't see much—the trail seemed to keep crossing a creek, which had repeatedly swelled up through the ice covering it and frozen in ugly, blob-like boils that spread out across the trail. Concealed, like everything else, by the fresh snow, they revealed themselves only as the sled suddenly twisted sideways like a rudderless boat. From time to time he broke through the ice, and water welled up past his ankles. To prepare for the climb, the musher wasn't wearing his waterproof boots, which had poor traction. Instead, he was wearing Lobbans, Norwegian quilted boots with rubber, sneaker-like soles. Although they didn't look it, they kept his feet warm . . . when they weren't wet. They were getting wet.

The lamp attached to his head lit up red-and-white reflective tape attached to the tops of metre-high stakes set up every hundred metres or so to guide him. It had been several hours since the team in front of him had left the checkpoint, and with the snowstorm, the trail was now completely concealed.

After a couple of hours, he noticed, as he began to climb, that the terrain was changing. The trees were getting shorter, farther apart, and stunted. He still couldn't see much, but the landscape was opening up as he came out of the river valley, terracing around what seemed to be a foothill.

With his left foot on the runner, he pumped against the snow with his right foot. He was trying to take some of the burden off the dogs, who were about to face the hardest part of the trail, that final, steep scrabble over the top of a mountain. There, the musher knew he would be pushing the sled, hunched over, arms pushed straight forward like piledrivers, with his head facing down between them as he and the dogs tried to get the 90-kilogram sled to the top.

It was his first time on the Quest, a race he had heard about only a couple of years ago, while chatting with fellow mushers in Colorado. The Quest was a race for purists, he was told. Not like the Iditarod—the same length, but as much a media spectacle as a race. The Quest was like a secret among the fellowship of dog people, and southerners like him were grudgingly allowed into the rite of passage on this, the trail of history itself, a path followed by adventurers and rogues who came to the land out of curiosity but became spiritually bound to the snow and the ice and the sky.

He had followed the Iditarod before, closely. There was nothing on the Iditarod Trail that looked like this.

A short time later, the musher snapped to attention, gripping the sled handlebar with both hands. Had he not been concentrating on the trail? It happens, after more than a week of sleep deprivation: some mushers hallucinate; all have trouble staying awake. The musher stopped the team and peered ahead. The snow wasn't as deep here, scoured from the ground by a scornful wind. It was still snowing, but the flakes were now sharp pellets that rattled against his cheeks.

There was no trail marker visible in the distance. He looked back, shining his headlamp down along the railway-line pattern dotted with paw prints, as it was quickly filled in by the blowing and falling snow. There were supposed to be flashing lights on the markers, too, he remembered. Evidently the batteries didn't last long enough for the back of the pack.

He pressed on. The going was quite steep now, and the dogs, used to seeing the trail markers reflected ahead, seemed less confident. They were moving slowly, sensing that the musher wasn't sure of himself. Over the last two weeks, spending every waking hour together, the man and his dogs had come to know each other through the tilt of the head, the grip of the hand, and the flick of the tail. Verbal communication was, usually, unnecessary.

He knew the risks of getting off the trail: he could easily head up and over the wrong pass, career down the other side, and wind up trapped in a nameless valley until help came along, which could take a long time. Earlier that year, a musher from Fairbanks had done just that in a race, and it had taken three days for him to get out.

He whistled, urging the dogs to carry on. But this time, the dogs said no. They had had enough of his uncertainty, they were tired, and they could sense that they weren't going in the right direction.

The musher, who had learned to trust their primordial logic, acquiesced. Walking forward, he cuddled each dog, unhooking their tuglines but leaving them attached to the gangline by the shorter lines connected to their collars. Not that they would go anywhere, anyway. Before he had finished unhooking the leaders, the wheel dogs, the ones at the back of the line, had already burrowed into the snow to sleep. They peered up at him now, their ice-frosted whiskers and curious eyes reflecting in the glow of his headlamp.

Tired, his feet wet, and his clothes drenched through with sweat from pushing the sled, the musher surveyed his circumstance. He thought he was somewhere near the top—at least he hoped he was. He got out his sleeping bag and lay down next to Jake, the blind dog, as was his custom when camping. Jake snuggled up, and the musher dozed off.

Minutes later he awoke, chilled, because the sleeping bag had melted the snow frozen on his toque and coat, and the dampness was cooling his body—the first stage in a downward hypothermic spiral. So he got up and decided to walk around to warm up, dry out, and perhaps find the trail markers.

He walked forward, into the blowing snow, and then turned right and continued on, stomping around in the drifts. Sometimes the snow was barely a crust on the surface, and through the soft soles of his boots he could feel the gorse and rocks that give Eagle Summit a strange, almost lunar appearance in the summer. Other times he would posthole, falling in almost to his waist. Once, as he slipped into deep snow, he fell backwards, twisting his leg painfully.

After an unsuccessful hour of searching for a marker, he realized, in his fatigued, cold brain, that he was walking around like a zombie, not really concentrating. He turned back, and stopped. His haphazard path had been swallowed by the blowing, drifting snow. He hunted around, trying to find his way back to the dogs, but he could see only a few metres of his trail. For another hour he wandered, calling out, straining his eyes and ears for a sign of his team. It was no use. For all he knew, he was spiralling farther and farther away. It was pitch black, three o'clock in the morning, and twenty degrees below zero.

Rule number one in mushing: Never, ever, leave your team. You might just never find them again.

The musher, who had entered the Yukon Quest International Sled Dog Race because he wanted to experience, firsthand, the spectacular, untrammelled landscape of Alaska and the Yukon, sat down in the snow near the top of Eagle Summit and rested his head in his hands. He was exhausted, alone, and lost.

THE TOUGHEST RACE
ON EARTH

EVERY FEBRUARY, under the cold flames of the aurora borealis and the brief, grey arctic sun, a small group of hardy men and women, each with an ash or aluminum sled and fourteen dogs, begins a long, lonely trek on and over a land and distance almost impossible to conceive: 1,640 kilometres of the least hospitable real estate on the planet, between Whitehorse, Yukon, and Fairbanks, Alaska. That is the distance from England to Africa. There are only eight checkpoints en route, which means that, on average, the distance the teams traverse between those checkpoint villages is equivalent to the breadth of Ireland. Most of those checkpoints, it's worth noting, are optional.

It is called "The Toughest Race on Earth," although it is a race only in the vaguest of terms. More aptly put, it is a test of psychological and physical stamina that pits those men and women and their dogs against some of the nastiest weather nature is capable of bestowing, in temperatures that can drop to more than sixty degrees below zero.

It is also an acute expression of the culture on which Canada— and, to a large extent, the United States—was built. Its trail follows that of the Klondike gold stampeders of a century ago, cutting through the heart of Jack London's "Northland," where, as poet Robert Service famously wrote in "The Spell of the Yukon," "the mountains are nameless / And the rivers all run God knows where; / There are lives that are erring and aimless, / And deaths that just hang by a hair . . ." Most important, the Quest is not a recreation of history; it is living history. This event is run not by otherwise-gentrified athletes looking to cross the next adventure off their list but by people whose lives and, in most cases, livelihoods are intertwined with their dogs.

Long-distance dog racing—races by dog team that are longer than 750 kilometres—begins (and ends, in the public consciousness, at least) with the Iditarod.

The origins of the name "Iditarod" are debated; it seems to come from a native American word, *Haiditarod,* which means either "clear water" or "distant place," depending on which expert you consult.

The "Last Great Race," as it is billed, is a homage to one of America's great legends, the 1925 diphtheria serum run from Anchorage to Nome. According to the story, in January 1925, a deadly diphtheria outbreak took hold of the tiny village of Nome, 1,700 kilometres from Anchorage on the windswept coast of the Bering Sea. The sole airplane capable of making the trip from Anchorage had been dismantled for the winter, and there was no reliable route connecting the two places.

The Alaska Railroad carried the medicine to Nenana, about one-quarter of the distance. From there, a relay of twenty dog teams was set up to carry the serum through more than a thousand kilometres of bush. When the final musher, Gunnar Kaasen, took to the trail, the conditions were terrible. At one point, according to the story, his sled was knocked down in a blizzard, its contents spilling into the deep snow. Barehanded, in temperatures hovering at fifty below, Kaasen scrabbled through the snow and managed to recover the serum.

But it was Kaasen's lead dog, Balto, who would become the most famous character of the trip. At one point, Balto saved the team when, sensing open water underneath a thin layer of snow, he refused to go forward, despite Kaasen's exhortations. When the black malemute led his team into Nome with the life-saving serum, he became the most famous dog in the world, and, the following year, a statue of Balto was erected in Central Park in New York City, where it remains today. The serum run, which had taken no more than six days and captivated the world's media, took its place among the frontier myths that pervade America's sense of identity. Kaasen, Balto, and some of the other dogs in the team later made a trip across the continental United States as part of a travelling show, and when Balto died, eight years after saving the children of Nome, his body was preserved and displayed in a museum in Cleveland, Ohio. The story was popularized in an animated feature in 1995.

In 1967 a sled dog driver named Joe Redington started a race to honour Leonard Seppala, the musher on the relay who travelled the greatest distance, some 400 kilometres. The race followed part of the same trail. In 1973, the trail was extended to reach Nome, and it followed most of the route taken by the serum-carrying mushers. It covered hallowed northern ground, once again capturing international attention, and the Iditarod, as it was called, soon became one of the best-known sporting events in the world.

The Yukon Quest and the Iditarod are the only two races of their kind. Both are approximately 1,600 kilometres long, depending on the routing of the trail, which can vary slightly depending on snow and weather conditions. This leads, among mushing types, to a debate about which is the more difficult of the two.

The Iditarod, because of its fame and its $1-million purse, attracts the best and wealthiest long-distance mushers in the world, the most sponsorship money, and the interest of hundreds of media outlets. The winner of the race earns $60,000 US plus a new truck. This represents, for most top mushers, only a fraction of their income, most of which comes from valuable endorsements from corporate sponsors like Eddie Bauer, Cabela's outdoor gear, or Timberland footwear. The race also has a $23-million impact on the state of Alaska.

It is an enormous mental challenge, run at a pace that forces competitors to be at their best all the time, aware that with, on average, twenty teams capable of winning, the slightest error in judgment can mean a drop of ten places in the standings and a commensurate loss of prize money. It runs both through mountainous terrain and along the northwest Alaska coast, which can bring both peril and unique challenges to dogs and their drivers.

However, where the Iditarod has twenty-three checkpoints over its course, the Quest has only eight. The Quest crosses four mountain passes—all of which are steeper than the sole pass on the Iditarod—and cuts through the cold, dry heart of the Yukon and Alaska. It is run several weeks earlier than the Iditarod, beginning in early February, farther from the sun in the Earth's axial tilt. Mushers are on their own in the Quest, with the exception of one thirty-six-hour mandatory layover in Dawson City, the halfway point, where handlers can step in and provide primary care for the dogs. You are allowed only one sled: if it happens to be damaged by a rampaging moose, which happens to a musher every few years or so, it means wandering into the woods to look for replacement parts.

The winner of the Yukon Quest gets $30,000 US, usually far less than the money it takes to maintain a kennel capable of winning.

Frank Turner, the sole Canadian-born musher to have won the race (setting the course record in 1995), finds himself today struggling to make ends meet, with no dog food sponsor and kennel expenses pushing $60,000 a year. Since winning, he has finished no worse than sixth, and has also come second, third, and fifth—statistics that make him a perennial contender and, in any other professional sport, would make him very attractive to sponsors. Yet Turner still gratefully accepts a nominal cheque from his octogenarian parents and paints their names on the side of his truck to recognize them.

In the race's seclusion also lies its glory. As hard as the terrain and terrible weather gets, there remains a spirit to the race that many say the Iditarod lost long ago, a spirit that allows a musher whose entire dog team cost him $250 to compete in the race. Where wealthy Europeans and Asians pay upwards of $30,000 US to lease a team and then have a handler guide them through the Iditarod—just so they can say they've done it, and move on to being guided up Mount Everest—most entrants in the Quest are there because they live and work with their dogs, and it is what they know best. Like the Scottish loggers who turned their skill in throwing felled trees across rivers into the caber toss contest, many mushers compete in the Quest because working with their dogs is what they do anyway, to earn a livelihood. The race provides an opportunity—for both person and dog—to get out on a long trip together and see just how well they can compete. Unlike the Iditarod contestants, not even most of the top Quest mushers would consider themselves professional racers.

The Iditarod, which has a slightly longer trail, is won in under nine days, whereas the Quest winner takes an average of more than eleven days to complete the course. This is partly because of the difficulty of the trail, but another important element in the race is a spirit of co-operation against a common enemy—ice and cold—that builds a community superseding the competition and provides an apt analogy for the principles that govern life in the North itself.

On the Quest trail, the same families have provided hot meals and water to mushers for nearly a generation, and mushers make a point of stopping, race be damned, because to disregard their hospitality and effort would be impolite. Iditarod mushers who have "come over" to the Quest are always staggered by the spirit of quiet community along the trail, a spirit that, on the Iditarod, has been obscured in the commercial fog of television cameras and corporate logos that descend heavily upon Anchorage and Nome—and the various villages in between—each March. America's "Last Great Race," an event formed to honour the spirit of the northern community, cast a spell over the American imagination when it began. Today, in a world filled with an all-consuming corporate thirst for the "real," it has become a victim of its own magic.

THE YUKON QUEST WAS BORN from a dissatisfaction with that corporate thirst, and from a few too many beers at a bar near Fairbanks.

In February 1983, two men, Roger Williams and Leroy Shank, were sitting in the Bull's Eye Saloon at the end of a race that had begun at Angel Creek, a lodge located some 100 kilometres east of Fairbanks by road. It was a shame, they said, that the race, along an engaging trail, had been so short. As the beers went down, the pair sketched out a new, thousand-mile race, one shielded from the media, with rules tough enough that only purists would participate.

From Angel Creek, their theoretical new event would extend to Chena Hot Springs, a resort several kilometres down the road. From there, it would traverse two steep mountain passes in the White Mountain range, connecting on the other side to another resort called Circle Hot Springs, near the mining town of Central, Alaska. Then it would wend north and east along Birch Creek, a mean-dering waterway once famous for its gold. Just beyond the end of

Birch Creek stands Circle, a town built around a gold find at the turn of the twentieth century that is now a mostly native village.

Circle is known as the gateway to the Yukon River, the fourth-largest drainage in North America, a well-used mushing highway, once the artery that connected to numerous stampedes for gold that announced the Yukon and Alaska to the rest of the world. At Circle, the Yukon River bends to the northwest, gathering turbid volume as it prepares to empty into the Bering Sea. In the other direction, 500 kilometres upstream, lies the home of the world's greatest gold rush, Dawson City, Yukon.

From here the discussion at the Bull's Eye became more fanciful.

If the race jumped onto the frozen Yukon River, Shank and Williams realized, it would become not just the celebration of a single event but a race over a historic route once travelled extensively by people whose lives were valued in troy ounces. Before that, the Yukon had acted as a centuries-old corridor connecting the first human inhabitants of this land. After the gold rush era, it remained the path of the mail carriers, who, until they were replaced by airplanes only as recently as the 1960s, brought news of the outside world to the isolated cabins and hamlets along the river. Even today, there are still year-round residents along the river, and a town, Eagle, that has no road access during the winter.

One thing has been common to the land in all eras: the central role played by dogs and sleds in getting from one place to another, to carry news of a potlatch, a love letter, or just a bottle of home-made wine to be shared by distant neighbours. Pass any cabin along the Yukon River today, and the chances are good you'll hear the reverberating blare of barking dogs.

Shank and Williams got excited about the idea of making the event international in scope—the Canada/U.S. border lies just east of Eagle—and realized that by extending the trail to the headwaters of the Yukon River at Whitehorse, the capital of the territory, it would be roughly equal in length to the Iditarod. (Several beers later, the trail stretched, reportedly, as far as Los Angeles.)

The discussion about the new race was largely forgotten with the following morning's hangover, but, several months later, when the pair was on a fishing trip, the subject came up again. This time they talked about the mechanics of the race, and how it might correct the "impurities" that had burrowed their way into the Iditarod.

There, outside assistance seemed rampant, even though the race's original rules forbade it. Mushers were permitted to switch sleds during their trip from Anchorage to Nome if one was damaged or if trail conditions favoured a different sled design. Often, dog handlers would help mushers care for the dogs at checkpoints. These indulgences, Shank felt, gave a nearly insurmountable advantage to those wealthy enough to afford to pay a handler to travel the distance along the trail.

So, mushers on the Quest would have only one sled. And there would be strict enforcement of the rule that no musher was allowed outside help, except at the one, mandatory stop in the race, in Dawson City. To be legal, any help offered to a team—like a new thermos from a general store or welding help from a mechanic's garage—had to be available to every other musher in the race. Breaking the rule would result in a time penalty or disqualification, depending on the severity of the infraction. This was supposed to help the little guy, the backwoods trapper who wanted to see what his dogs were capable of. The Quest would be an annual coming together of mushers who, thrown into a perverse winter world with their canine companions, would have, at times, to work together to survive.

The Quest would also emphasize proper and humane dog care and would limit the number of dogs allowed on a single team to fourteen, two fewer than the Iditarod's limit. That way, mushers could spend more time looking after individual dogs.

Perhaps as important, it wasn't to be an "extreme" event tailored for television ratings. It was to be the exercise of a privilege granted to those who have endured extreme circumstance, a competition among guides, trappers, and the other, mostly north-ern residents who are a link to a world where, for thousands of generations, northern people lived with, worked with, and relied on their dogs in an ancient and untrustworthy land that does not suffer fools.

The pair recruited other volunteers and found that people in the small towns like Central, Eagle, and Carmacks (a Yukon River community north of Whitehorse) were ready to embrace a race that brought teams through their towns. Money came in from unlikely sources. A hardware store in Fairbanks donated $10,000. A middle-aged widow, about to undergo serious surgery, gave them $1,000. By the time Pecos Humphries took off from the start line on February 25, 1984, followed by twenty-five other brave mushers, the Quest could guarantee a total purse of $50,000, the money raised from the mushers' $500 entry fee and other donations. Nearly two weeks later, a thiry-four-year-old, hippyish-looking construction worker named Sonny Lindner crossed the finish line in first place, collecting $15,000 for his—and his dogs'—effort.

The 2001 race still holds true to Shanks's and Williams's ideal. Some of the Quest's mushers were born up here, but most, like their antecedents a century ago, were lured to this country for its harsh beauty, open space and the freedom to live shorn from the constraints and claustrophobia that characterize the temperate world.

The Yukon Quest has remained, over nearly twenty years, an event that few people in North America outside of the Yukon and Alaska seem to notice or care about. Strangely, however, this is not the case in northern Europe or Japan. The race has been filmed, live, with hours of daily footage, by the massive Eurosport channel. *Paris-Match* has covered the race. One year, journalists from Switzerland outnumbered the Canadians and Americans put together. But the race has received daily national coverage in Canada only once, when the editors at the *National Post* (most of whom were European transplants) were convinced that the event warranted a series of stories.

The Yukon Quest reflects the image of Canada popularly held around the world (though not at home) as a harsh but spectacular land, which perhaps explains the media's fascination. Sadly, most Canadians can't remember the capital of the Yukon, confusing it with Yellowknife, the capital of the Northwest Territories. For most Canadians, the Yukon is a remote, cold backwater, somewhere up near Alaska, that makes it into the news a couple of times a year whenever something happens that, well, confirms the fact that it is cold or a backwater.

This, however, suits most Quest supporters just fine.

FIRST AVENUE IS USUALLY THE EMPTIEST street in Whitehorse. Bordered on one side by the unheralded left bank of the Yukon River, it is home to several warehouses, a small museum, a fenced-in power transformer and, as it crosses the foot of Main Street, the Yukon capital's main drag, several small shops.

It wasn't always thus; the city's train station once lay there, in the post-gold-rush days, when the narrow-gauge railway used to carry people and goods between Whitehorse and Skagway, Alaska. But the railway, crossing the treacherous White Pass in the Coast Mountains, was difficult to maintain, so the trains no longer reach Whitehorse and instead carry tourists and tired hikers back from the end of the Chilkoot Trail, some 100 kilometres southeast of Whitehorse.

Now, the White Pass and Yukon Route building houses the nondescript office of the Yukon Quest International Sled Dog Race, a largely volunteer-driven organization. On this Sunday, February 11, 2001, you can't even get close to the office for the three thousand or so people lining the street in a colourful array of Gore-Tex and fleece and wool.

It is the start of the eighteenth Yukon Quest, the biggest event in the winter Whitehorse calendar. Every year, because the direction in which the race is run alternates, the Quest either begins or ends here.

Although the thermometer reads something like twenty-four below—not particularly chilly weather for Whitehorse in February—it feels a lot colder. There is a stiff breeze, which stings cheekbones and noses and quickly freezes ink. If you want to take notes, it's pencil weather.

Directly in front of the office is a yellow banner, strung across the street, and two rows of red plastic snow fencing that stretch out for several hundred metres on both sides of the road. The pavement on either side of the banner is covered by snow, piles of it, flattened out; snow that has, in the last week, been dumped on the usually bare street by front-end loaders emptying dump trucks filled in undeveloped areas around Whitehorse. The packed-down snow forms a flat, white highway leading along First Avenue until it drops down to the Yukon River half a kilometre away.

Behind the banner, and on several side streets closed to traffic and the public, sit an array of pickup trucks with large, mostly wooden boxes attached to their beds. Some of the boxes have a row of small doors cut into them; others open at the back to reveal shelves piled with straw. Many of the trucks are festooned with local logos: Nuway Crushing, Princess Construction, The Bonanza Gold Motel, North Country Bison. One truck has a big, red AC/DC sign, for the Australian rock band. The trucks are almost universally filthy, especially the tires and hubcaps, which are lined with frozen yellow rivulets. Yellow icicles drip from the tailpipes and bumpers.

The reasons for this, and for everything going on this sunny Sunday afternoon in Whitehorse, are attached to the trucks on long chains or cables that run the length of the sides. Some sit quietly, looking a little perplexed. Others horse around, wrestling with their neighbours. Some are contributing to the aforementioned yellow streaks. Most, however, are barking, continuously and loudly. Barking at each other, at people walking by, and at nothing in particular. For these dogs, it is the day they have been waiting for, the day they were promised. Beginning soon, every two minutes, a team of fourteen will pull a sled filled with a few hundred kilograms of musher and supplies northward along the Yukon River towards Fairbanks, Alaska, over 1,600 kilometres away.

Somewhere near each of the thirty-one teams of dogs, a man or a woman is fretting, loading sleeping bags, dog kibble, bits of rope, coolers, Thermoses, clothing, and saucepans into an open canvas bag slung inside the dog sled.

There is a schoolteacher from Fairbanks who has financed his Quest attempt by driving a taxi; a part-time swim instructor; and a woman who owns a very successful air-taxi company, flying tourists and mountaineers in and out of Denali National Park and to the Mount McKinley base camp. There is a coal miner. There is a man who lives year-round in a circular, Mongolian tent called a yurt. There is a lawyer from Nome, and a former professional soccer player and professional wrestler from Germany who now lives in Alaska. There is a trapper whose cabin, alone on the Yukon River north of Dawson City, is overloaded with books, but who has no electricity, plumbing, or telephone. There is a rumour that one of the mushers is an FBI agent.

One or two live in large, log homes with employees to help them train in excess of one hundred dogs, which are chauffeured around on the backs of four-wheel-drive, crew-cabbed trucks. Others live in tiny cabins and had to borrow a neighbour's dog or two to make a complete team. One, destitute, had to hitchhike 1,300 kilometres with his dogs to get to the start line. Some own kennels with a six-figure annual operating budget; others paid less than $300 for their entire dog team. Most are somewhere in between.

They are held together by a common thread: all of them live with their dogs, year-round, and their dogs are the central focus of their lives. To be a musher capable of completing this frozen passage demands nothing less.

Frank Turner, Canada's most famous long-distance musher, and, at times, its most absent-minded, has forgotten his lunch and the special neck-warming collars he gives some of the dogs on his team in cold temperatures. His start, in third position, is in about an hour, and it's about a half-hour trip each way to his kennel and home, forty kilometres or so from downtown Whitehorse. One of his crew of handlers is dispatched to test the resolve of the highway patrol. He makes it back with the neck-warmers in time. Turner's lunch, it turns out, was in his sled all along. When you're worried about readying fourteen dogs for two weeks' worth of trudging over snow, ice, and river overflow, a ham sandwich might slip your mind.

STAFF SERGEANT DOUG HARRIS, the head of narcotics investigations for the Whitehorse detachment of the Royal Canadian Mounted Police—and the race marshal for the Yukon Quest—awaits the first team's entrance to the starting chute, a cordoned-off area underneath the yellow banner. Harris, who has run the Quest several times himself, has earned the respect of most mushers for his even-handed but strong, dogs-first approach to running the race.

In the Quest, the rules are there to ensure, generally, two things: that no musher gains help from any sort of illegal outside interference, and that the dogs are treated humanely. Each musher must have already completed a recognized race at least 300 kilometres long, to demonstrate that he or she is capable of looking after the dogs while travelling in remote wilderness.

Dog care is paramount, and any indication that dogs have been pushed too hard or too far is dealt with harshly by the race marshal and the veterinarians on the trail. A veterinarian may ask a team to stay longer at a checkpoint, and, if a musher is obviously negligent towards his dogs by, say, not treating injuries properly or not feeding them enough, he can be disqualified.

There are no rules concerning the kind of abuse mushers might impose upon themselves. There are eleven race veterinarians. There is no race doctor.

Harris, frost building on his moustache, stands in the starting chute with a battery of officials whose job it will be to hold the team in place on the start line for a minute or so before it is allowed to depart. With the excitement, the training, and the strength of fifty-six well-muscled legs, the team's power far exceeds the musher's ability to hold it back, and thus a dozen people are involved with holding the sled and gangline in place while the dogs jump, bark, and strain at their harnesses.

As Turner arrives at the start line, he sets a gnarled piece of metal in the snow that acts as an anchor, although its placement comes from force of habit; there's no way it will hold a team this ornery. Harris steps on the brake between the runners so Turner can walk along the length of his team. There are eight people, heels dug in, holding onto the gangline, the sectioned rope that all the dogs are attached to. It's necessary: Carrie Farr, the musher who left immediately before Turner, didn't have enough help restraining her team and it shot several metres past the start line before enough people grabbed it and held on. The team had to be backed up, a difficult thing to do with fourteen dogs whose breeding and training impels them forward.

Safely at the line, Turner stops at each dog in turn, kneels down, and looks into its eyes with his hands cupping the sides of its head. Latte, when Turner approaches, stops barking and gazes lovingly back at him, tapping his front paws up and down in expectation of a tender touch. Turner pulls Latte's head close to his chest, whispers in his ear, and rubs the length of his back. Then it's on to the rest of the dogs: Birch, Rudi, Decaf, Minto, Kirby, Tank, Spencer, Bozo, Albert, Alder, Terror, Brandy, and Ella all get several seconds of last-minute TLC.

When he's gone through the entire team, and with about ten seconds left, as he's done seventeen times before—every edition of the Yukon Quest, in fact—he steps back on the runners. The din, with the dog's barks, the announcer counting down the remaining seconds, and the crowd cheering for a hometown favourite, is tremendous. As the count reaches zero, Turner quietly—and unnecessarily—whistles, a noise audible only to those standing within a few metres. The hook is pulled, the handlers let go, and Frank Turner and Co. are gone, a rooster tail of snow arcing high behind them as they recede through the tunnel of spectators and well-wishers.

Rich or poor, experienced or rookie, nearly half of the thirty teams won't make it to the finish line in Fairbanks, their race cut short by attrition from ice, snow, and the screaming echoes of doubt inside a cold, tired mind.

The Yukon Quest has begun.

GRANDMA

I WOULD LIKE TO SAY THAT I was drawn to the Yukon by the Homeric tales of life in the North I read as a boy, stories by Jack London, poetry by Robert Service, or the booming voice of Sergeant Preston as he commanded his faithful dog, Rex. It's not true, though. I recall, vaguely, learning "The Cremation of Sam McGee" in school, but don't remember it having any dramatic effect on my ambition, at the time, to be a veterinarian. Worse, I'm somewhat embarrassed to say that I didn't actually read *The Call of the Wild* until 1998, when I had already stopped living there and had moved to Winnipeg. Sergeant Preston was brought to my attention at a bar in Brooklyn, New York, by a bartender who was intrigued that someone who lived in the Yukon would actually come to New York City.

In fact, I moved to the Yukon more for what it wasn't than what it was. From Toronto, it was the farthest capital city I could drive to and stay in Canada. And, at the time—I was twenty-four years old, with limited job prospects in the big city and an urge to live near mountains—it seemed a perfectly reasonably way to spend a summer.

I arrived in June 1994, after a seven-day Volkswagen Rabbit trip from Toronto that took me through the pastel sunsets over Agawa Bay on the north shore of Lake Superior, past the over-buoyant sulphur Lake of Manitou, Saskatchewan, halfway up Mount Robson in the Rockies, and beyond the Moby Dick Inn in Prince Rupert, British Columbia.

None of it prepared me for what I would find when I crossed the sixtieth parallel.

The otherness that is the Yukon first struck me just as I crossed into it on the then-unpaved, rutted Cassiar Highway, the route to the North avoided by all but a few of the thousands of motorhomes that wend their way in pilgrimage each summer along the Alaska Highway. It is Winnebago-free with good reason: logging trucks treat the narrow, mucky road like a private superhighway. Cars, whose roofs barely reach the bumpers of these log-laden monsters, are best advised to get off the road when a logging truck approaches, which, depending on the day, can be every few minutes. There is no centre line on much of the road, and the trucks use it to their advantage. (It is impossible to get windshield insurance in the Yukon, and most vehicles possess a web of cracks from the errant rocks pitched by the tire treads of passing trucks.)

I stopped to camp at Boya Lake, set up the tent, and watched, transfixed, as the sun shed strips of purpling magenta over the stilled surface of the water. It was 1:00 a.m., on the twenty-first of June—the summer solstice—and I could still read by the daylight.

Whitehorse, when you approach it by highway, is not a terribly impressive sight. You know you're getting close when the bill-boards start to appear, promoting local campgrounds, hotels, restaurants, and tire stores. Most are held up on steel poles. This is because some people object to the advertisements and have a habit of taking a chainsaw to any supports made of wood. During one territorial election, a candidate had his billboard sawn down three times. (He lost.)

In Whitehorse, it is easy to notice how the people who live there aren't the average sort you might find in other towns its size. Not long after I arrived, I was in the Capitol, a bar, and a man sat down next to me. His name was August, he said, and he was at least six-foot four. He had been released that day from the Whitehorse Correctional Centre, he told me. I forget what he was there for—defending his brother, I think he said—but he was glad to be out. Next, he related how he would kill someone if he was paid enough money to do so. I didn't ask him what he thought might be a suitable fee, I just nodded my head. He bought me a beer. I bought him a beer. Then he sauntered outside.

The next day, they pulled a dead body from the Yukon River. Two days later, my companion was arrested for murder. (He was eventually released when the Mounties charged somebody else.)

In the same bar, I once watched as the Yukon director of the Public Service Alliance of Canada, while in a scuffle, had a good chunk of his bushy beard ripped from his face.

It is a place of contradictions. A town of 20,000, it has the best-educated populace of any capital city in Canada, perhaps because its largest employer, by an overwhelming margin, is the territorial government. It also has the highest number of bars, per capita, of all Canadian capitals. Yukoners drink more beer than the residents of any other Canadian jurisdiction.

The territory is a political conundrum, traditionally a no-holds-barred battle between the far right and the far left, the latter supported by the descendants of hippie squatters and draft dodgers who moved there in the 1960s and early '70s as a way to escape the socially rigid conservative mores still controlling the rest of the continent. The former are descendants of those who moved there seeing it as a frontier, an escape from the seeping liberalism of the aging twentieth century. The Yukon is a universal New Jerusalem, fortunately big enough to accommodate divergent rules of Paradise. The legislative result is a curious mix. The Yukon was the first jurisdiction in Canada to formally ban discrimination based on sexual orientation, and it is a leader in recognizing aboriginal claims to independent self-government. It is also, as a matter of policy, bitterly opposed to firearms registration. And, in one session, Whitehorse city councillors couldn't even pass a bylaw making their own offices smoke-free, much less any other public space.

But both sides manage, usually, to coexist peacefully. Whatever their politics, residents of the Yukon agree on one thing: it is different, in spirit and body, from the rest of Canada and the world, which is a place called "Outside," be it British Columbia, Botswana, or any place in between.

Modern Whitehorse, which sprang out of an army base and resupply depot for the engineers building the Alaska Highway in the 1950s, is a town with more than its fair share of talented people: There are two theatre companies (one professional) and several dance troupes, and the territory is home to some of Canada's most successful artists. There are two newspapers, a publishing house, and a modern, impressive arts centre, where Margaret Atwood launched her Booker Prize–winning Novel, *The Blind Assassin*. Not bad for a population that couldn't fill one-third of a modern football stadium.

The reason for the disproportionate number of talented people is, I believe, because Whitehorse is in the sort of location that people find on a map, point to, and say, "I want to live *there*," which wouldn't be the case for most places of a similar size in southern Canada or the United States.

This was all beyond me as I arrived in the early Yukon summer, where snow was just about gone from the squat, rounded mountains that frame the Yukon River valley.

I FIRST MET FRANK TURNER several days after arriving in Whitehorse. It was at the Yukon International Storytelling Festival, an annual gathering to honour the ancient art of spinning a yarn, which attracts storytellers from all over the world and especially the northern circumpolar region. The festival is organized, in large measure, by Anne Tayler, Frank's wife. I was volunteering to help serve food, in exchange for a free pass to the events.

Turner, wearing a greasy Canadian Tire baseball cap, was changing a propane cylinder on a cook stove that was heating giant pots of stew for the participants.

"That's Frank Turner," I was told. "He's a musher." We were introduced, shook hands, and he went on his way. I remember noticing how short he was.

I had been offered a job writing speeches for the Council of Yukon Indians, an administrative body that gave a collective voice to the fourteen Yukon First Nations (before several inter-tribal arguments broke out and the agency was fractured). So, with the promise of paid work, I decided to stay the winter.

As the leaves on the birch and alder turned bright yellow—in August—and the snow line began creeping down the mountainsides—in September—there was a dramatic change in the way Whitehorse people interacted. In summer, the town is overrun with tourists and seasonal workers, which dilutes, to a certain extent, the community atmosphere that pervades Whitehorse at other times. In winter, which more or less corresponds to the school year (minus June) the weather is colder, the days are shorter, and the community huddles together.

And although it can pop into the news at any time, it is around Christmas that stories about the Yukon Quest begin to show up: who's signed up this year, if the route will be changed, what the river conditions are like, and so on.

I remember watching the start of the 1995 edition of the Quest. It was cold, pushing thirty below, but there must have been three thousand people out to to watch, toddlers sitting atop their fathers' shoulders, wearing bright orange fleece toques, craning for a glimpse of the dogs as they charged in a spray of snow through this human tunnel.

I had brought my camera gear, and I remember getting a nice photograph of a bearded, sunglassed musher wearing bright orange gloves as he waved to the crowd while roaring down the starting chute. It was, I later found out, Frank Turner.

I saw him again that day, as the Quest trail wound right past the small, two-room cabin near the Takhini River I had rented for the winter, about thirty kilometres north of Whitehorse. I was transfixed for several hours as team after team chugged along on the trail that ran parallel to the road, the dogs trotting, tongues lolling out, the mushers, beards greyed by the frozen vapour of their breath, waving every few moments to the well-wishers dotted along the trail.

FOR THE NEXT TWO WEEKS or so, the race consumed much of the two newspapers in Whitehorse, and I followed the morning and evening Quest reports on CBC Radio religiously, imagining what Larry "Cowboy" Smith, a tough, no-nonsense musher from Dawson City, looked like as he held the lead for most of the race. Everywhere I went in Whitehorse, people were talking about the Quest, and not just because a Canadian was leading it. It seemed to bring the community together, stopping people from pulling each other's beards out. I would learn that the arrival of the Quest, in mid-February, also signifies, timorously, the beginning of the end of winter, however distant.

Late in the race, at a place called Eagle Summit, a mere 200 kilometres from the finish line, Larry Smith faltered; his dogs decided they'd had enough and lay down. He was passed, left to convalesce on the mountainside knowing that, although he had made it that far in record time, he'd pushed his dogs beyond their capabilities.

Jim Wilson, the man who first passed Smith as he camped 200 metres from the top of Eagle Summit, was looking over his shoulder as he approached the last checkpoint, Angel Creek. He had good reason. Another team was gaining on him, and, just before he arrived at Angel Creek, he, too, was passed. By the time he reached the finish line in Fairbanks, he had fallen nearly an hour behind.

The man who had passed him was Frank Turner. He had waited, patiently, until just before the end to make his move. He was rewarded by winning the Yukon Quest in a record time that still stands today: ten days, sixteen hours and twenty minutes. Anne Tayler can recite the time as if it were her social insurance number.

Frank was received back in Whitehorse with a gusto more typically reserved for war heroes. He was the first Canadian-born musher to win the race. It made it into the newspapers in southern Canada. (He was even featured, along with Buck, his best lead dog, on the popular television program "Canada A.M.," where Buck stole the show by first burying his head under a cushion on the sofa and then licking his testicles.)

The victory, however, was somewhat overcast by sponsorship difficulties, which meant that the first-place prize was only $15,000, $10,000 less than the norm and half what a musher earns today for winning the race. Moreover, only the top ten finishers earned money, as opposed to the top fifteen, as was the custom. But that didn't seem to bother Turner much. He wasn't doing it for the money.

I went on to work for the *Yukon News,* for which I covered the race as a photographer in 1998. I got to see all the checkpoints, and how the communities and cabin-dwellers along the trail really came alive when the Quest passed through. The media that covers the Quest is traditionally a small group, especially once the race gets beyond Whitehorse or Fairbanks. The close-knit group carpools to the checkpoints that are accessible by road, and, when the race travels some 500 kilometres through the bush, it gets to checkpoints by air, on small planes like Cessnas and Super Cubs. It was an experience I will never forget, and I was hooked.

The following year I was working at the *National Post* and living in Winnipeg. I went back to cover the race as a reporter, the first time the race had been given daily national coverage in any medium. The stories I sent back from the trail were sufficiently well read that, in December 1999, the editors at the *Post* asked me, naively, if I would volunteer to enter the following year's race and write about it from that perspective.

Considering that I had barely spent any time on a dogsled, and that I utterly lacked the outdoor skills necessary to survive outside for two weeks at forty degrees below zero, I turned them down. In any case, no musher would have considered renting out his dogs to someone as obviously inexperienced as I was. So I offered to do the next best thing. I said I would try to get work as a dog handler for one of the mushers.

A WEEK BEFORE THE RACE, I showed up at Muktuk Kennels, a.k.a. Frank Turner's house, ready to learn how to be a dog handler.

Real dog handlers (as opposed to dilettantes) who work at large kennels like Turner's (that year, he had eighty dogs in his yard) are the unsung heroes of sled dog racing. They shovel the poop, feed the dogs, repair their houses, train the dogs, and repair the sleds, harnesses, and lines. They are generally paid with room and board.

Many are in the process of building their own teams and aspire to be racing mushers themselves. It's the best way to learn.

Working as a dog handler on the Quest, however, is a different thing. The Quest was founded on principles of self-sufficiency, so the handlers are allowed to do very little while the race is on. Except at Dawson City, where handlers take over for the thirty-six-hour layover and provide primary dog care—so the musher can get some proper sleep for the first time in nearly a week—they are not allowed to touch the dogs during the race.

The handlers on the Quest play an entirely hands-off, supporting role. They have to be at each road-accessible checkpoint in case the musher decides to drop a dog that is injured, sick, or sore and needs to be cared for by the handler after the musher has moved on. The handlers clean up the straw and the dog poop that is left behind when musher and team leave the checkpoint, as well as any equipment he might have decided to leave behind. The handlers listen and take notes when the musher is talking about the condition of the dogs or things that need to be attended to in Dawson City. The handlers do not get to fly on small planes to Eagle, the checkpoint that is inaccessible by road, because they are driving the truck some 1,600 kilometres across the Yukon and Alaska from Dawson City to Circle, the next checkpoint with road access. The highway system in the Yukon and Alaska is not terribly well developed, especially in the winter. So where the musher travels 500 kilometres between Dawson City and Circle on the Yukon River, the handlers drive three times that distance by road to get to the same place.

All this was explained to me the day I arrived. In case I forgot, I was handed a blue binder, the *Muktuk Kennels Handlers' Manual,* which detailed the handler's responsibilities. And Frank Turner very generously agreed to take me on, the greenest of rookies, as a handler on 2000 Quest.

On paper, it seemed to me that I would have about ten minutes' worth of work at each checkpoint, and a lot of driving to do. Turned out I was right about the driving. Much of the time during the race was spent sitting and waiting. Most of the trail is deserted, and few reports come in, so the handlers sit around at checkpoints drinking stale coffee and trying to guess when their musher might arrive. And, when Frank did arrive, there seemed to be things to do, like standing there listening to him mutter as he fed and looked after the dogs, that occupied the entire time he was there. Then, when he left, it was back in the truck and on to the next checkpoint, trying to catch some sleep and maybe eat a diner-style meal before he arrived.

I worked out that I actually got about thirty-seven hours sleep in the twelve days he was on the course that year. I had three showers. I wore my heavy Sorel boots, without taking them off, for three days straight at one point, and I wore the same pair of Carhartt insulated work overalls—the unofficial handler's uniform—for the entire race, despite the fact that Jet, one of Frank's dogs, peed all over them the day after I arrived. I spent one night with a dog in my bed, after he had been dropped because he'd developed an eye infection. Alexander, who hitherto had spent virtually his entire life outdoors, made the transition quite easily, it's worth pointing out. I once fed an adult dog cat food. Frank, never one to censor his emotions, hugged me sometimes, cursed at me sometimes, and once swore he'd never speak to me again.

At the end of that Quest, I was exhausted, smelled of stale urine and dog dander, and was badly in need of some vitamin C. I came out of it with a lifelong friend in Frank Turner, fourteen new furry buddies, and a burgeoning addiction to mushing.

AT THE BEGINNING OF JANUARY 2001, I turned once again down Frank Turner's driveway, this time to learn the ins and outs of running dogs before donning the mantle of a journalist to cover the race again. He and Anne had offered to put me up for a couple of months in exchange for chopping some wood, shovelling some dog poop, and making Caesar salads.

Frank Turner's dog yard is a cleared-out field on a bend in the Takhini River, a tributary of the Yukon, that contains some ninety plywood huts caked in urine-jaundiced ice. To almost every hut is attached a smallish, noisy dog. The yard, along with the Turners' new two-storey log home and several one-room guest cabins, is about five kilometres off the Alaska Highway, far enough from neighbours that the sound of eighty-five barking dogs is more an efficient alarm system than an aural imposition.

When I pulled into the clearing, he was out among his dogs, scooping food from a big white bucket into each of the dented aluminum bowls.

Frank Turner is short. He has been described in print as "jockey-sized," "gnomish," and "diminutive." With his biblical beard and twinkling dark eyes, he bears a resemblance to Dom DeLuise. He is Jewish, from Etobicoke, in the west end of Toronto, and has a squeaky voice. He is garrulous in the extreme, and possessed of a dry wit. Fifty-three years old, Frank likes to drink Grand Marnier, and his favourite breakfast food is mayonnaise on toast. From a distance, wearing his tiny, circular, wireless spectacles, he looks as though he should be a rabbi. But one look at his hands gives him away: stubby, blackened little digits that look shorter than they ought to be, scarred by years of rubbing ointment into dogs' leathery paws, pockmarked by hours of working barehanded at forty degrees below zero.

He has the hands of a musher.

His are the only hands that have steered a dogsled out of every single Yukon Quest starting chute, eighteen times including this year. Nine times from Whitehorse to Fairbanks, and nine times, in alternate years, the other way around.

Anne Tayler, the logistical brains behind his eighty-five-dog operation, is his second wife. His first marriage ended when he was forced to choose between that and the dogs. The dogs won.

His is a household name in the Yukon, and, in Fairbanks, the dog-mushing capital of the world, Turner is treated like royalty, held with the regard reserved in southern Canada and the lower forty-eight (how Alaskans refer to the continental United States) for hockey heroes and football stars. Attendants at gas stations wave and offer him luck, and people on the street whisper to their children and point at him.

Turner never wanted to move to the Yukon. After graduating from university with a master's degree in social work in 1973, his plan was to move to Mexico. His friend wanted to come to the Yukon. They flipped a coin. Frank lost.

He got his first dog while squatting on some land near Whitehorse. After a couple of years, he had enough critters to enter—reluctantly—a short, six-dog race during Rendezvous, Whitehorse's annual winter festival, where dog races are held among the chainsaw-throwing competitions and flour-packing contests.

By 1984 he had moved to Pelly Crossing, a native community 300 kilometres north of Whitehorse, where he worked as the Selkirk Indian band's manager and lived in a cabin. He had just enough dogs to enter the inaugural Yukon Quest. The race, run from Fairbanks to Whitehorse, took him almost two weeks. He came fourteenth out of the nineteen teams that finished the race, earning $600. The next year he was sixteenth, but out of twenty-eight finishers. Then he failed to finish two years in a row. By the early 1990s, he was hitting the top ten; between 1995 and 2000, he finished no worse than fifth, and placed second and third.

On the trail, they call him Grandma. He has a reputation for offering an opinion on everything, and being somewhat of a busy-body. (Once, in a hotel room, after spending five days on the trail in forty below temperatures without access to running water, he criticized the way I brushed my teeth.) But his maternal moniker is something he came by honestly: there are few, if any, mushers who provide better care for their dogs. He is the only musher I have ever met who, when he travels with his dogs, carries a Fisher-Price baby monitor with him so he can always listen to what's going on in the dog truck. He is held up as an example to mushers whose dog care is found lacking.

The doghouses in Frank's yard are arranged in paired rows, and each dog's line is long enough that he or she can play with at least three neighbours. The chains are looped around posts so they can twist about without getting tangled up. His dogs are friendly. The day I arrived, most of them hopped onto the flat roofs of their houses to greet me, or jumped up, putting their legs on my chest, straining to get a lick in at my nose. Most were just about tall enough to make contact.

We went inside, to the workshop. For Frank, this is a garage attached to his home, which comes complete with solar panels and a faulty, experimental, heat-sink boiler system that generates little more than expletives.

Harnesses hang from hooks and dog booties are strung out in long rows to dry. Along the back wall is a cluttered workbench, beside which is a closet that holds Frank's assorted collection of parkas, snow pants, gloves, and other outerwear. Along the opposite wall is a rack of old, disused parkas, most bearing the logos of former sponsors. These are donned, periodically, by throngs of Japanese tourists who come out from Whitehorse in minibuses for a tour of the dog yard and a twenty-minute "express" ride in the basket of a sled pulled by six dogs.

The operation looks more like a farm than a kennel, and has a budget to match. The Turners spend around $30,000 a year on dog food alone. They have two full-time handlers who live rent-free in a cabin on the property in exchange for the work they do feeding, training, and shovelling poop (about thirty kilograms a day).

There are three other cabins on their attractive property, which are often rented out to tourists who come for week-long "rookie ranch" crash (literally) courses on dog mushing. It's a fledgling business—Frank recently gave up social policy consulting to work as a guide and musher full time—but they are optimistic. Other money—most of it, in fact—comes from Anne's salary at Yukon College, and from sponsors, most of whom provide services in kind like food shipping, deworming medication, and the like. The Quest, generally the only race Frank enters every year, is their industry, their currency. Even for a musher of Turner's quality, though, it's generally a money-losing proposition. Even if Frank were to win the race and the $30,000 US that waits in the winners' circle, he would barely cover what it costs him just to enter.

Preparing to go out with a dog team involves more that just jumping on a sled and going. It's a procedure that takes at least an hour or two. After sorting through the blue, red, and yellow webbing, Frank picked out eight harnesses and handed them to me. We went back outside.

Putting a dog into a harness is easy, assuming the dog co-operates and you know what you are doing. However, there seems to be a direct relationship between the two: the less you know what you are doing, the less the dog co-operates.

In simple terms, the harness is several pieces of webbing stitched together so that, after it is looped under each front leg, it forms an "X" shape across the dog's back, evenly distributing the weight of the load. At the end of the "X" is a loop to which will be attached a metre-long piece of rope called a tugline. The other end of the tugline clips onto the gangline, which is the long, central piece of rope that attaches to the sled and runs the length of the team.

To put the harness on, I was told to straddle the dog as if I were going to sit down on it and ask for a ride. Then, if it stayed between my legs—which, generally, they do not—I would bend down, with the harness scrunched up so that the hole where the dog's head goes through is ready, and slide it over the dog's head. Then I would unhook the chain attaching the dog to its post, slide its collar underneath the harness so the harness is behind it, and reattach the chain so the dog can't run away. ("Come, boy" is not part of the sled dog lexicon. Nor is "sit," "heel," or "stay.")

After this was done, I would then lift up one of the dog's front paws and slide its leg into the leg loop of the harness, as though I were putting a knapsack on it. Then the other leg, and I'd almost be there. Pull the harness straight along its back, and make sure there's space between the harness and the collar so they don't rub together, and ensure that the shoulder straps that go under the dogs forelegs aren't twisted, and I'd be ready to go.

In theory.

The first dog I approached, Rascal, a big black-and-brown fellow, ran straight back into his house and hid. Despite repeated exhortations, he seemed resolved to stay there. He's a bit shy, I was told.

I tried Shilo, who seemed eager. About half the size of Rascal, she had dug a moat around her doghouse. But every time I tried to stand behind her she turned and faced me, so we chased each other around in a circle for thirty seconds. Great fun. Eventually I grabbed her by the collar, and held her in place.

By now the harness, which I had neatly prepared so her head would go through the head hole and not the leg hole, had become a tangled ball of webbing, and while trying to untangle it I had to let go of her collar. She turned around again. This time I got the harness straightened out, jumped behind her, and lassoed her with the neck hole. It was actually the leg hole, though, so I had to start again. This time it went on. When I unclipped her collar to slide it up I accidentally let go of her, but I managed to grab her before she could take off. By the time the harness was on properly, it had taken me the better part of ten minutes. Frank had harnessed his entire team.

Once the team was harnessed, they had to have booties put on. These are small, nylon socks that attach with an elasticized Velcro strap. They protect the dogs' pads from ice and snow, which in some conditions can ball up or get caught between their toes and rub, causing irritation.

Dogs, as a general rule, don't like having their feet grabbed, so just getting hold of one of their feet was an accomplishment.

Three times I managed to get a bootie on, and three times the dog shook her foot free and sent the bootie flying. It was frustrating, I could feel myself getting angry, and I began to suspect that the dog—in this case, Tango, a friendly, brindle female—was doing it deliberately. But I knew she wasn't. It tickles, having a bootie put on, and she was reacting just as I would if someone was trying to put a sock on my bare foot. There is an art to properly "bootieing up," getting the booties on tight enough that they don't fly off within fifty metres—which about 80 percent of mine do—but not so tight that they restrict circulation to the dogs' feet.

Now, with the team harnessed and bootied, it was time to attach the dogs to the gangline.

The gangline isn't actually a single line. It's a series of lines, each about two metres long, with a loop at each end. A two- or four-dog team uses one section, and beyond that a new section is added for every pair of dogs. The dogs attach to the gangline in two places. First they are linked by a short, thirty-centimetre line called a neckline, which clips onto the loop in their collars and a loop on the gangline. These are often elastic, like a bungee cord, so that when the matching dog on the other side of the gangline pulls to one side to sniff at something or take a mouthful of snow, his partner doesn't get pulled with him.

There is also a loop at the back end of the harness, near the dog's tail on the top of its back. From there, a longer, metre-long line vees out from the gangline and connects the pulling end of the dog to the team. Called a tugline, it gives a clear indication of whether a dog is properly pulling its weight. If the tugline is taut, the dog is contributing. If it is slack, he's just running along for the ride.

The gangline is securely attached to the front of the sled by at least one pair of heavy-duty clips or carabiners, locked opposite ways, so even if one comes open the other stays shut. If a gangline separates from a sled, it spells disaster, because not only is the musher left standing there while the unencumbered dog team carries on, but also the dogs themselves will inevitably get into a potentially life-threatening tangle.

There are usually several loops of elasticized cord between the gangline and the sled to dampen the vibration and movement of the sled so that the wheel dogs, those closest to the sled, don't get jerked around by a heavy sled bouncing on ice.

Getting a harnessed, bootied dog from its house to the gangline proved an adventure in itself. Rocky, who was to be my leader, was ready to go. The leaders—the pair of dogs in front—get attached first, so, theoretically at least, they (being, supposedly, the smartest dogs in the team) will keep the line straight while the other dogs are hooked up.

I grabbed Rocky, who was very excited at the prospect of going for a run, and unclipped her from her chain. Although she weighed only about twenty kilograms, as soon as she got free she pulled me so hard I tripped on the snow. Frank smiled. That, I suppose, is why huskies make good sled dogs. They can pull very hard. Especially when they have four legs on the snow. He suggested I lift Rocky's front legs off the ground by pulling her collar up, so that she could sort of hop to the sled. It worked better, although, even on just her hind legs, she was very strong.

We walked (or, more correctly, did a stumbling dance) through the dog yard, past the houses of other dogs, to where my sled was set up, and I got her tugline hooked on. Out in front, the lead dogs' necklines don't attach to the gangline; instead, they are attached to each other by a single line.

I got Devil, another small female (with the exception of Rascal, my whole team was female, which didn't mean anything at all, except that they're a little smaller), and the pair of them were now standing at the front of the line, barking. "Keep it tight!" I shouted, as instructed, which they were supposed to understand meant to stay in one place and not go exploring all over the dog yard, getting tangled up.

Together—I obviously missed the nod and wink—they moved off to one side to explore an empty dog food bowl and got tangled up.

I came back. "Keep it tight," I said, again. Off they went again. This happened several times, until I gave up and got the rest of the dogs hooked up as quickly as I could.

Finally, all eight dogs were in harness, in a straight line, and the sled was held fast in the yard by a secure knot wrapped three times around a stout post. The eight-dog team stretched out almost as long as a semi truck and trailer. They were barking and jumping. With each pair of dogs that jumped, the sled yanked against the knot, jerking back and forth.

A dogsled is a piece of transportation wizardry that, beyond the advent of lighter, stronger construction materials, has evolved little in the hundreds, even thousands of years it has been around. The one I was about to get on was made of ash, like a wooden hockey stick, and had been handmade in Fairbanks by Ray Mackler, an octogenarian carpenter who fought in the South Pacific campaign in the U.S. Army during the Second World War. It takes Ray several months to build a sled, using wood, gut, laminates, and a lot of craftsmanship. The result is a nearly bombproof sled that holds up on the Yukon Quest when aluminum, carbon fibre, and other space-age alloys fail.

A dogsled is about a metre and a half long. It sits on two runners that curve up in the front and extend half a metre behind the sled. Where they stick out at the back, they have plastic, slip-proof pads attached, which is where the musher spends most of his time. The sled is protected at the front by a rounded, V-shaped piece of laminate called a brush bow, which is kind of like a cowcatcher on an old steam locomotive. It's designed to knock branches out of the way, and when the sled hits a tree—which it will—its shape helps deflect anything more than a glancing blow. The runners are connected by a smooth piece of laminate that, depending on how far above the snow it sits, makes the sled either like a toboggan or a basket. A toboggan sled has its base just a few centimetres above the snow, which gives it a lower centre of gravity and makes it easier to balance. Because the basket is solidly attached to the runners, however, it has a stiff, bouncy ride. A basket-style sled has, usually, a series of pivots between the runners and the base, which raises it considerably and makes travel through deep snow easier. This leaves it tippier, but the pivots, which work much like shock absorbers, offer a smoother, back-saving ride for the driver. The shock absorption is limited, however. Go off a metre-high drop and it will still hurt to land.

The sides of the sled slope or curve gradually up to about a metre off the snow, where they meet the rear stanchions. The handlebar is a piece of wood that curves between the two stanchions, which are securely attached to the runners and the sides. Lines of gut are tied between the base of the sled and the sides to form the basket, which, when filled, will hold several hundred kilograms of gear.

A canvas sled bag fits in the basket, and closes with Velcro straps. Between the runners, at the back of the sled, is a spring-loaded, curved piece of aluminum with screws pointing downward from the bottom. Pushing down on this acts as a brake to slow the sled quickly, stop the sled, or hold it fast. As soon as you lift your foot, the brake is released. Behind the brake, sitting on the snow between the runners, is a piece of snow-machine tread, a flat piece of steel-reinforced rubber called a drag. You step on this to slow the team down by adding resistance to the sled. The drag is used primarily at the beginning of a run when the dogs are excited; once they settle down to a normal, trotting pace the drag can be lifted off the snow and hooked onto the back of the sled.

There is one other crucial piece of equipment: at the end of a two-metre-long rope coming back from the carabiners holding the gangline is a gnarled, medieval-looking, shiny curled claw. Called the snow hook, its job is to act as an anchor when a musher wants to hold a team in place and get off the sled. When the team has stopped, the snow hook is dropped on the snow and stamped into it.

They don't always work, and woe betide the musher who is standing several metres behind his sled when the snow hook pops out. She could be in for a long, lonely walk.

After ensuring that everyone was lined up and untangled, the sled bag was Velcroed closed, my gloves were on, and my parka was done up, I was about ready to go.

Frank gave me a brief clinic on how to drive a dogsled. He stood on the runners and pointed out how the sled would turn like a pair of skis if I shifted my weight properly. "If you want to turn wide," he said, "put both feet on the outside runner." To turn tight, he added, I should stand on the inside runner. "Stay loose," he instructed, crouching casually and jumping back and forth. "Oh, and stay relaxed. Don't yell at the dogs."

He walked over to his waiting team, in the next row over, smiled, and waved. Then he vanished in a puff of snow.

I got on the sled. The noise was deafening. My dogs were barking. The other seventy or so dogs were barking too, jumping, standing on the roofs of their houses. It was time to go.

This is what happens.

I pull the slip knot, but the dogs, not looking back, haven't quite noticed. About one-third of a second later, they do. Slowly, agonizingly slowly, the loops around the post unravel. One. Two. As the third loop comes loose, the sled moves forward, slowly, taking up the slack.

Then, a little faster, the third loop unwinds, and, like the Starship *Enterprise* stretching itself to warp speed, the rope releases, the sled is free, and the power of all potential seems to hang in the air for an instant.

Then all hell breaks loose.

The barking has, all at once, stopped. These dogs are down to business. Which means instead of taking turns lurching and diving forward against the secured sled, all the dogs, in eight-part harmony, dig their nails into the snow, and, with thirty-two muscular legs rippling, yank the sled forward with the pent-up power of a slingshot.

Before I can even find the brake with my boot, I have cleared, in a blur, the twenty-five-metre laneway leading past the rest of the dogs, all standing on the rooftops of their houses. I catch merely snapshots, frozen, as I shoot past: a tooth here, a lolling tongue there, a pair of eyes, mournful at the prospect of being left behind.

Then the first challenge: crossing the driveway.

Actually, crossing the driveway and getting across the ditch on the other side. As the sled comes onto the smooth, ploughed road, it starts to slide sideways as well as forward. By the time I register this, we are airborne over the ditch. As it lands on the other side, the sled jerks back into a straight line, and my feet slip off the runners. Now I'm balancing on the drag, the piece of snow-machine tread between the runners that is designed to slow the team down. Somebody forgot to tell the dogs this, I note wryly. The sled, on the rough trail, is bouncing around all over the place, making it difficult to get one foot up on a runner again. Eventually I succeed, and the team begins moving faster still, now unencumbered by the drag. I'm barely hanging on, trying to figure out how to keep one foot on the brake and the other on the runner or the snow-machine tread, and suddenly I feel like I can't remember anything, and this is a problem because there is a turn coming up very quickly so I should stop looking down at my feet and start looking at the ninety-degree corner ahead.

It is too late. The dogs have turned the corner, which takes me through a mogul-ridden path leading to the Takhini River. The unsteered sled does not turn. Rather, it takes a diagonal path through some clusters of weeds and grass sticking up through the snow, which collect in clumps on the claws of the brake.

I never quite get my balance. The moguls, after the turn, are too much. I slip off the one runner I've been managing to stand on, and, painfully, land on my knees between the runners. The pain is brief, about as brief as the time on my knees, which, being kind of pointy, don't slide very well, so my position soon becomes sort of a combination slide on the side of my right knee and the right side of my chest. I'm trying to hang on, honest. But the sled keeps charging along, and my arm is growing longer by the second. Now there is another corner coming, this one more serious, because it is at the bottom of a steep, metre-high drop. As we go over it, the sled, free of any downward pressure to keep it earthbound, leaps up briefly and slams down at the bottom of the hill. Gamely, so do I.

Now, of course, the dogs, who seem to be enjoying this, are moving east while the sled is still going north. But not for long. Violently, as the sled spins to the left, the whiplash heels it hard to the right. It tips over, almost in slow motion. Holding on with my right hand, I'm rolled over on my back, feeling like a cowboy being dragged by a galloping horse. "Never let go of the sled," I mutter through gritted teeth.

I let go.

My head digs into the snow at the bottom of the drop. Suddenly, the world is very quiet, and I begin to admire the form of the unique, tiny snow crystals all over my face, caught on my eyelashes and glinting in the sun. It is the very definition of sublime.

No, it isn't.

It is cold, really, just cold, especially the bits that are now up my sleeves, in the cuffs of my gloves, and down my thermal undershirt.

Sound now re-enters my sphere of consciousness. The first noise I make out is howling. Not laughter, as you might suspect, but the aggrieved howls of the seventy or so dogs left behind in the dog yard, wailing at the disappointment of not being picked for the team. Then, ahead of me, about ten metres or so, is my team, standing, wagging their tails in the brilliant sunlight. Rocky and Devil, the lead dogs, look back at me impatiently. Anna and Shilo jump against their harnesses, anxious to go, as do Chinook and Fox. Tango rolls in the snow, taking mouthfuls. Rascal just stands there, his tongue lolling out. He, I am sure, is laughing.

I get up, stumble back to the sled, and pull it upright. The dogs immediately take off again, but this time, on the nice, smooth trail, I'm able to dig in the brake and stop them while I catch my breath.

Frank, about a hundred metres ahead, looks back and waves. I wave back, slowly releasing the brake. As the dogs settle down to a trot, I realize, as the sun reflects yellow off the steep, snow-covered cliffs that line the river, that this is more fun than I could possibly have imagined.

Here I am, ghosting along the snow on a frozen river, mountains all around, with eight critters who are so clearly pleased to be pulling the sled that they can't bear to stand still. I'm travelling over the same ground, using the same technology, as people did a hundred, even a thousand years ago.

I shut my eyes, and I can feel the runners moving independently across the snow. All is silent but for the hiss of the runners and the dogs' rhythmic breathing.

At one point, a raven swoops down in front of the dogs, goading them into a chase. They happily oblige, and for twenty minutes we charge along, the raven almost allowing the lead dogs to nip at its tail feathers before zooming back into the sky.

At one point, we stop to give the dogs a snack: frozen chunks of salmon. The sled is tied off on a fence post, and I take a moment to look around. We are kilometres from the nearest house, the sky is clear, and there isn't a breath of wind.

Standing still, I suddenly notice the quiet.

Sound travels better through the denser molecules of cold air, casting into stark relief the silence in between: when the clinking of the dogs' collars has stopped, boots no longer crunch in the snow but stand still, and when the wind stops rustling the trembling aspen branches, the absence of noise is breathtaking. It's that silence, Robert Service wrote in the last verse of "The Spell of the Yukon," "that fills me with wonder, and the stillness that fills me with peace."

Two hours later, we were back. The dogs were fed, the harnesses hung to dry, there were steaks on the barbecue, home-made Caesar salad in the bowl, and Yukon Arctic Red beer in the fridge. It had been a perfect day.

After dinner, I retired to my four-metre by four-metre cabin on the perimeter of the dog yard to a pattern that would become familiar.

I sat down to write, stripping off layers of clothing as the over-torqued stove heated up. The stove, which I could not seem to control, belted out its dry heat relentlessly, causing everything in the room—especially me—to perspire. Most nights I ended up sitting naked to the bubbly hiss of a Coleman naphtha gas lantern in the oppressive heat before sweatily lying above the covers on the bottom of the bunk bed. At 4:00 a.m., of course, I would wake up seeing my breath against the upper bunk, now the victim of my zealous damping down of the stove. I would then spend half an hour trying to coax flames from the greying embers. There was no phone, no electricity, and no running water. I filled steel dog food bowls with snow and placed them on the stove in an attempt to moisturize the stove-baked air, which had seized upon my skin and, starting excruciatingly with my scalp, had begun stripping it from my body several hundred flakes at a time. I took to rubbing snow on my head in fits of naked, psoriasitic rage. In less than a month, I came to understand the true meaning of cabin fever. It's not isolation. It's dandruff.

Having said that, there was something pleasant about standing naked in the cabin doorway, leaning against stacked cordwood as I peed off to the side of the steps. Orion stared down from the top left of the sky, above the curve of the Big Dipper's handle. If it was clear, the northern lights were often dancing around nearby, usually in a pale shade of green. Sometimes they were white. Rarely, they appeared in a spectacular magenta stream, sliding across the night sky like a school of iridescent eels. One night, well after midnight, I stepped out to my urinary ritual and, as I stood there, heard the distinct sound of footfalls in the snow. I grabbed my headlamp from the wall. The Turners' two horses were standing against the paddock fence, about ten metres away, watching my indiscretion.

IT WAS MORNING, and Anne and Frank were having an argument, something about paying for part of their house construction. Maybe it was about the guy who bulldozed the driveway. I left the room, noting that there was more to being a musher than getting on the runners and reciting Robert Service. It's an expensive habit.

Or at least I thought it was an expensive habit, until I met Hugh Neff, who showed up at the Turners' kitchen to make himself a ham sandwich the day before the Quest started.

Neff, who, it seems, makes a virtue out of poverty, managed to get himself—and his fourteen dogs—to Whitehorse from Fairbanks by hitchhiking. It's a fifteen-hour drive.

He had nowhere to stay when he arrived, so he went to a bar, where he met the members of a Whitehorse band called Fish Head Stew and managed to cajole an invitation to bring his dogs to one of the band members' homes.

He still had no way to get his team to the start, however, which was then less than twenty-four hours away. You can't exactly fit 400 kilograms of living, squirming dog into the back of a taxi, even if you have the cash for the fare. So Neff was here, at the Turners', to see if he could borrow a dog truck. One of Frank's sponsors is a local truck dealership, which lends him a new truck every winter for the mushing season. Neff, by contrast, had only one sponsor, the Good Karma Tattoo Parlor. He got a free tattoo in exchange for putting their logo on his sled. So Frank agreed to lend his own truck, an old Toyota 4X4, to Neff.

Hugh Neff was born September 1, 1967, in Tennessee. He grew up, however, in Evanston, a suburb of Chicago, and he came to Alaska, incongruously, to be a golf caddy, a career that didn't last very long.

His story, besides the caddying part, is typical: he read Jack London and Robert Service as a youth. He fell in love with the state after reading James Michener's epic tome *Alaska*. "That's where I wanted to go. Alaska, the freedom of it all," he pronounced. "Mushing, it's all about unconditional love, and having dated a few girls and everything, I saw with the dogs that they never went away and they never stopped loving you." His sentiment echoes a bumper sticker common in the Yukon and Alaska: "The more people I meet, the more I like my dog."

He flew up for several summers, working in construction, canning fish, each time returning to the lower forty-eight when he ran out of money.

Planning to move permanently to Alaska, he started to drive up one summer from Chicago, but he ran out of money in Oregon and spent the winter there before going home to Illinois again.

He was, however, determined to get to Alaska. Finally, on October 3, 1995, he stepped off a plane in Anchorage with two dogs, bought a station wagon, and drove up to Fairbanks. It was the day O. J. Simpson was acquitted of killing Nicole Brown Simpson, he pointed out. There, as winter closed in and the temperature dropped often to thirty below, he lived in the back of the station wagon. Each day, he went to Cold Spot Feeds, a Fairbanks mushing supply store, to see if anyone needed help as a handler. He wrote a letter to Rick Swenson, the five-time winner of the Iditarod, asking him for advice, and Swenson told him to watch the mushing magazines.

Eventually Neff found work in the dog yards of Curtis Erhart, a top Alaskan sprint-musher raised in the native village of Tanana in the central part of the state. Ramy Brooks, another native musher, who would go on the win the Yukon Quest in 1999, also offered him work cleaning up his dog yard. Instead of making money, he was paid in dogs. Within a year, he had thirty.

Neff signed up for the Quest in 2000 because, he said, he couldn't afford to do the Iditarod. "I didn't know what the Quest was until I got up here. All I heard in Chicago was, 'Iditarod, Iditarod, Iditarod.' But the Quest is the cooler of the two races, as far as I'm concerned. Old-school mushing without the corporate influence."

"Old school" is an expression Hugh Neff uses a lot. It's a term, you sense, he would love to hear applied to him, even though he has been living in the North and mushing for a scant few years. He does his best to look the part: his clothing is old and worn, and he lets his hair do its own thing, to put it charitably. He is forever going on about how much money he doesn't have, which is, to him, a point of valour. He seems to aspire to be a bush-hardened dog man, and he's come a long way towards it. In his first Quest, the 2000 edition, Neff was handed the Challenge of the North Award, which is given to the musher who best displays the spirit of the race. Struggling to a ninth-place finish after running most of the race with only nine dogs, he seemed awestruck by the beauty of the trail and the communion with his dogs. Genuinely moved, he wrote a poem, and read it aloud at the finishing banquet.

Frank was impressed with him, enough that he offered to help him out if he needed any assistance. Hence the dog truck.

When he showed up in the Turners' kitchen in 2001, though, I barely recognized Neff. His attitude had changed dramatically. Last year, he said, he had talked too much. "I was like a kid in a candy store." This year, he said, he would be more serious. "I'm still a wild child," he added. "I just want to put on a good show, and spread some joy around. This is a celebration of life more than anything, and I have a major respect and reverence towards this land and the whole sport, so to me these are like the best days of my life. I'll just have to see what the sun brings me."

Now there was something of the didactic Jack London about him. He railed against the freeze-dried, lightweight, high-calorie food mushers take with them along the trail to feed their dogs. It's too expensive, he said, calling it "yuppie food," even though it was developed and made by Charlie Champagne, the patriarch of one of Alaska's premier native mushing families, who has likely never lived in an urban centre in his life.

Neff took his ham sandwich outside and eyed one of Frank's sleds. "I couldn't afford to pay the guy that was making a sled for me the money up front, so I'm having to use a sled that's more of a mid-distance-type sled. More like being on a surfboard than driving a car." He didn't mention that the mid-distance sled was given to him, free, by Ray Mackler, who also made Frank's sleds. According to Mackler, Neff never did properly thank him for the donation. It's something that Mackler, a quiet man who thinks before he speaks, hasn't forgotten.

LIGHTS IN THE SKY

Occupying the cabin next to mine in Frank Turner's dog yard was a sixty-one-year-old Japanese adventurer named Kazuo Kojima. He and Turner met more than a decade ago when they ran together in the Hope race, an annual sled dog "rally" that runs through both Siberia and Alaska, and they have been friends ever since. Kojima, who is well known in Japan as a mountaineer and as the first Asian to enter the Iditarod (he's competed in the race seven times), was in Whitehorse staging the second-last leg of what has become the biggest adventure of his life. For four years, he has been on the longest solo sled dog trip ever attempted, during which he has become the first person to cross the Arctic eastward from Mongolia to the east coast of Greenland, a journey more than 30,000 kilometres long.

With an ever-present Camel cigarette in his mouth and a fondness for single-malt whisky, Kojima has a mischievous sense of humour and an infectious laugh. He's also very tough.

His passage, called the "Last Great Expedition on Earth," was designed to trace the theoretical migratory route of the Mongolian people as they moved northeast across Siberia, over the Bering Land Bridge into Alaska, and through the Canadian Arctic to Greenland, spreading civilization as they went and peopling much of Asia, modern Canada and the United States, and Greenland.

His trip has been controversial, and, interestingly, his biggest challenges have come not from the land or climate but from people, most notably the Siberian secret police, who detained him for a month and a half, believing he was a CIA spy. He wasn't, and he eventually convinced his captors of this, but not before they had taken his laptop computer, satellite telephone, GPS, and several of his dogs.

He returned the following year to pick up where he'd left off, and each winter he has managed to travel several thousand kilometres. By the end of 2001, he'd reached Grise Fiord, on the southeast coast of Ellesmere Island, several hundred kilometres west of Greenland.

Kojima's trip might not be historically accurate, since there is no known record of dogs used in harness dating back quite that far. The use of dogs as draught animals seems to have originated in eastern Siberia, northern Alaska and Canada roughly a thousand years ago, according to archaeological evidence, although dogs were used domestically by Arctic people for several millennia before that.

Written references to sled dogs first appear in tenth-century Arabic texts about Siberia. Marco Polo also referred to dogs used in harness in the thirteenth century.

In the 1675 edition of English explorer Martin Frobisher's *Historic Navigations,* there is an illustration of a dog in harness pulling what looks like a kayak over the snow. On his 1577 trip to Greenland, Frobisher also reported seeing a dog used as a draught animal.

The Chuckchi people of Siberia are known to have bred smallish, thick-coated dogs that they used for herding reindeer (caribou) and pulling loads from place to place as they migrated. Although the dogs couldn't pull very large loads, they were fast and could cover great distances.

In neighbouring Alaska, the Mahlemuit people, Inuit who lived around the Anvil River, used a larger dog to haul game meat from the bush to the wilderness. The malemute, as it came to be called, was in great demand as a pack animal during the gold rush era around the turn of the twentieth century, and the Siberian husky was brought from Russia into North America around the same time.

Indeed, when horses were first brought to North America for domestic use, some aboriginals called them "elk dogs," apparently in reference to their physique and use.

The Mounties began dog-team patrols in the Yukon in 1873, and later, in the nineteenth and early twentieth centuries, explorers such as Roald Amundsen, Ernest Shackleton, and Robert Peary used sled dogs from northern Canada and Alaska as they sought the north and south poles and other polar firsts. In those days, rather than modern "X-back" style, harnesses were modelled after horse tack and were leather traces that ran down the dogs' sides from their collars.

The first sled dog race is said to have taken place in 1908. The All-Alaska Sweepstakes provided a diversion for miners and others who used their dogs for carrying gear and supplies. Sled dog racing was officially made a sport in the Yukon Territory in the same year, before hockey made it onto the official list.

Sled dogs were also used in the eastern Canadian Arctic, but, perhaps because of the geography of the northern Canadian archipelago, the eastern Inuit style of harnessing a team varied from that of their land-based cousins to the west. Where dogs were harnessed in single file in the western Arctic, and later two-by-two, the nature of travelling over sea ice dictated a fan-shaped string. With the dogs in this configuration, should one or two of the animals break through the ice, the rest of the team can pull them out. The more heavily wooded Western Arctic, however, with narrow trails, makes a fan-shaped string impossible.

Although they rarely travel over sea ice, modern Western Arctic mushers still travel over water; the Yukon Quest runs largely along the Yukon River and crosses numerous lakes. While cold and nasty weather is the most obvious hazard mushers must deal with on the trail, there are few spectres mushers fear more than plunging through weak ice, the dogs tied to their fate along the gangline.

In November 1993, Bruce Johnson, a former Quest champion (also Frank Turner's training partner and one of his best friends) was alone with his dogs crossing Little Atlin Lake, about 100 kilometres south of Whitehorse, on a training run for that winter's race. With little warning—perhaps only a rumbling, cracking noise—the snow underneath him shuddered and fell away as the ice that supported it broke into a kaleidoscope of irregular, shattered chunks in a cigar-shaped pattern around his sled and dogs.

The sled, the heaviest part, with Johnson standing on the runners, plunged into the icy, deep water, dragging the dogs, two by two, down into the water with it. The coat Johnson was wearing turned from an insulating layer into a bulky straitjacket; the harnesses, necklines, and tuglines on the dogs became an entangling web.

As he bobbed in the frigid water, Johnson tried to grab at the ice beside and behind him, straining for purchase. Each piece he grabbed broke off in his hand. If he reached farther forward onto the ice to try to pull himself up, he couldn't grip the ice, and his hands slid back. All around him, the dogs, panicked, tried to do the same thing, leading to a cacophony of desperate barking as they frantically trod water in a losing battle to stay afloat.

Eventually, as the cold seeped through Johnson's parka and thermal under-layers, into his boots, and down his back, it numbed his ability to struggle. As his metabolism slowed, he gradually gave up the fight.

He had given it a good go: when the Mounties recovered his body, his fingertips had been worn to the bone from scratching against the ice.

At the opening banquet of this year's Quest, Frank Turner and Genille Johnson, Bruce's wife, announced the Bruce Johnson Memorial Award, which would go to the community along the trail that mushers felt offered the best hospitality in the spirit of the race.

FROM WHITEHORSE, the Yukon Quest trail covers about 170 kilometres to Braeburn Lodge, a lonely highway roadhouse that serves as the first checkpoint in the race.

After leaving the melee of the start line, the trail flops down onto the Yukon River, where most of the race is run. In Whitehorse, the river is about 150 metres wide, and it travels sufficiently quickly that it rarely freezes over completely—even during the several forty-below cold snaps that hit the city every winter—so the trail tends to go along the edge of the river, darting in and out from the shoreline to avoid occasional stretches of open water, called leads.

Whitehorse is generally the mildest area of the trail, and, in some years, especially when it is at the end of the race, the finish line is moved northward, to avoid the Whitehorse section of the river.

This year, with a mild winter, rumours have abounded about where the race might start: perhaps forty kilometres north, at Takhini Hot Springs (well, warmish pools at best), or above the town, on the other side of the Alaska Highway, so it might avoid the still-open Yukon River completely.

However, as they almost always do, the rumours died out about a week before the race, when the front-end loaders began dumping snow on First Avenue.

Initially, the trail follows the Yukon River for just a few kilometres before it turns left, onto the narrower but shallower Takhini River, which drains a series of lakes east of Kluane National Park in the southwest corner of the Yukon. At this intersection, which has pushed the Yukon River into a wide, clay-terraced bight, if it is warm enough, mushers will run into one of the most challenging, and potentially dangerous, aspects of the sport.

When one river, or creek, flows into a larger one, or when a single river or creek bed narrows, the influx of water creates pressure where the two streams meet. If the surface is frozen, there is nowhere for that water to go, so it will well up through cracks in the ice or around the sides of the stream, causing overflow. The result, if it is warm, can be a layer of open water up to half a metre deep on top of the frozen surface of the river. Although there is not usually a danger of falling in, running through it is an unpleasant task. The musher will be soaked up to the knees, and, for the dogs, it means wading—or even swimming—through chest-high cold water.

After going through overflow, most teams must stop to replace dog booties, which will freeze into ice-encrusted lumps. The bottom of the sled bag will freeze too, and ice can build up dangerously on the brake and around the runners on the sled.

If the musher knows what to expect, he'll wear his waterproof "bunny boots," once the army's standard issue winter footwear, and probably the warmest boots ever mass-produced. They have no pile insulation; instead, based on a simple design, they are lined with two layers of thick, impermeable rubber, which trap a layer of air between them that is heated by the foot inside and kept warm. As long as that air pocket remains intact, the feet inside are well protected. Moreover, if the boots are left outside, or freeze, then all the musher has to do to warm them up is pour hot water into the boot, wait a minute, dump the water out, and dry it with a paper towel.

Unfortunately it becomes distressingly obvious several days into the race that what succeeds in keeping the weather out also keeps the odours and other microclimates created by unbathed feet inside. The stories of people wearing their bunny boots too long are legion, and probably myth. One famous tale involves a bush pilot finding a man who spent most of the summer in a tent in the bush without removing his bunny boots. When the pilot came upon the man, he was unable to walk because his feet had begun to rot inside the boots, and he had worn them so long that when he did try to take them off, they were sealed to his feet. Amputation was required when the man reached medical help.

If the weather is cold enough, overflow freezes after it wells up, creating, over time, layers of frozen lumps that stick up in blobs at creek intersections. These "glaciers," as mushers call them, are perilous because they are very slippery, and shaped in such a way that the sled will tend to pivot and slide sideways as it passes over them, with no way to regain control until it slides off the ice and hits snow, or a tree, or whatever else is alongside.

The Yukon Quest trail follows the Takhini River for eighteen kilometres, past Frank Turner's house and around a series of oxbow turns framed by hoodooed, eroding clay cliffs, until it makes a sharp right onto the historic Dawson Trail, the original overland route connecting Whitehorse and Dawson City.

During the Klondike gold rush, and for some time after, convenient travel between Dawson City and Whitehorse was on sternwheeler boats that plied the 600-kilometre stretch of the Yukon River between the two cities. However, once the ice closed in for winter, obviously, the boats couldn't travel, and the trip between the two centres was limited to mushers, or those brave enough to attempt to walk on snowshoes. Even by dog team, as Jack London documented in *The Call of the Wild*, it would take several weeks.

In a territory that has always been ruled by its weather, winter travel was long, exhausting, cold, and, not surprisingly, uncommon. Dawson City, 25,000 strong and the largest city west of Winnipeg and north of San Francisco, was virtually cut off for eight months of the year.

In the early days of the Klondike gold rush, until the turn of the century, dog teams were used to carry mail and light freight along the river between Dawson City and Whitehorse. Starting in 1901, however, the dogs were gradually replaced by horses.

The following year, the Canadian government contracted the White Pass and Yukon Route Company to build an overland route between the two towns, and, after a summer and fall of construction, the roughly 400-kilometre Overland Trail was finished. It cost $129,000, and was a shorter route than the highway in use today. The road opened Dawson City to coach travel year-round, and much improved the selection of goods and services available in the town.

Eventually, a highway was built from Whitehorse to Mayo, a mining and aboriginal town about 350 kilometres north, and a spur was built off that highway linking Dawson City. The new highway had a flatter, better-quality surface more suitable for cars.

Today, in summer, the Overland Trail is a living museum, with deteriorating bits and pieces of carriages and tack lining the route, as well as derelict cabins that once served as popular roadhouses. Because of the swamps, rivers, and small lakes that have reclaimed the trail in the last hundred years, it is navigable only in winter, although in summer it is popular with hikers, mountain bikers, and ATV enthusiasts. In 1996, it became part of the Trans-Canada Trail, an ambitious federal government program designating a path from coast to coast, adopting old railway beds, existing trails, and derelict roads.

Mushers on this part of the trail in the Yukon Quest travel over a long section of small, stumpy hills with creeks at the bottom and cross several lakes. Although there are no long hills, the short, steep drops mean that mushers must stay alert for sudden, narrow twists along what is generally a fast trail.

Eventually the terrain flattens out somewhat, the trail pops out behind Braeburn Lodge, and mushers have made it to the first checkpoint in the race.

DRIVING NORTHWARD ON THE KLONDIKE HIGHWAY, it is easy to miss Braeburn Lodge if you're looking the other way. A squat collection of buildings and a pair of nondescript gas pumps, it is a highway stop like many others in the Yukon and Alaska. There are clapboard outbuildings that seem to be living on borrowed time, surrounded by the detritus of self-sufficient remote living: vehicle parts, water tanks, pallets, fuel containers, and trailers. It has its own airstrip, which runs parallel to the Klondike Highway. The main lodge has been rebuilt with a pleasant milled-log exterior.

Even if it weren't the only commercial building within at least a seventy-five-kilometre radius, it would be remarkable for two things: its legendarily large food—especially the cinnamon buns—and Steve Watson, the man who makes it. Watson is an ex-biker. He doesn't have to tell you this: there's something about his black T-shirt, ample girth, and long, grey hair pulled back over his balding pate that gives it away—not to mention the panoramic photograph hanging above the restaurant counter of some fifty-one Harley-Davidson riders side by side astride their machines. He used to own the lodge with his wife, but now he is apparently the sole proprietor. He handed me a business card, then took it away again, uncapped a pen, and crossed out his wife's name before giving it back. He didn't offer an explanation, and I didn't press him.

To a casual observer, he's a scary-looking fellow, and there is a rumour that he once chased a restaurant sanitation inspector out of his lodge brandishing a gun. I don't believe it's true, though. Even here, it's still Canada: you can't wave firearms around with impunity. In fact, Watson is as pleasant as anyone you could meet. He loves to chat, and his face is crinkled from years of smiling in the cold, dry weather. The two days the Quest spends passing through are his busiest of the year. He keeps the restaurant open all night and stays up to greet every musher, many of whom know him by name. It's a pattern that's repeated all the way down the trail, as mushers, handlers, officials, reporters, and photographers descend on and wake up normally sleepy places in what becomes a travelling circus. A couple of days later, the troupe has moved on, sending local proprietors back to sleep with a little extra spare change in their pockets and something other than the weather to talk about.

The interior of Braeburn Lodge is as forgettable as its exterior aspect, with flickering fluorescent lights casting a greenish glow on the faux-wood panelling. There are collections of the *National Enquirer* that are at least a year out of date, as well as copies of the *Lost Whole Moose Catalogue,* a compendium of tips to living in the Yukon containing anecdotal stories and cultural missives by local writers. Week-old copies of the *Yukon News* and the *Whitehorse Star,* the territory's two main newspapers, are also stacked near the wood stove.

The simple plywood floors are worn dark and shiny, and the urinal in the men's washroom is enclosed by a garbage bag held fast with red plastic tape. "Out of Order," reads the redundant sign above. A new washroom, it appears, is under construction on the other side of a temporary wall, along with other refurbishing projects.

For all its cosmetic shortcomings, however, Braeburn Lodge is a haven of warmth for the crammed-in mushers and spectators. The single room has eight tables, in a space about ten metres square. There is nowhere for the media and other observers to sleep (mushers are given a separate area to sleep in), and the air in the dining area, at times, becomes thick with smoke. Eyeglasses steam over as mushers and others make the forty-degree transition from outdoors to in. Every chair is concealed by a parka, and there are numerous other piles of colourful outerwear lining the walls along the floor. A bright-blue pay telephone is this year's addition to the decor. Previously, with only a radio for outside contact, journalists and others had to drive to Whitehorse or use a satellite telephone to get race information out or do live radio hits.

Mushers are treated to a free hamburger, which is a term loosely applied. It measures at least twenty centimeters in diameter and comes sliced in half. Similarly, a BLT is half as large as a laptop computer, and the cinnamon buns—as if anyone would have room for dessert—weigh about a kilogram each.

Braeburn Lodge also figures in one of the stranger, and less well known, events in Yukon history. It was a gathering point for a group of people who watched a football-field-sized UFO follow the Yukon Quest trail. All but one of the witnesses wished to remain anonymous. The one person who would use his name was Steve Watson.

On December 11, 1996, between 7:00 p.m. and 8:30 p.m., twenty-two people witnessed a UFO along a 216-kilometre stretch of the Klondike Highway between Fox Lake, just east of the Dawson Trail. It carried on towards Braeburn, Carmacks, and Pelly Crossing. According to observers, it was between 800 and 1,800 metres in length.

People travelling on the highway reported seeing rows and rows of lights illuminating a curved surface that was silently drifting across Fox Lake, which is an elongated, flooded valley along which the Klondike Highway travels for some twenty kilometres.

Around the same time, a trapper in Pelly Crossing saw a similar row of lights. When he cupped his hand over his flashlight to avoid being seen, the object came towards him very rapidly and stopped 300 metres in front of him, sending out a sweeping searchlight. Another family in Carmacks reported seeing the lights out their window, and the children said they thought, since it was just two weeks before Christmas, that it might have been Santa Claus out on a trial run. After being in the sky for all this time, the family then reported that it vanished, one light at a time, as if it were passing behind a mountain, but there was no mountain to conceal the lights.

The spaceship, or whatever it was, never returned.

ON THIS NIGHT, FEBRUARY 16, 2001, there are also about twenty-two people standing outside Braeburn Lodge, although nobody is looking up at the sky. They are peering intently up the Yukon Quest trail towards Whitehorse as it fades into an inky night. It's a ritual that is repeated at every checkpoint on the race, where people stamp their feet in the snow and speculate about whose dogs might be the first to show up.

It is one o'clock in the morning, a dozen hours after the Yukon Quest has started, and the coffee is flowing thick from Steve Watson's urn. Outside, there is a brief flash of light from among the trees, the sight of which causes a mumble through the crowd assembled under the race banner behind the lodge. The banner has fallen down twice already; now it's being held up by two men. The volume of vapour escaping the assembled mouths seems to triple as speculative murmurs grow. Then, as the light becomes constant and grows stronger, the faint sound of rhythmic huffing wafts into the crowd, a sound balanced by the percussion of clinking clasps on collars.

"Team!" shouts the checker, a tall man wearing a Day-Glo orange vest with "QUEST" spelled out on it in black permanent marker, whose job it is to record the time each musher arrives at the checkpoint. He shouts with a grave sense of self-importance; it's the only time in the race he commands the attention of any of the spectators.

Coming along the final straightaway, the dogs' eyes glow in the reflection from the generator-fired lamps lighting the checkpoint.

Sticking nearly straight up, their wagging tails are silhouetted against the glare of the musher's headlamp and their own eerie, vaporous breath. "Whoa," comes a soft male voice from the back of the sled, from an amorphous lump shrouded in layers of Gore-Tex and fur and snow and ice. The dogs trot to a stop underneath the banner and stand there, with frost-crusted whiskers and lolling tongues. Two dogs roll over, legs straight up, wriggling their their backs against the hard-packed trail, and then sit back up, expectantly. The temperature is more than twenty degrees below zero. The team has just travelled 172 kilometres in less than half a day, but you wouldn't guess it by looking at them. They seem to be smiling.

Bill Pinkham, the musher now at the centre of everyone's attention, stands on the runners, chatting with Doug Harris, the race marshal. A rookie, he is surprised to be here first. Harris is surprised to see him, too.

Forty-two years old, Bill Pinkham is originally from Washington, D.C., although he grew up in suburban New Jersey. "I hated it," he explains, bluntly. After getting a liberal arts degree from college, he set out on his motorcycle to cross the United States to California and travel with his guitar.

He is a world-class rugby player, and, although he didn't play for the U.S. national team when in his prime (he was too busy travelling and exploring, he says), he now plays for the thirty-five-and-over national side.

He is tall, big, balding, and sports a soul-patch goatee. His voice, however, is soft as a feather, with that gentle, west-coast American accent.

From California, he wound up in Colorado, where, in 1994, he began working for a wilderness guide who had sled dogs, and the critters began to take over his life. After doing tours for a few years, he decided that he really wanted his own dogs, to do his own thing and try to learn how to race.

He went to Montana in 1998 and bought ten adult dogs and two puppies. The dogs started breeding. Within a year, he had thirty dogs, then forty-six, and his neighbours were starting to get annoyed. He bought out a nearby kennel, raising his total number of dogs to eighty-two, which is comparable to the size of Frank Turner's kennel. But where Turner employs two people to help him care for the dogs over the winter, Pinkham does it all by himself. He operates a tour business of his own. The Quest is only his fifth race ever, and certainly the longest.

For Pinkham, entering the Quest was a way to distract himself from the pain of life in the non-mushing world. He was divorced from his wife, Kristin, last August. Like Frank Turner's first marriage, it succumbed to the commitments of raising, training, and caring for dogs. It was a choice she forced him to make: the dogs or me, he likes to joke. Dogs, two; wives, zero.

Having decided to enter the Yukon Quest, he trained through the fall and early winter, occupying his mind and time running his dogs and preparing food—grinding meat and fish and separating them into Ziploc packages that would be sent out, along with other supplies and straw, to all the checkpoints well before the race started.

He admitted he had no idea what to expect. The Quest was three times as long as any other race he'd entered, and his first in the Yukon and Alaska.

"When they call me a rookie, I really am a rookie, a different standard than some of the other rookies that go into a race like this," he says, smiling.

And now he has found himself in the lead.

The fact that his is the first team into Braeburn is an accident, more than anything, the result of an unusual training regimen. His dogs, he says, are used to doing long, slow runs, with prolonged breaks in between. Where other teams stopped for a significant rest en route to the checkpoint and ran in shorter segments, he did the whole trip in one go, and he now plans to take a rest equalling the time he's spent running on the trail.

As Pinkham chats to Harris, he opens the flap of his sled bag and begins rooting through it. There are a number of items that mushers must carry with them at all times, most of which are practical things aimed at ensuring safety and proper dog care: an axe, snowshoes, a sleeping bag, dog booties, and a veterinary logbook. When the race official or checker is satisfied that the musher is carrying all the required gear, another official gets on the runners to steer the sled while the musher runs to the front to guide the team to a suitable parking spot. The musher's handler usually walks behind, watching.

The checkpoint routine is similar among most mushers: he lets the team settle down, unclipping their tuglines and their booties (generally the dogs are tired and quite willing to stop running), and fills his cooler with hot water. He walks over and gets his drop bags, which, marked with his name and sent out prior to the race, contain dog food, dry clothing, new booties, and fuel for the camp stove he uses to melt snow for water out on the trail. He dumps the dog food into the water to allow it to soak before serving it to the dogs. This kills two birds with one stone: it means the dogs are getting hydrated as well as fed, and a warm, mushy meal takes less energy to digest than cold, hard food.

While the food is soaking, which takes about twenty minutes, he will collect his straw and spread it out in piles underneath the dogs. As fast as he's laid out a dog's straw bed, the dog will get on it and begin to burrow in. A good insulator, the straw traps heat between the dogs and the snow, allowing the animal to conserve energy as it sleeps.

He then examines each dog closely, shining his headlamp on its paws to make sure they haven't been cut or irritated. He checks each dog's chest and shoulders for harness rub, and gives each one a massage. Sometimes he will rub a healing antibiotic ointment into the dogs' feet.

If a dog is sick or injured, he will call one of the trail veterinarians over to examine it; if the injury or illness is deemed serious, he will drop the dog from the team, passing it to the handler, who will help the dog recuperate. Dropped dogs cannot be put back in the team, and no dogs can be replaced. Once a musher has dropped a dog, his team size is reduced for the rest of the race.

Once the dogs have eaten, the musher will take their bowls away—some dogs like to chew on them—and leave them to sleep. How long they sleep depends on their condition and how long they have just run. The formula is simple: for every hour they run, they should have one hour of rest.

An efficient musher takes about half an hour to do all this, knowing that the longer the dogs are left alone, the more rest they will get. To this end, whatever the temperature, most mushers will do all their chores barehanded; it increases their dexterity and speed.

Only when the dogs are down does the musher go inside, sit down to a hot meal, and, if he wants, talk to the media. Then he will try to get some sleep himself. When you add up the hour or so he spends after arriving, and the two hours or so it takes to get ready to go (the dogs are fed again, massaged, re-bootied, and so on before the musher leaves), a musher is lucky if he gets two or three hours' sleep on a six-hour rest.

Bill Pinkham sits at a table, politely fielding questions, insisting that he was not going out too fast, and that he was going to stay at Braeburn Lodge for a good eight hours. Flushed from the exertion of looking after his dogs, and with his goatee still dripping, he shuffles off to get some sleep.

Outside, six more teams have arrived before Steve Watson has cleared the leftovers of Pinkham's giant hamburger.

THE FINEST ATHLETES
IN THE WORLD

IT WAS EARLY DAWN, before 7:00 a.m., and the first musher was getting ready to leave Braeburn Lodge. It wasn't Pinkham, who, along with his dogs, was still sleeping.

It was still dark, and would be for some time, and as he pulled his snow hook, William Kleedehn's headlamp shone a white streak into the darkness.

William Kleedehn has the whitest teeth and biggest forearms I have ever seen. The former is good, because he smiles a lot. The latter is even better, because he, more than any other musher, has to be able to hold on to his sled.

William Kleedehn only has one leg.

And of the Canadian mushers in the 2001 Quest, he clearly had the best team.

William Kleedehn grew up near a small farming village east of Hanover, in Germany. His parents had a mixed grain, potatoes, and sugar beet farm, plus dairy cows. "It was basically a labour camp," Kleedehn recalls, smiling again. He, his two brothers, and one sister, "Every holiday, all we did was work there. There was just no end. I remember once we got back to school after summer break, in grade two or three, and the teacher asked us where we went on holiday—but he used a different word, not holiday, he used a certain German word, and I'd never heard this word before. I didn't know what he was talking about."

After he finished high school, he decided he wanted to learn a trade. The closest business to his family's home was a mechanic's shop, so that's where he went. He hated it, but his father told him it would be a useful skill for fixing farm equipment. He thought he'd rather be outside.

Shortly after he began working for the mechanic—while continuing to work on the farm—he left a bar, early, after one beer, because it was his turn to milk the cows the following morning. He got on his motorcycle for the short trip along the rural, southern German roads. He was eighteen, and it was 1978.

Riding along, he figured he saw another motorcycle approaching in the middle of the road. As it got closer, though, he saw the reflection of his own bike in the front grille of a car, on the wrong side of the road, with only one headlight.

The road, like most in Europe, had trees growing right on the shoulder, so there was only so far over he could manoeuvre past the car. His shoulder was skimming the trees as he tried to slow down, hoping the driver would see him and swerve back into the proper lane. There wasn't much time. "I was going maybe fifty, sixty miles an hour, and the guy was going probably the same, so everything happened really quickly."

At the last minute, he tried to avoid the car, whose driver was clearly asleep at the wheel. He couldn't. The car hit him head on. The impact sent Kleedehn flying over the car's roof.

The driver, evidently awakened, drove off.

He remembers hitting the car and then coming to, a minute or so later, in the ditch. His leg was broken into pieces, with arteries cut wide open, spewing blood. He could see bones sticking out in several places. His whole left side was smashed, and his hand, pulverized, was dangling from his wrist.

That was just what he could see. "It was so dark there—it was spring and clouded over. I couldn't even tell where the road was, and I figured that for some reason I couldn't see the full extent of the injuries. But I figured I was going to be in big trouble."

His helmet had flown off. Some of his teeth were missing, too. He knew he was in a remote area, with little traffic. He could see the trees against the sky, and he crawled towards them, leaving a trail of blood. He stopped, he says, when he reached the middle of the road.

"Then I just had nothing but luck. Soon another car came, a bunch of guys with CB radios—they actually knew me, too— realizing that I was in big, big trouble. They didn't know what to do but they called SOS, and then an emergency doctor that was within a few miles on a different side road, he heard that, he rushed over and he was able to stop the bleeding."

He'd already lost a lot of blood, the doctor said, enough, he thought, to cause significant brain damage.

"That," he notes, smiling again, "could have been the reason I started mushing dogs."

An ambulance came and took Kleedehn to hospital. It was the first time he'd ever been to one. He was there for seven weeks, at first, and then had numerous operations afterward. Surgeons rebuilt his shattered hip, and they removed part of his other hip to make a graft for his leg. They repaired his arm.

His left leg was amputated at the knee.

Police found the driver of the car by matching paint chips found embedded in Kleedehn's leg with those of a suspect car that was being repainted in a garage. The driver turned out to have been drunk at the time of the accident.

Kleedehn's long-term prognosis wasn't good. "This damn old nurse would come in the room once in a while, she was a physiotherapist, and she was an old, rough woman. She must have been in World War II. She was telling me, 'All right, my friend, one thing you might as well know, you're not going to make money in your life with physical work any more, or anything like that. You've got to get your shit together and go to college and get an office job.'

"And I just told her, 'I don't think that anybody is telling me, at this point, what the hell I am going to be doing.' I was more polite than that, but that was what I was thinking."

He kept leaving the hospital when he wasn't supposed to. "I made them give me crutches, right away. They said that I couldn't use them. But whenever nobody was looking I was trying to get going. I just can't handle staying indoors, for any amount of time." He believes that trying hard to use the crutches played a large part in rehabilitating his hand. "Otherwise they would have had to rip it apart, and try to line up the bones, wire them all up, and whether it would turn out, they didn't know."

He walked out for the last time before the stump from his leg had healed and returned to the hospital only to change bandages.

He came home, and looked at the newspaper. There, on the front page, was a story about the Iditarod, and how two mushers—Dick Mackey and Rick Swenson—had duelled over 1,600 kilometres, finishing in first and second place one second apart.

The margin of victory, the closest ever in a 1,600-kilometre race, was less impressive to Kleedehn than the sheer distance the teams had covered. "And I was just reading this. I couldn't believe it, and my Dad comes in there too, and we both read it. When he was a young boy he always trained his own sheepdogs to herd sheep and cattle. We were wondering, 'What kind of guys were those guys?'"

The old nurse, it turned out, was right about one thing: Workers' Compensation in Germany prevented Kleedehn, even on full recovery, from working in any kind of a shop, or anywhere where he would have to climb a ladder or where he could be slipping on oil. So much for being a mechanic.

Instead, Kleedehn took the money he was given in the accident insurance settlement, about $30,000, and bought himself a one-way ticket to Canada. He'd never been to Canada, and didn't know much about it, so he picked Winnipeg, about as close to the geographical centre of the country as he could get.

His father, who revealed that he'd always dreamed of moving to Canada, came along too. His parents bought a chicken farm near Emerson, Manitoba. Kleedehn helped him fix it up, but, once that was done, he got bored.

He got married, and with his wife, Claudia, and his father, he bought a motel, restaurant, and gas station near Kenora on the Trans-Canada Highway. Most winters the motel was closed. With nothing to do, Kleedehn began learning to mush dogs.

You can't spend too much time in that part of northern Ontario, Manitoba, and Minnesota without noticing the dog trucks. Kleedehn got to know one family from The Pas, Manitoba, who would stop at the gas station each time they passed through. Kleedehn told them about his interest in running dogs, and they told him they had some retired dogs that he could have to start out. He went to pick them up, and they threw in an old, used sled.

Kleedehn spent several years "cruising around the bushes," as he put it, never even thinking about entering a race. Then he went to a feed store to buy some dog food and saw *Everything I Know About Training and Racing Sled Dogs,* by the legendary Alaskan musher George Attla.

Attla, one of the pioneers in breeding the Alaskan husky, was not a writer, and the book is essentially a series of questions and answers. "I read that book over and over again," Keedehn recalls. It became his training manual.

He watched a couple of races, and then, in 1987, entered some middle-distance events—160 to 500 kilometres long—in Minnesota and Wisconsin. In his first race he placed second. The next race he won. His third race he was second again. For the next three years, Kleedehn and his ten former retirees never fared worse than second place.

He went back to the family and asked them if they had any more dogs they didn't want. "I got mostly dogs with mental problems, but those are the best dogs with which to learn. Problem dogs."

In 1990, Kleedehn decided to enter the Yukon Quest. He'd never been to the Yukon or Alaska before, but he knew it was the centre of the sled dog universe. He'd watched a video of the race, and once, in Idaho, met a musher who had competed in the Quest.

"I had a hell of a good dog team. Nothing short of a top-ten dog team. Maybe top-eight. But the musher didn't know what the hell he was doing. Absolutely no clue," he recalls, laughing. "I didn't know heck from all."

He got caught in a snowstorm that blew the roof off a cabin. He lost the trail. "We were out there for hours just trying to find the markers. We totally got bogged down." Eventually, an airplane pilot spotted them and race officials sent out a snow machine to guide them back onto the trail. "We were totally lost."

He was eating ice cream at Stepping Stone, 500 kilometres from the finish line, when he heard the winner, Vern Halter, being interviewed on CBC Radio. "I had forgotten about the fact that it was a race. There was a race going on and I was just sitting there eating ice cream."

He finished seventeenth, in a field of twenty-six finishers. But he completed the course, where thirteen mushers did not.

Kleedehn's trip north had made him an addict, and both he and Claudia were tiring of their Trans-Canada highway motel. Claudia issued an ultimatum: he'd better have the place sold by the time he turned thirty.

By his thirty-first birthday, they were living in the Yukon, south of Whitehorse, in a house Kleedehn had built himself. He'd bought the property from his neighbour, who'd asked him what kind of a house he planned to build. He said he didn't know; he'd never built a house before. "I'll show you mine," the neighbour said. "You can do it, because I did it, and I'd never built a house before." So William copied his neighbour's house, to the letter, and now has a wonderful, spacious, milled-log home, powered partially by the sun and the wind.

Claudia and William later divorced. She moved to Whitehorse, and Kleedehn now occupies his house alone, except when he's looking after their eleven- and nine-year-old sons. The place could use a woman's touch. Kleedehn is an unabashed AC/DC fan, and nearly every exposed piece of log wall is adorned with a poster, LP record sleeve, or some other piece of paraphernalia related to the heavy metal band.

Outside, about a hundred metres away, Kleedehn's dogs live in a compound bordered by a grove of pine trees.

Kleedehn has small, fast dogs. Most weigh less than twenty-five kilograms. By comparison, Frank Turner has a dog named Decaf—one of his best leaders—that weighs almost thirty-five kilograms. But that's the nature of the Alaskan husky, a cleverly husbanded mongrel whose pedigree and appearance is less a defining factor than its performance.

A so-called purpose-bred breed, the Alaskan husky, the dog of choice for the Yukon Quest and the Iditarod, is bred for what it does, not for what it looks like. And what it does, extremely well, is run quickly, pulling large loads over long distances in extreme weather. Depriving a sled dog of the privilege of pulling a sled for hundreds of kilometres is like depriving your Labrador retriever of the opportunity to chase a stick. It takes only one trip to a dog yard to understand this, one listen to the cacophony of excited barks when a sled is hauled out and, perhaps more telling, the morose howls of the dogs left behind after the chosen team has left. They are furry dynamos.

There are many breeds of northern dogs, animals that are loosely called sled dogs. Malemutes are large, strong dogs capable of pulling big loads slowly, but they have weaker feet and lack the work ethic of an Alaskan husky. Greenlands, Samoyeds, and Canadian Eskimo dogs, all registered breeds, are bigger, have wider chests and bigger heads, and are stronger than Alaskan huskies, but, like the malemutes, they aren't as fast.

The Siberian husky—the dog most people think of when they hear "sled dog"—is smaller than the Alaskan husky and neither as strong, nor as fast. It also lacks the incredible endurance the Alaskan possesses.

There is no such thing as a purebred Alaskan husky. The traits possessed by the breed—strength, speed, and endurance—come from years of experimental crossbreeding with other types of dogs.

The original Alaskan huskies came from remote native villages in central and northern Alaska, and are said to have descended from wolves tamed by aboriginal hunters. Natives would breed their dogs with any that came into the village to add a hybrid vigour to lines that, because of their isolation, inevitably were plagued with inbreeding. Airedales, spaniels, Irish setters, Labrador retrievers, and German shepherds have all been bred into sled dogs.

When sled dog racing took off, breeders began looking for genes that added speed and endurance to the Alaskan husky. In recent years, greyhounds and German short-haired pointers have been added to the mix. The result, today, is a very athletic animal that can weigh anywhere between fifteen and thirty-five kilograms with a narrow, deep chest, muscular thighs, and tough feet.

Some are all white, some all black, most a mix, with brindle, grey, spots, and even red thrown in. Some have ears that stick up, others that flop over. Many have one of each. The test of the dog was never what it looked like, but how it performed, which also meant how well it ate and drank, and whether it could handle living outside in the extreme temperatures of Alaska and the Yukon.

Several traits are common. A thick (but not necessarily long) coat of fur and dander. Tough, pigmented feet that are slightly webbed. Lean, long legs. Endurance that goes beyond belief. These dogs are athletes, the canine equivalent of the Kenyan or Ethiopian marathon runners. Fast, strong, and endowed with such a natural set of gifts that they make running 160 kilometres a day seem effortless.

Indeed, if you fear that running sled dogs such great distances is cruel, you are being anthropomorphic. Humans, even the most athletic among us, could not contemplate the kind of exertion long-distance sled dogs are capable of performing as part of a day's work. Physiologically, we are a vastly inferior species. The dogs are fitter than us, process food better than us, are kilo-for-kilo stronger than us, and are tougher than us. A sled dog is, in almost all ways, perfectly designed to run and pull for extremely long distances.

Consider first that the average sled dog is capable of converting oxygen into energy at a rate three times faster than even the fittest humans.

We measure endurance—cardiovascular or aerobic fitness—by evaluating the maximum rate at which our lungs can channel the oxygen we breathe into our bloodstream, so it can supply that oxygen to working muscles and allow them a steady source of fuel. The standard test—called a maximum volume of oxygen uptake test, or VO_2 max, for short—is conducted in a laboratory, and it is measures how many millilitres of oxygen per kilogram of body mass we can process per minute. An average, moderately active man in his thirties would have a VO_2 max of around 40 to 45 millilitres per kilogram per minute, which decreases with age. A typical Olympic-calibre marathon runner would score between 70 and 80 millilitres. A thoroughbred horse would peak at around 150.

An average sled dog scores 240.

This means much more than simply being able to run three times as far as a top human marathoner. It means that dogs operate at a physical comfort level far above that of humans. They are, simply, the finest endurance athletes in the world.

If we run too fast, for too long, then eventually our need for energy outstrips our ability to provide aerobic—oxygen-based—power, which comes from the result of a reaction between oxygen and the simple sugar called glucose we draw from the food we eat. Sprinting, flat out, an average person would last a couple of hundred metres at most. When we outpace our ability to provide oxygen to our muscles, our body switches to anaerobic, non-oxygen-based, forms of energy that come from a complex set of chemical reactions. Although anaerobic power is tremendous—this is what fuels weightlifters and other strength-intensive athletes—it is grossly inefficient and useful only for a very short time.

Once we start using anaerobic energy and go into oxygen debt, our blood sugar levels begin to drop rapidly, and our perception of effort increases dramatically. We slow down as both brain and muscle run out of energy. Moreover, if we press on, the waste products from anaerobic activity will eventually stop us from moving, as our ability to remove the waste products at the cellular level is overwhelmed. One of the waste products is acid, and the body uses lactate to buffer the acid and pull it out. There is, however, a limit to how quickly the cell can do that, and the lactic acid concentration builds up, causing cramps, nausea, and eventually rendering muscles so inoperable that they tie up. This is what causes runners to stumble and collapse, often heartbreakingly close to the finish line.

An elite human athlete running six-minute miles—a world-class marathon pace—is running at 70 percent of his or her VO2 max, a figure that increases as he or she becomes more exhausted. A dog running at the same pace (about the average pace of a strong team in the Yukon Quest) is running at only 30 percent of its maximum capability. Extremely fit humans running on good pavement or a track can maintain a six-minute mile for roughly the distance of a marathon before hitting the wall. A dog running at a similar pace on the Quest can do so for ten to twelve hours a day, ten days in a row, over a rough surface of loose snow or chunky ice, all the while pulling a sled and person with a combined weight exceeding 150 kilograms.

A well-conditioned sprint team can run for 40 kilometres at a pace faster than Michael Johnson sustains during a 400-metre sprint. Beyond several hundred metres at that pace, even the fittest human would build up so much lactic acid in their muscles from anaerobic output that they would be virtually unable to move. Dogs, however, because they perform at a much higher efficiency, can sustain tremendous speed and run for a much longer time than humans can. As a result, with rare exceptions, they don't dip into oxygen debt.

Moreover, a dog's physiology dictates different requirements for nutrition; for example, they are able to manufacture their own vitamin C (a good thing, since, as carnivores, citrus fruits and potatoes are not high on most dogs' lists of favourite foods). More important, for energy, they have a capacity three times as great as ours to draw energy from fat; so, there is no need for sled dogs to "carbo-load" before a big race, the way a triathlete might down several pounds of pasta the day before an event.

A result of getting so much energy from fat—which is easier to digest and contains more calories than carbohydrates—is that dogs are able to process and use much more energy over a given time period, and sustain this energy production over a long period of effort. For every gram of fat a dog consumes, it gets two-and-a-half times the amount of calories it would from a gram of carbohydrates or protein.

Cyclists in the three-week-long Tour de France—arguably the most gruelling endurance race for human athletes, and the only event approximating the sustained effort of a long-distance sled dog race—consume between 4,000 and 5,000 calories each twenty-four-hour period in order to satisfy the energy requirements of travelling around 200 kilometres per day. A dog on the Yukon Quest—which weighs about a quarter of the average professional cyclist—consumes 11,000 calories per day. Kilo for kilo, a sled dog is eating eight times what a Tour de France cyclist is consuming—more than twice as many calories a day, while weighing a quarter as much. To match that intake, an average, seventy-kilogram man would be eating twenty cheeseburger and fries specials a day at about 500 calories a burger.

It's not surprising, then, that the biggest challenge for mushers—and dogs—in a race like the Quest lies in coming up with a food that contains enough calories to match the energy requirements of the dogs, whose stomachs are roughly the size of a human fist, without overtaxing their robust, but smallish, digestive systems.

It's also a challenge to get as many calories from fat without short-changing protein, because protein is necessary for maintaining the dog's muscle mass, red blood cell mass, and plasma volume, all of which help prevent injuries and maintain a healthy immune system.

Enter Arleigh Reynolds, who, in the early 1980s, became bored with his life as a run-of-the-mill veterinarian and began studying canine exercise physiology, earning his Ph.D. from Cornell and ultimately lecturing there. He began studying greyhounds, until he began reading about sled dogs and realized that they, because they ran for a lot longer than just forty seconds at a time, offered a good opportunity to study the relationship between nutrition and performance.

There are few scientists in the world who know more about the way sled dogs work than Reynolds.

In 1998, he moved to Fairbanks, where he now works as a senior scientist developing high-performance dog food for Ralston Purina. "Initially, the dogs were just something that I did as part of my job studying them, but the more I worked with them, the more they became the centre of my life. That's why I moved to Alaska."

He is now one of the best sprint-mushers in the world, regularly winning events between thirty and sixty kilometres long.

Best of all, his studying consists almost entirely of observing the dogs doing what they love to do. "Most of the sled dogs I study have no idea that they're actually research animals. They think they're just regular old sled dogs."

Prior to Reynolds's research, mushers carried great blocks of frozen fat and meat and fish, but they could rarely get as much food into the dogs as they were capable of processing. As a result, dogs either ran more slowly or gradually lost weight as the race progressed. It wasn't uncommon for mushers to try to add several kilograms of weight to each dog prior to the race to buffer the weight loss. Worse, the loads they had to pull were much heavier because mushers had to carry so much bulky food.

Now, however, racing dog food is so sophisticated that, unless there is a storm or the dogs pick up a virus, many dogs actually gain weight during the race. Although it looks like regular kibble—dense, brown chunks that dogs happily eat loose on the ground—this is not food for regular dogs, because it contains several times the calories, along with carbohydrates and vitamins and minerals. It is generally available only to mushers with high-performance kennels, through veterinarians.

In a sprint race like the kind Reynolds competes in, which is over in several hours, feeding and storing energy reserves can be done well in advance, and mushers make sure their dogs have expelled the waste before a sprint race starts. (Feces add considerable weight, and are akin to a racehorse carrying a nine kilogram handicap, which is significant in an event where competitors pay $150 an ounce for runner wax that will make a several-second difference.) Running a race like the Yukon Quest, however, which lasts almost two weeks, means that the dogs must be able to digest and defecate while running at 16 kilometres an hour. Fortunately, because they are so fit, the dogs are running at such a low physical intensity that they can pull it off. Mushers abet this by carefully monitoring exactly how much food a dog needs. Various supplements are added to the mix to boost immunity and recovery from injury, although anything that might mask pain—like aspirin or ibuprofen—is strictly forbidden. Each dog competing in the Quest must also be examined thoroughly by a veterinarian a week before the race start; a microchip is implanted into the scruff of its neck to ensure that a musher cannot sneak another dog into his team during the race. Like most athletes in elite-level events, Quest dogs are subjected to random drug tests at the end of the race.

With proper care and the right genes, a sled dog can have a long, satisfying career on the trail. Unlike greyounds, whose racing career is usually over by their second birthday, a long-distance sled dog doesn't usually hit its racing prime until it is four or five years old; many dogs are still racing in their second decade. Frank Turner has one dog in his team, Bozo, who has competed in—and completed—the last seven Quests in a row, without ever suffering an injury. Another Quest musher, Jim Hendrick, has a retired sled dog who lords around his yard like a wizened queen. She's twenty-three years old, still happily trotting, and doesn't look a day over fourteen.

COMING OUT OF BRAEBURN, the teams, protected by a road marshal and flashing construction lights, cross the Klondike Highway and the airfield that runs parallel to it opposite the lodge. The trail climbs a hill, makes a gradual turn to the left, and heads eastward for some twenty kilometres until it reaches Coghlan Lake, a long, finger-like body of water that is the start of a 60-kilometre chain of lakes that mushers cross one after the other on the way to Carmacks, some 170 kilometres away. Between the chain of lakes and Carmacks lies Pinball Alley, a forested section of hills that have seen the death of many a sled. The 1987 Quest, for example, featured thirty-nine teams; at Carmacks thirty-seven had broken runners. One musher had his sled caught so inextricably— among three trees—that one of the trees had to be cut down in order to free it.

Although the trail has been rerouted around the worst parts of of the section, the densely wooded, hilly terrain makes driving a dog team that stretches out twenty metres a challenge. In this part of the Quest, the bark has been worn away from trees, and it is one section of trail where the rhythmic sounds of a dog team are punctuated by expletives and the noise of splintering ash. Travelling through twisty, tree-lined trails requires a musher to run, jump from runner to runner, and, sometimes, to duck.

SOFT SNOW

CARMACKS IS A STEREOTYPICAL ONE-HORSE TOWN. Well, actually, it's a two-horse town, cleaved in half by an oxbowing Yukon River. On one side of the river are the municipal offices, the municipal community centre, and most of the homes of the hundred or so non-native residents of the town.

On the other side of the river is the Little Salmon/Carmacks First Nation, one of fourteen native bands in the territory. Here there's a band office, community centre, and the homes of most of the native residents of the town.

It's a pattern that is, for better or worse—but usually for worse—matched in most rural communities in the Yukon, like

Haines Junction, Ross River, Beaver Creek, Mayo, Teslin, Watson Lake, and so on. Carmacks is different, however, in that the native side of town seems considerably more upmarket than its counterpart on the other side of the river. This year, the First Nation was hosting the checkpoint, and homemade stew and bannock were the order of the day for the soggy, snow-covered mushers who arrived there, beginning mid-evening.

Long before gold-seekers and other rogues arrived in the Yukon, the land around Carmacks was part of the traditional territory of the Northern Tutchone people, of which the Little Salmon First Nation is part. There were fishing camps dotting the Yukon River during the late summer, when salmon were running, and, later in the year, the same camps were used when caribou herds converged to cross the river.

It evolved into a trading centre where the Northern Tutchone would meet the Southern Tutchone from the southwest corner of the territory. From the south and east would come the Tagish people and the Tlingit (pronounced *klink-it*), inland relatives of the coastal Haida natives.

The area was first "officially" explored by an American army lieutenant, Frederick Schwatka, who was charged with the responsibility of learning the geography of Alaska. He named many of the mountains in the area—or renamed them from their aboriginal titles—including Tantalus Butte, the steep-sided hill south of Carmacks in the Yukon River that was later found to hold significant coal deposits.

Indeed, within several years, after extensive logging had depleted wood supplies, coal from the Carmacks area would power the riverboats that plied the Yukon River, as well as provide electricity for Dawson City in its heyday.

George Carmack is one of the men credited with making the gold strike at Rabbit Creek near Dawson City that unleashed the Klondike gold rush. But years before he struck gold in that creek (which was renamed Bonanza), he discovered coal in and around the town that would come to bear his name. He built a cabin there, which eventually became a trading post. During the gold rush, Carmack's Landing became a riverboat stop. The North West Mounted Police (precursor to the modern Mounties) built a detachment there. The Dominion Telegraph Line between Dawson City and Whitehorse also passed through Carmack's Landing, and the company set up an office there. The Dawson Overland Trail was routed through the settlement in 1901, and it became a popular overnight stop.

The truncated name "Carmacks" was reportedly coined by one Seymour Rowlinson, who owned "Roadhouse Number Six" (the sixth roadhouse out from Whitehorse), a well-adorned hostel with beds for twenty people over a dining area that held up to fifty. An acquaintance of George Carmack's, Rowlinson apparently ordered a sign that read "Carmack" for the side of his roadhouse. The painter mistakenly added an "s," which has never been dropped.

Today, the roadhouses are gone, replaced by the town's one hotel and the Goldpanner restaurant, the sole place to get a hot meal. There are a couple of gas stations and convenience stores, and not much else. Hiking and cycling trails wind around many of the bluffs that buttress the town, and a recently built boardwalk curls along the river's edge.

ON THE THIRD NIGHT OF THE RACE, it was really snowing—big white flakes that settled on sleeping dogs, blanketing them so that, at times, only a pair of eyes peered out from beneath a white mantle. The dogs don't mind; in mild weather like this, the snow is an insulating layer. When it comes time to leave, they rise, shake off a miniature blizzard, and look up at the musher expectantly.

Outside the centre hall were two barrels filled with water, and two men were holding blowtorches to the barrels' sides to heat up the water for the mushers.

Inside, there were rows of long tables set up, the kind with the legs that fold up underneath.

Outside, in the snow, a strange sight presented itself to the assembled race officials: lumbering up the hill to the checkpoint was a crazily overloaded sled, tippy, top-loaded, almost hiding the musher driving it.

It was Joran Freeman, a thirty-eight-year-old rookie, an ex–beach volleyball player, and probably the best-looking guy in the race. Normally, he smiles and flirts with the female reporters. Not that night, though. He'd had a pretty bad day.

Freeman comes from a long line of adventure-seekers. His great aunt, Dora Keane, was the first woman to climb Mount Blackburn, one of the highest peaks in Alaska, and she climbed it even before nearby Mount McKinley, Alaska's highest, had been climbed at all. To this day, no other climber has climbed the mountain by the route she took.

Freeman has longish, brown hair, and a soft voice that tends to quaver. He speaks slowly and deliberately, and is possessed of an understated common sense.

Born in Berkeley, California, in 1962, Joran is old enough to remember when the riots happened. His family were Swedish immigrants, some of whom were doctors and some of whom were founders of the city of Philadelphia. Joran went to Berkeley High, and then on to Santa Cruz, where he attended Cabrio College. There, he became a champion beach volleyball player. At times, he thought about learning a profession, like engineering, but he found the beach and surf scene too time-consuming and interesting. He spent most of his time socializing, living, as he recalls, "carefree, in a day-to-day existence." In 1980, approaching twenty years old, he figured he might as well have fun while he could: by forty, he figured, he would have bought into contemporary society and be raising a family, with a nine-to-five job. This would be fine, he concluded, by then. First, however, he had some ambitions to take care of. "I had this urge," he says, "to continue to be curious and spontaneous and figure out a bit more about what I really wanted to do for my own self."

After a couple more years in California, he had had enough. The freewheeling beach volleyball scene was being polluted by overflow from the nouveaux riches of nearby Silicon Valley. He didn't wear the right clothes, or drive the right car. In fact, he didn't drive a car at all. So he left, and went travelling through Mexico and the South Pacific.

In 1989, while back in Berkeley, he grabbed his bicycle, threw it on top of the Green Tortoise—the famous "alternative" bus that provides inexpensive travel across North and Central America—and headed north. He got off in Washington state and rode his bike up to Vancouver, British Columbia.

He carried on, still on his bicycle, up the Fraser River valley and northwest to the tiny town of Hyder, on the tip of the Alaska Panhandle. He took the ferry back to Vancouver Island and rode his bike back to Washington.

But he was haunted by his tiny taste of Alaska, and the following year, he hitchhiked to Anchorage with a fellow who was planning to climb Mount McKinley. Finding like-minded people in McKinley Village, many of whom were refugees from an expanding corporate southern American culture, he got a job driving a bus for a whitewater river-rafting company. He spent every hour of his spare time on the river learning to kayak and pilot a raft. By the end of the summer, he was guiding his own trips.

The following year, bitten by the travel bug again, he toured Australia, New Zealand, and Tasmania. He then went back to California, and, while working as a river guide in Six Rivers National Forest, enrolled in engineering school at Humbolt State College.

As soon as he had earned his degree in environmental engineering, Freeman returned to Alaska to scour the newspaper classifieds for engineering jobs. In the meantime, he worked as a river guide in Denali National Park and spent the winter house-sitting in Healy, a small town on the north end of the park.

Over the course of his time in Denali, he came to know Jim Hendrick, another summer river guide. In the winters Hendrick was a musher, and he regularly entered the Yukon Quest. During February, while he would be away on the race, Hendrick asked Freeman to look after the rest of his dogs.

As he left, he told Freeman—who had never stood on a dog sled before—that, if he felt confident, he could take a couple of dogs and a sled and run them on a one-mile loop around the house. Freeman took Hendrick up on his offer, and, after a few wipeouts, found that travelling by dog team was at least as fun as shooting rapids in a kayak.

Eventually, in 1996, Freeman found a job as an environmental engineer in Nome, on the remote, western coast of Alaska, where the Iditarod finishes. The land around Nome, swept cold by wind off the Bering Sea, is featureless. For outdoor fun, there are really only two things to do: ride a snow machine or a dog sled. Freeman hated snow machines, so he started handling for a local musher and former president of the Iditarod Trail Committee, Matt DeSalernos, who had twenty-four dogs. He helped DeSalernos look after his dogs for one season, learning the ropes, so to speak, and then went looking for some dogs of his own.

The following year, he met a woman whose son also had twenty-four dogs but was away at college. He worked out a deal with her: he would run them and look after them if he could enter some races with them, and be in charge of their care. She agreed. At the same time, he started accepting retirees and other dogs from friends and began to build a kennel of his own.

His first race was the Council 200, a 300-kilometre contest that starts in Nome, with no dog drops, food drops, or mandatory stops. It's known as a race that's hard on mushers and dogs. Five teams finished the race. Freeman came fifth.

This wouldn't be the last of his "red lanterns," as the trophy for finishing last is called (a term borrowed from the traditional light on the back of a caboose), but he was hooked. "Travelling was exciting," he recalls. "Just to be able to be on a trail, going some-place that I'd never been before, with dogs that I'd worked with and I'd developed this camaraderie with, a relationship that was truly unique. Something that I hadn't discovered before."

His next race, the 500-kilometre-long Kuskokwim 300, is a very competitive race that is used by several top kennels as a tune-up for the Iditarod. For Freeman, it was a matter of trying to learn all he could about racing and mushing at the same time, which is a challenge in a race, because most competitive mushers tend to keep their strategies close to their chests. Though nobody, while the race was on, went out of their way to offer him advice, he discovered that, if he asked, people would offer suggestions and tips. Mushers are generally like that, he found: quiet, introspective people, glad to help if asked, but not intrusive with unwanted advice.

Late in the race, he took a wrong turn. He finished in last place.

In his next race, the Kobuck 440, he came fifth, and, after several people he'd passed dropped out, he found himself in last place again.

After running dogs with Matt DeSalernos, however, and having seen the Iditarod consume the village, he decided his real goal would be to compete in the Iditarod. After one winter of racing, his growing red lantern collection notwithstanding, he was deter-mined to give the long-distance race a shot. Running the Quest didn't occur to him; Fairbanks is a long way from Nome, to say nothing of Whitehorse. Logistically and financially it made sense for Freeman to run the Iditarod.

He signed up for the 2000 Iditarod, along with more than eighty other mushers, the largest field ever assembled. He was still running the same dogs, which, he estimated, had cost him $200. Half came from the dogs he had been training in Nome, and eventually bought, and the rest had been given to him by friends. "They just didn't see the potential in some of these dogs. I didn't either, but I took them and tried them out, and they've stuck with me ever since," he recalls, smiling.

Much of his family came up to help him start the Iditarod. He felt euphoric at the start line, with supporters in Nome rallying behind him. He was in the most famous sled dog race in the world, and he was going home.

Once the euphoria ended, though, Freeman found himself in a tough race. His sled came apart, and he had to repair it. He finished the race, he said, running on perseverance. When he arrived to a cheering home crowd in Nome, only thirty-one teams had finished ahead of him. His was the second-fastest time posted by a rookie. He'd had a tremendous time with his team travelling across a remote, great distance. And, most important, he saw that he had been learning as a musher, and that his training had paid off.

But he also found something disconcerting about the Iditarod. The media seemed to outnumber the mushers ten to one. The top-ranking teams were kennels with millions of dollars to develop extensive husbandry programs. "It kind of turned me off," he says.

Meanwhile, Freeman's work as an engineer in Nome had run its course. The limited work was getting boring, and life in Nome wasn't quite as exciting as he'd hoped it might be.

He began looking for somewhere else to live in Alaska—an area that had good potential for work, with lots of trails for running dogs. That spring, he quit his job in Nome and moved, with his ten dogs, to Fairbanks. He bought some property off the Chena Hot Springs road, about fifty kilometres east of Fairbanks, in an area loosely called Two Rivers.

The slightly swampy, forested land is, in the winter, right alongside an extensive network of mushing trails. In the summer, it is a perfect home for several million mosquitoes.

He began cutting down trees and cleared enough space for his house: a yurt that he bought in a kit for $4,000. A yurt is a sort of permanent Mongolian tent, round, with a canvas roof raised in the middle for a chimney to pass through. The yurt takes some getting used to. Counters have to be curved, and, obviously, pictures and the bed don't sit properly against the wall. But it's toasty when the wood stove is lit. Freeman is clearly an expert at living minimally.

If Fairbanks is the mushing capital of the world, then Two Rivers is the mushing capital of Fairbanks, with the highest concentration of dog kennels in the known universe. Houses, cabins, and more than one yurt lie scattered around, and the swampy area is dissected by a seemingly endless network of dog trails. Two Quest mushers, Tony Blanford and Tim Mowry, are Freeman's neighbours. The air in Two Rivers, it seems, is never silent for the sound of barking dogs.

There was another bonus for Freeman in moving to Fairbanks: it was the finish line for another 1,600-kilometre race, this one without the corporate affluence and media influence, a race for purists. "I liked the fact that the Quest had longer distances, more winter conditions, and that it was just a more remote race." He also liked the idea of mushing home again to a town that, despite being many times the size of Nome, embraced the race with familial vigour. Indeed, the Quest trail, as it comes through Two Rivers on its way to the finish line, passes several hundred metres from Freeman's yurt.

Because Quest teams generally start with fourteen dogs, and Freeman had only ten, he set about, casually, looking for more. "I wasn't really desperate to find any. I just figured the dogs would come if I really needed them."

Looking at a bulletin board at the post office in Ester, a village on the northern outskirts of Fairbanks, he saw a free-to-a-good-home advertisement for a dog called Alta. The dog had been in harness twice on a skijoring trip—where one or two dogs are harnessed to a cross-country skier—but the family told him that the dog had too much energy and might be better suited for a sled dog team.

Freeman brought the dog home and tried him out in the team. Alta performed brilliantly.

He later found two more dogs for free, and someone he knew in Nome was asking $200 for a dog called Sam. He now had enough dogs, he figured, to start the Quest.

In the several months before the Quest, however, two of his dogs got minor, but nagging, injuries. He was down to eleven. Enter the Two Rivers mushing fraternity. Tony Blanford, who had signed up for the Quest but ended up changing his plans, lent three of his Quest dogs to Freeman. Now he had a full dog team, and he was ready to go.

The problems started even before he crossed the start line. Dario Daniels, an Italian-born Alaskan musher—who was planning to continue beyond the finish line in Fairbanks to Nome, another 2,000 kilometres distance—missed his cue to start, causing confusion. The rule is simple: if you miss your allotted start time, you have to wait until all the other teams have gone. Freeman, who had been waiting for Daniels to go, thought he had more time than he did, and, in the confusion at the start line, officials didn't call out his name. Looking at his watch, Freeman realized that it was almost time for him to go, and that Daniels had obviously missed his chance. With the help of several onlookers, he got his team quickly harnessed up and arrived in the chute with just enough time to smile at the television cameras. Before the dogs had even stopped moving, he ordered the eight or so people holding the gangline to let go.

He felt a moment, a split second, of exhilaration. He tuned in to each dog on the team within the space of a heartbeat. Then, in an explosion of snow, Freeman's dogs took off at a speed of about thirty kilometres an hour.

Half an hour later, the exhilaration of the fast start fell to the ground and shattered. Cobra, a four-year-old dog in the prime of his career, started labouring, a sign he was overheating in the mid-afternoon sun. Freeman stopped the team, nervously, because they were still excited from their start, and looked at the dog. As well as overheating, his foot seemed a bit sore. Freeman was shocked that a dog of his calibre—he had been counting on Cobra to be one of the stars of his team—had faded so quickly.

Unhooking Cobra from the gangline, he walked him back to the sled. When a dog gets injured on the trail, the musher must carry the dog to the next checkpoint, where he can officially "drop" the dog and have it examined by a veterinarian, and then leave it with a handler to recuperate.

Carrying a dog in the basket is no easy task, especially at the beginning of a leg—and, worse, the beginning of a race—when the sled bag is pretty much full of food and extra supplies. This was especially true for Freeman, who had what veterans call the "rookie bulge" in his sled bag, resulting from an overly cautious estimate of needs during the race. In an empty sled bag, a dog, or even two, will fit quite neatly, and, clipped by their necklines to the side of the sled, can be reasonably stable. But a mere eight kilometres into the race, there was certainly no space in the sled for Cobra, who weighed more than twenty-two kilograms, so he had to be balanced on top, moving the centre of gravity of the sled considerably higher.

After about eighty kilometres, Freeman took a four-hour rest stop, and by the time he'd left, it was dark and considerably cooler. Cobra could safely go back into the team for the remaining eighty kilometres to Braeburn.

As he got closer, he could see that Happy, a ten-year-old dog, was getting tired and running stiffly. Arthritic, she had been with Freeman since he'd begun mushing, and he knew that to have left her in the dog yard at Two Rivers would have broken her heart. Freeman had brought her along for the chance to run with the excited team and to be part of the action, knowing she would probably retire for good at the first checkpoint.

At 3:32 a.m., thirteen and a half hours after he left the start line, Freeman turned a corner and came into the brightly lit parking lot of Braeburn Lodge. He was in eighth place. After the team was given a clean bill of health by the veterinarians, Happy, feeling decidedly unhappy, was led away to the dog truck to convalesce, her racing career over.

At Braeburn Lodge, Joran Freeman had decided against dropping Cobra, because he seemed to have recovered from his sore foot and overheating problems. He pulled out, and shortly after coming over the first hill, just as he was turning northward towards the chain of lakes, barely three kilometres from the highway crossing, Sockeye, a twenty-five-kilogram wheel dog, started to limp. Freeman stopped.

Should he turn back? It would be faster than having to carry a dog for the next 125 kilometres, the distance to Carmacks. But returning to a checkpoint is a risky psychological gambit. If the dogs get the sense that they are allowed to return to a checkpoint, they might decide that every time they leave a checkpoint they can stop, turn around, and go back for the piles of straw in which they had comfortably rested for hours. Besides, given a rest, perhaps Sockeye would be okay later on. Freeman put Sockeye in the spot occupied by Cobra for most of the first leg and carried on.

Thirteen kilometres later, Cobra was hurt again, limping. Freeman picked him up and put him into the basket. If the sled was top-heavy with twenty-five kilograms of dog in the basket, he now had more than forty-five kilograms riding on the very top of his load. Cobra and Sockeye were sitting quietly, at least—that was lucky, because many dogs don't like to ride in a sled—but Freeman kept having to take one hand off the handlebar to steady the dogs as he went around corners, to prevent the sled from tipping over and the dogs from falling off.

Sixteen kilometres further on, things went from worse to disastrous. Rooster, one of Freeman's most dependable leaders, had somehow twisted his back. He joined Sockeye and Cobra on the sled. Carrying one dog on a full sled is challenging. Two is extremely difficult. Three, however, is an accident waiting to happen. Especially since Rooster, unlike his sled-mates, had no intention of staying in the basket. He was fidgeting constantly, looking for any opportunity to get out.

Trying to hold three dogs in the basket, Freeman could barely steer, and, worse, the possibility of further injury was high if one of the dogs fell under the sled when it tipped over. And he was crashing into trees at nearly every turn, dumping the sled over and over again. The snow on both sides was deep and soft, making it very difficult to get enough leverage to pick up the 150-kilogram sled and its contents each time. Rooster's back was too sore for him to be put into harness again, though, so Freeman had no choice but to try and soldier on.

The weather was rapidly deteriorating. Although the temperature was relatively mild, about minus fifteen, it had started snowing: big fluffy feather flakes, leaving the sides of the trail softer still and making it nearly impossible to see more than a few metres down the trail.

For another seventy kilometres Freeman struggled along, tipping and spilling dogs every few metres. He decided it was easier and safer to try to hold Rooster in place by his collar while he squirmed around, rather than attach his neckline to the sled and risk a tangle with the other dogs' necklines.

He wiped out again, and, getting up and shaking the snow out of his eyes, he got the sled upright and back on the trail. He set the snow hook, as he'd done a hundred times in the last five hours, and put the two clipped dogs back in the basket. Rooster, however, was now two metres behind the sled, lying down and burrowing himself into the fresh snow, preparing to take a nap.

There is a simple rule that most mushers observe: if you drop something behind you, forget about it, unless there is another team in front of you to catch your sled when it takes off. Freeman had a dilemma. Rooster had no intention of walking back to the sled to get back on his uncomfortable ride, but the musher couldn't reach him while standing on the brake. The snow hook was secure, but, in the soft snow, it could easily pop out if all ten dogs pulled simultaneously. As it was, they were barking, eager to go, annoyed by the constant interruptions in what should have been a pleasant run.

Freeman pondered his circumstance. He could go forward, and unhook all of the tuglines of the dogs. They would be unlikely to have sufficient strength to pop the hook without the direct power transmission the tuglines provided. On the other hand, Rooster was only three steps behind the sled, and grabbing him would take less than five seconds. He could grab him before the rest of the team even noticed he had stepped off the brake.

Freeman was already in a pretty bad mood, having lost, he figured, several hours, slowed down by the extra weight on the sled and the constant wipeouts. He was soaked with sweat and snow. Unhooking and re-hooking the tuglines would have taken several minutes.

He decided to take the chance.

Looking behind, he quickly stepped off the brake, spun around, and pounced on Rooster, grabbing him by the collar. He turned, took one step towards the sled, and, as he lunged to grab the handlebar, the hook popped out. The dogs were gone, the driver-less sled bouncing behind them as they charged around a corner.

Freeman stood there, the falling snow collecting on his shoulders, surrounded by the silent forest. It was just past 2:00 a.m., and he was thirty kilometres from Carmacks. It had been two hours since he'd last passed a team, and it had been travelling much more slowly than his. He was getting cold, exhausted from bouncing off trees and landing in deep snow and collecting sprawling dogs.

He looked down at Rooster, who, apparently oblivious, resumed his burrowing in the snow. The sight of his sled disappearing in the distance—and the accompanying despair he felt, alone in a suddenly silent, cold landscape—would become an unforgettable image from his race. With the dogs, he felt like part of a group, a collective working together to survive. Now, with one injured dog beside him, he felt alone. This was, he realized, about as far as you could get from playing beach volleyball in Santa Cruz.

After several minutes of reflection, he hoisted Rooster onto his shoulders, fireman-style, so that the dog's legs dangled on either side of his head. Then, wearing his twenty-five-kilogram Alaskan husky stole, he started a long, lonely trek.

The snow was already up to his knees, and it was getting deeper as he walked. After several struggling minutes, he rounded a corner and started to climb a steep hill. Halfway up the hill, he came across his dog team, stopped, wagging their tails. They were looking back, impatiently, as if they were wondering what had taken him so long to catch up. Freeman didn't know whether to feel happy or angry.

Two hours later, after making the acquaintance of several more trees, Joran Freeman, with ten dogs running in front and three along for the ride, ran up the steep bank of the Yukon River to the checkpoint banner at Carmacks and the waiting clipboard of Doug Harris, the race marshal. "This is just the most wonderful checkpoint I've ever seen," he said as he pulled off his gloves. His adventure had cost him five places, and, after he took a much deserved nine-hour rest, he would leave the checkpoint in fifteenth place with ten dogs.

WILLIAM KLEEDEHN HAD BEEN THE FIRST to arrive in Carmacks, having maintained his position in the front of the pack since leaving Braeburn Lodge. Speaking to the media shortly after arriving, Kleedehn, never one to say anything less than what is on his mind, issued a stern message to the rest of the mushers. He was here to race, he said, not to cruise along in a group, as he described it, until the final section of the trail and then sprint to the finish line, as is the general pattern of the event. Kleedehn wanted to throw the unofficial race motto—"Survive First, Race Second"—out the window. He accused his competitors of hanging around in a "kaffeeklatsch" all the way to Angel Creek, the final checkpoint before Fairbanks.

"This is supposed to be a sled dog race," he told reporters inside the community centre, his sweaty hair sticking up in different directions. "So let's race."

AS KLEEDEHN WAS MAKING HIS PRONOUNCEMENT to the media, Andrew Lesh was struggling up the riverbank to the checkpoint, having run the last sixty kilometres with a broken sled runner.

A decade ago, Andrew Lesh was teaching high school English and social studies in Brooklyn, and he kept hearing great things about Alaska. He decided to come for a summer visit. The following year, he transferred his teaching certificate to Alaska and moved from New York City, population 10 million, to Gaseegklit, Alaska, an Inuit village on the western corner of the state, population 300. He stayed there for seven years.

In his second winter, he began mushing with a three-dog team. He had fun with the dogs: it kept him outside and exercised, and gave him something to do in a remote and, compared to New York City, very quiet place.

As the story so often goes, by the next year he had seven dogs. The year after that, he had seventeen dogs in his yard.

After seven years in Gaseegklit, however, Lesh had had enough. As a single man, aged thirty-eight, he wanted to seep gradually back into western culture. Perhaps more important, he wanted to find someone to marry him, and suitable candidates where he was teaching were in short supply. He decided to move to Fairbanks, where, like Joran Freeman, he could still mush dogs but have better employment—and matrimonial—prospects. But just before he left, he met Patricia Caruso, another teacher who worked in a nearby village, and the pair started dating.

Lesh was already committed to moving to Fairbanks, however. In the summer before the 2001 Quest, he came for two weeks, found a half-built house north of town near the mushers' hall (which, in Fairbanks, is much like the Legion or Elks Lodge), and moved in. He and Patricia were married in November 2000, although she remained in western Alaska until after her teaching contract expired, after the 2001 Quest.

Patricia's absence was painfully obvious at their home. It was still, to put it charitably, half built, and it was cluttered with winter gear, dog supplies, and other "musherly" equipment. It's not that it was dirty, although there was at least a week's worth of dishes stacked in various spots around the kitchen. There were books and CDs and unidentifiable paraphernalia on nearly every flat surface, and some sitting precariously on curved surfaces, too.

Lesh talks dramatically, waving his arms with a flourish when he makes a point, which is usually punctuated with his self-deprecating, dry wit. When he smiles, his eyes crinkle up, and you can't help smiling along with him. He has, it seems, a constant five o'clock shadow.

In Fairbanks, he couldn't get a job teaching, at least not with the commitment of training for the Yukon Quest full time. So he began driving a taxi part time to pay some of the bills.

Lesh was intrigued by the Quest because of its reputation as a tough race, in the dead of winter, that was less competitive and more relaxed than the Iditarod. It's a little cheaper, too, and less intimidating.

It also, he admitted with a sly grin, impressed the folks back home in Westchester County, New Jersey, to whom he sends a newsletter every few months. They are his cheering squad, he says, even if they think he's a little nuts and don't quite grasp what it means to compete in the Yukon Quest.

During the race, an article about the terrible ice conditions on the Yukon River wound up in the hands of his mother, back in New Jersey.

Panicked, she called up Patricia. "Has Andrew crossed the Yukon River yet?"

"Well," she replied, "he's not exactly crossing it. He's running on it for 210 miles."

There was silence at the other end of the line. "Oh, my God," Andrew's mother said. "It didn't say that."

The 2001 Quest was Lesh's third effort at the trail, after finishing tenth last year and fourteenth in 1997, and, he's promised, it will be his last. He never had any plans to become a professional musher, and he would rather spend most of his time travelling casually with his dog team.

He has already agreed to sell several of the dogs on his team, and he'll sell most of the rest of them after the race is over, keeping only his younger, more recreational dogs.

"If you want to do it well, it takes everything you've got, and that doesn't leave much for anything else, I think," he explains, thoughtfully. "I had a life last year, this whole year preparing for the race, but my life was mushing. And there's more to my life than mushing, and I need to sort of rediscover that. I haven't read a book since August. A friend of mine said, 'Well, that's not all it's cracked up to be,' and I said, 'Man, you're not reading the right books!'"

As he arrived in Carmacks, however, he was wondering how much fun this actually was. He'd had a rough start. First of all, upon arriving in Whitehorse for the start of the race, he realized he'd forgotten much of the personal food, including seal oil, that he'd planned to carry with him in his sled bag. He'd left it on his porch at home.

Obviously, unlike Frank Turner, who could send someone back to his house, Lesh couldn't possibly make the thirty-hour return trip to Fairbanks. So he would rely solely on the food in his dropped bags, which, really, wasn't that bad: Kentucky Fried Chicken, jumbo shrimp with garlic sauce from a restaurant in Fairbanks, gorp, and homemade burritos.

Twenty kilometres into the race, Nitro, an eight-year-old leader, tore his Achilles tendon and couldn't even walk. Lesh had to carry him the rest of the way to Braeburn Lodge, where he was treated by a veterinarian. (Before the end of the race two more of his dogs would suffer muscle tears, which are very unusual. Eventually, he would track the cause down to an antibiotic they were taking that weakened the muscles.)

At Braeburn Lodge, Lesh bumped into Bruce Lee, the 1998 Quest champion and one of the best-known and most respected mushers in the North. Lee, who lives in Denali Park, Alaska, was on his way back from a stage race in Wyoming, and he stopped in to watch the Quest go by.

Lesh had purchased several dogs from Lee, and he was running one of them in his team. Lee pulled Lesh aside and told him that the runners on sleds like his were falling apart in the race he was just at.

The runners on a sled are more complex than they appear. Lesh's sled, like William Kleedehn's and those of most top mushers, is made from aluminum. The runners are also aluminum, and, along the very bottom, they have a narrow plastic rail that runs their entire length. Sliding on that rail is a long piece of removable plastic, with a surface like the bottom of a ski, that actually makes contact with the snow.

There are several different kinds of plastic for different snow conditions, and mushers will replace their runner plastic several times during a single race as conditions change or the plastic gets scratched or damaged. Removing and replacing it can be tricky; usually, it will peel off the rail, and then, after the edges of the rail have been cleared of snow, a new piece of plastic can be slid on.

Lee told Lesh that the rails were snapping either when hitting a solid object or when the plastic was being peeled off. If this happens, and the musher doesn't have a spare, it is impossible to put the plastic on. With no plastic attached, the runner itself will scrape against the snow and ice and eventually break—a race-ending catastrophe.

Lesh had to change his plastic. He gingerly tapped the old plastic off. A tiny piece of the rail broke off; not enough to alter its performance. He peeled the rest off very carefully.

After crossing the chain of lakes on the trail towards Carmacks, Lesh hit a section of trail that, in a wooded, forested area, has numerous small hills with tree stumps, twists, and turns: the remnants of Pinball Alley.

Bouncing down a twisting hill, he slammed into a tree stump at the bottom. The rail on his runner snapped in half, leaving the plastic lying on the snow, a curled, yellow tendril spread across the trail. He had no choice but to try to carry on, riding on the bare aluminum underneath the sled. But without the plastic to protect it and reduce the runner's resistance over the snow, a rock or tree branch lying on the trail could end his race by breaking the runner in half.

It was sixty kilometres to Carmacks, and Lesh winced at every bump and knock on the trail. He made it to the checkpoint, but he still faced a problem when he arrived. He had no replacement rail, and there was no way he could run the rest of the race without one. With some of the worst ice conditions just ahead, he wouldn't even make it halfway to the next checkpoint before his sled runner snapped completely.

An hour after Lesh arrived, Bill Steyer, a friend and occasional training partner from Fairbanks, pulled in. Steyer had a similar sled to Lesh's. Miraculously, he also had a spare runner, but it was in his dog truck.

Yukon Quest Race Rule #2: ". . . Items relative to the safety of dog teams and drivers (i.e., sled brakes, mittens, etc.) may be replaced with the race marshal or race judge's approval and the thirty (30) minute time penalty assessed at the last mandatory stop."

The rules of the Quest are designed to force mushers to honour the tradition of northern self-sufficiency. Borrowing a rail from another musher on the trail is fine. But the only time mushers are allowed to use supplies from their dog trucks is in Dawson City, the halfway point of the race, still 500 kilometres away.

Lesh walked over to Doug Harris, the race marshal, and told him his predicament. Had he been carrying a spare rail in his sled, or in his dropped gear at the checkpoint, then all would have been fine. But Lesh didn't have a spare rail—he knew of no musher who actually carried one along the trail, as they rarely break—so to get one would force a penalty.

Harris said he would allow Lesh to borrow a rail from Steyer's handlers, but that he would be penalized thirty minutes for doing so. The penalty time would have to be served, according to the rules, at the last mandatory checkpoint on the trail.

Lesh shrugged and accepted Harris's decision. Thirty minutes was a small price to pay, he thought, for the opportunity to continue in the race, and Angel Creek, the last mandatory checkpoint, just before Fairbanks, was a long way off. He would rather have served the penalty in Dawson City, during the mandatory thirty-six-hour layover there, but he understood the rules.

He pushed it out of his mind, happy to be able to carry on.

GENERALLY, WILLIAM KLEEDEHN'S PRONOUNCEMENTS notwithstanding, there is a feeling of camaraderie among the mushers in the Quest which draws from a shared experience against a hostile landscape. But at times there are disagreements among drivers, spats that, looked at from the dispassionate vantage of an armchair, might seem petty and ridiculous. You have to remember that when you've gone forty-eight hours with very little sleep, minor irritations can become major controversies.

Frank Turner arrived tenth into Carmacks, three hours after Kleedehn. He fed the dogs and sent Albert and Terror home; both were suffering from sore shoulders. He bedded the rest of the team down on straw and went into the community hall to eat and chat with Anne and the media. After dinner, he went to an area of the hall reserved for mushers to sleep, found an empty sofa, lay down, and fell asleep. An hour later he woke up and had to go to the bathroom. He left his hat, gloves, and a sweater on the sofa, to make it clear he was sleeping there.

Dave Dalton, a Willow, Alaska, musher whose claim to fame, among other things, is that he's sponsored by Reflections, a Fairbanks strip club, had arrived about an hour after Frank. While Frank was in the bathroom, Dalton climbed onto the couch and took his spot.

When Frank returned from the bathroom, he was shocked to see Dalton on the sofa. "I'm sleeping there," he said. "I left my stuff there."

Dalton refused to move, and, after some argument about trail etiquette, another musher—probably to get them to shut up—offered Frank his spot. He refused and went to sleep on the floor. "There's kind of a protocol when you're out there. When somebody's there before you, they kind of establish rights, and your sleeping spot comes with getting there first. The same way you wouldn't interfere with somebody's dogs, or somebody's sled, you don't interfere with their space as well. It's just the way you do things," Frank said later. "It's something that I'm not going to forget. I'm not going to hold a grudge, but I certainly wouldn't go out of my way in terms of providing assistance."

Joran Freeman, watching all this from his sleeping bag less than a metre away, would later say that the argument opened his eyes, literally and figuratively. "It kind of brought the Quest down to earth. These iconic mushers were bickering about what I thought to be a trivial matter, but to both of them it was important. It brought a little humility into the race."

ICE

IT IS ABOUT 115 KILOMETRES from Carmacks to Pelly Crossing, the next official checkpoint. However, for years, a farmer just over halfway along that route, Jerry Kruse, has been opening his land and an outbuilding for mushers as a rest stop. McCabe Creek is now an official Quest dog drop, which means that, although mushers do not have to stop there or sign in and out, there are veterinarians on hand, hot water is available, and, if they have a dog that is sick or injured, they can leave it in a handler's care instead of carrying it on to Pelly Crossing.

When the race is run from Fairbanks to Whitehorse, few competitive mushers stop at Kruse's farm, and those that do don't stay very long. They are nearing the home stretch. But coming from Whitehorse, not even one-quarter of the way into the race, the atmosphere at McCabe Creek is usually jovial. And this year, thanks to some nasty trail that fatigued dogs and battered mushers, the atmosphere of relief—and gratitude for a break and a warm pot of chili—was tangible. It was mild, there was neither a breath of wind nor a cloud in the sky, and the farmyard was soon full of dogs, dozing on beds of straw.

Heading out of Carmacks, teams run along a road for about twenty kilometres before dropping down once again on to the Yukon River. The trail weaves its way on and off the river, criss-crossing it several times.

The winter of 2000–2001 was a particularly strange one for the Yukon River. In October it froze over, but warm weather at the end of the month meant it partially thawed. As the ice thawed, it broke into massive slabs that began to float downstream. In November, when the temperature dropped again, the slabs were frozen in place, forced upwards under the pressure of the newly forming ice below. A week or so later, it broke up again, only to refreeze at the end of the month, where it stayed.

The result is called jumble ice, something that looks like a bomb blast frozen in mid-explosion. The riverscape became a field of outcroppings, boulders, and chunks of ice that ranged from the size of a breadbox to a decent-sized bungalow. It looked like a bizarre, white-and-blue cubist nightmare.

"Mushers are facing the worst trail conditions in the history of the race," Leo Olesen, the race manager, said before the race started.

The river near McCabe Creek brought to mind the images sent back from the Mars lander. Standing out in the middle of the river, which is about 300 metres wide there, you could hear the ice grumbling under the weight of its own enormity.

Somehow, the Canadian Rangers, a northern, volunteer division of the Canadian Armed Forces, travelling by snow machine, had managed to cut a trail for the Canadian half of the Yukon Quest, using axes, chainsaws, and a lot of elbow grease. It wasn't fun. They don't get paid, and, worse, they have to use their own chainsaws and snow machines.

Sergeant Brian Murrell, who cut much of the trail between Braeburn Lodge and Pelly Crossing, explained his process of "trail-making by revenge": "When your machine comes upside down on you, you get off, you take your axe, and you beat the piece of ice that flipped your machine over and you try to smooth it out. You actually pulverize it like with a sledgehammer until it's nice and flat so it doesn't happen again. Eventually you get all the worst ones knocked down, and hopefully the snow will fill in all the extra little divots." Marking trail on the off-river portions is no piece of cake either. In the area around Carmacks and Pelly Crossing, the route is dotted with hundreds of small lakes, on which the ice can be dangerously thin. "I don't really want to stop on the lakes," Murrell says. "I'm going fifty miles an hour and I'm up on the back of my seat, looking for the trailhead. If I see water, I'll keep it at fifty—to clear the water—and hit the bush at whatever speed."

Besides cutting the trail several weeks before the race starts, the Canadian Rangers also travel just ahead of the leading mushers to make sure markers are still in place. Not only do they get knocked down by the wind, but wolves, it seems, have acquired a taste for them and tend to chew them off. The Rangers also reroute the trail around any new patches of open water. Through the bush, a dog team can actually travel faster than a snow machine, so, unlike the pace car in a motor race, the Rangers try to stay at least two hours ahead of the leading team.

The team coming over the treacherous jumble ice was, amazingly, William Kleedehn's.

In almost any other sport, Kleedehn would be competing in a separate category. But the Quest makes no allowances for ability, gender, or any other differences among people, which, not surprisingly, Kleedehn prefers.

His prosthetic leg is not the modern, plastic, high-tech sort you see on disabled athletes today. It is an ancient, leather-and-wood contraption that attaches, with straps, below his left knee. It is nearly rigid when it's properly attached, so when he walks under normal circumstances he can't really bend the leg at all; he sort of swings it out and around, while his right leg bends normally.

This isn't particularly useful for dog mushing, which is an athletic exercise of balancing, pivoting, and leaning in different directions to counteract the forces of gravity on the sled. So, to increase his range of motion, Kleedehn wears a carpenter's tool belt around his waist, underneath his clothing, to which he attaches several bungee cords. Then he attaches his prosthetic leg to the bungee cords without firmly connecting it to his knee.

The result is that he keeps the prosthesis loose, so he can bend it further and increase his mobility. The downside of this, of course, is that, when he's engaged in heavy physical activity, it tends to bounce against the stump, rubbing it raw and making it bleed. For Kleedehn, it is a painful occupational reality, but one that allows him to mush dogs and work on highway crews in the summer.

Even though, by modifying his wooden leg, he has increased his mobility, he is still at a tremendous disadvantage on difficult terrain like jumble ice, which requires the musher to be in constant motion, jumping from one side of the sled to another, running behind it and pushing it forward.

He still often loses his balance and has learned to compensate by doing what he calls a "volunteer" crash: seconds before he is about to hit a piece of jumble ice, he twists the sled over so it is almost, but not quite, on its side, and runs behind it while holding on with his hands. He then hits the piece of ice with the airborne runner, which is more durable than the side of the sled. "That's how I protect my sled," he says. "I always hit everything with those aluminum runners first. I make sure of that." He also reinforces the sides of his sled with thick plastic, which prevents the individual stanchions from getting caught up on a jagged piece of ice.

If he can't avoid or control a crash, he has one plan of last resort, which explains why he has such big forearms: "I just never let go. I never let that handlebar go. I only need to put one hand around there, that's enough." With just one of his immense forearms, he can twist a 150 kilogram sled upright, an incredible feat of strength that most mushers find difficult with both arms. "Sometimes," he adds, "you really get banged. Then I just call the dogs to stop."

On the jumble ice between Carmacks and McCabe Creek, Kleedehn was crashing all over the place. It was still snowing heavily, which, mercifully, cushioned the impact when bouncing along the ice and filled in some of the larger cracks and divots in the surface, saving Kleedehn—and his dogs—from injury.

When he arrived at Jerry Kruse's farm, early in the morning, his arms, kidneys, and hips were bruised. He needed a good, long rest.

So, it turned out, did everybody. Soon, the little hut at the farm was brimming with mushers, some trying to sleep on the floor or on the bare wooden pallets stacked along the wall in makeshift bunks. The conversation, after the hell of the trail the night before, was convivial, the chili was excellent, and the coffee was hot. "This," said one musher, "is what the Quest is all about." Even William Kleedehn seemed to enjoy the environment, which looked suspiciously like the kaffeeklatsch he had railed against only the night before.

Kleedehn had been caught by two other mushers, both of whom had come to the Quest from the Iditarod, expecting to win. One was Tim Osmar, a bearded, thirty-four-year-old fisherman from Alaska's Kenai peninsula. This was Osmar's second Quest—he'd run it for the first time when he was nineteen and finished third. Osmar—the closest thing there is to a professional musher—was planning to run in the Iditarod, a race he is much more familiar with, just a week after the crossing the Quest's finish line. The other musher was David Sawatzky, a coal miner from Healy, Alaska, who hadn't raced in the Quest since 1994.

WHILE WILLIAM KLEEDEHN, Tim Osmar, and David Sawatzky were enjoying Jerry Kruse's hospitality, Joran Freeman, down to ten dogs, was labouring through the jumble ice, covered now by a thick layer of fresh snow.

Leaving Carmacks, at least all his dogs were pulling in front of him. However, an hour after leaving the checkpoint, Rocky began limping and favouring his shoulder. Sore feet are one thing—with good care they will heal as the race goes on—but an injured shoulder isn't likely to improve, and may well get worse. So, in a now-familiar routine, he stopped, unhooked Rocky, carried him back to the sled, and clipped him in.

He continued along until he noticed that Clive, one of the dogs he'd borrowed from Tony Blanford, was urinating blood. This, in itself, can mean a host of things, not all of them serious, but Freeman also noticed that Clive's demeanour was off; he seemed to lack confidence. Then, the dog started to wobble, suggesting, at worst, that it was close to collapsing.

Freeman stopped immediately, picked Clive up, and packed him along with Rocky.

Bashing into trees once again, he tried to continue, and, once on the Yukon River, he spilled dogs every time he bounced off one of the ice chunks. At one point, the ice tore the runner plastic off the bottom of his sled. He had to stop and, carefully, replace it.

Freeman's Quest was quickly becoming a major fiasco. He had had a successful training season, and in a tune-up race for the Quest his dogs had performed well. He knew he had a decent team: fast enough, he believed, to finish among the top five teams. But now, when typical middle-of-the-pack mushers were passing him like he was standing still, despair was gnawing at his faith in his dogs and himself. For the first time in his mushing career, he wondered why he was bothering to compete.

Somehow he navigated his way through the jumble ice on the Yukon River crossings and made his way up McCabe Creek to the Kruse homestead, seventy kilometres from Carmacks. He arrived in the middle of the afternoon, just as William Kleedehn was packing up and getting ready to go after resting there for nearly nine hours.

Freeman was 300 kilometres into the race and had lost nearly half his dog team. The leaders of the race were all still running either thirteen or fourteen dogs, a considerable horsepower advantage, particularly with the Black Hills, Eureka, and King Solomon's Dome—the highest point in the race—coming up in another couple of hundred kilometres. It didn't bode well.

He could see no way to continue competitively, and he had come to race. Earlier, he had talked to other mushers who had scratched in previous Quests. Their advice: wait one day. If you still want to give up then, okay, but a mind can change given distance from disaster.

"I know that anything can happen in a dog race," he said, repeating an oft-heard mantra on the Quest, "that you have to make the best of whatever you have, but even so, just being behind and feeling like I am not a part of that front-running race is real hard on me."

He decided to wait nine hours, let his eight dogs sleep well, and then re-evaluate.

THE TRAIL FROM MCCABE CREEK to Pelly Crossing runs along the Kruse driveway for several kilometres before crossing the Klondike Highway and travelling in the roadside ditch for several more kilometres. Then the trail leaves the road, travelling through the Pelly Burn, a hilly, wooded section of trail with swamps and lakes.

It's an eerie landscape that provides a stark reminder of the powerful immediacy of nature in the North.

In June 1995, three massive forest fires burned between Carmacks and Pelly Crossing, all of them started by lightning. Pelly Crossing was evacuated, but only five cabins were destroyed. By the end of the summer, 140,000 hectares of forest—nearly 900 square kilometres—had been burned to a crisp, and the Canadian Department of Northern Affairs had spent $3.7 million to fight the fires.

What was once a pleasant, spruce-filled landscape, home to thousands of birds, black bears, and wolves, had become a collection of blackened spires standing on a bed of grey ash, the sounds of wildlife silenced.

The following winter, accusations were levelled that not enough work had been done to protect the five cabins that were lost, and that few resources had been made available to fight the blaze. A report revealed the fact that senior fire officials had been taking their holidays at the height of the fire season, and even area residents who had offered their own earth-moving equipment, like Jerry Kruse, had received no response to their willingness to help.

Although fires in remote areas should burn naturally—it's part of the natural regeneration of an aging forest—the report supported the accusations that insufficient action had been taken to protect aboriginal land. Nearly a quarter of the territory of the Selkirk First Nation, based in Pelly Crossing, was destroyed.

In the end, however, the area inhabitants probably came out ahead: a bumper crop of morel mushrooms, which thrive in scorched soil, grew on the forest floor. The mushrooms drew pickers from across the world and earned the First Nation a tidy sum from exports to buyers in France and other European countries. Brightly coloured tents and aging Airstream trailers were parked alongside the Klondike Highway for weeks.

Several years on, the forest is finally growing back, with saplings sprouting underneath the still-standing husks and brilliant pink fireweed blossoming every spring. In the winter, however, when snow covers the regenerating forest floor, it presents a stark, sterile, savage beauty.

Pelly Crossing has been the home of the central Northern Tutchone, whose Yukon roots stretch back thousands of years, for only about fifty years. It has a school, a curling rink, a community centre, and no restaurant, except in the summer, when a roadside hamburger stand opens up. But about sixty kilometres west of Pelly Crossing, the Quest trail passes within several hundred metres of what must surely be the spiritual home of the people who now live where the Klondike Highway crosses the Pelly River.

Fort Selkirk, at the confluence of the Yukon and Pelly Rivers, is the oldest known permanent settlement in the Yukon, and probably its most historically significant. It is accessible only by water or air—or dog team—which probably explains why the abandoned buildings are so well preserved. Stone tools have been found dating back 10,000 years, and 1.3-million-year-old fossilized caribou bones have been discovered nearby. There are, these days, fewer than a thousand visitors a year to the site.

As far back as anyone can remember, and longer, this has been a meeting and trading place. The coastal Tlingit Chilkat people, who lived on the Alaska Panhandle, would travel up through what is now Kluane National Park to exchange goods with the Northern Tutchone. They brought walrus ivory, shells, seal fat, and clams in exchange for furs, hides, and clothing. Starting in 1790, they also brought European guns, tea, and tobacco—half a century before the Northern Tutchone would encounter European traders face to face.

The first white man arrived there in 1848. Robert Campbell, a trader with the Hudson's Bay Company, paddled down the Pelly River and established a trading post there, naming the site for the fifth Earl of Selkirk. He began receiving supplies from Fort Yukon, a Gwich'in settlement farther down the Yukon River, above the Arctic Circle, and, as a result, he began, inadvertently, to compete with the Chilkat for trade with the Northern Tutchone. This apparently didn't sit very well with the Chilkat: they pillaged the fort in 1852, tied Campbell to a raft, and sent him floating, helpless, down the river.

He was rescued by the Selkirk chief, but the experience evidently soured Campbell on the Yukon. So much so, in fact, that he donned a pair of snowshoes and walked all the way to Minnesota. He eventually wound up in Montreal.

Appropriately, there is a highway in the Yukon named after him.

No European returned to trade with the Northern Tutchone there for forty years, until an American named Arthur Harper opened shop. The Hudson's Bay Company returned in 1938, only to shut down thirteen years later when the fort was abandoned following the construction of a new highway connecting Whitehorse and Dawson City. The highway signalled the end of the sternwheelers that had stopped at Fort Selkirk on their trips between the first and second cities of the territory.

At the turn of the century, Anglican and Catholic missions and schools were established, and the North West Mounted Police and Yukon Field Force arrived to keep order among the rowdy Klondike stampeders. Fort Selkirk was a well-run town with a mixed European and native culture, which is more than can be said for Dawson City, where natives were relegated to slums on the outskirts.

By the 1950s, pretty much all of the residents of Fort Selkirk had moved to Pelly Crossing. One of the last to leave was Maria Van Bibber. Maria had been born there in the town's heyday, when there were even rumours that Fort Selkirk was going to be made the capital of the Yukon. Indeed, in 1898, as the sternwheelers docked at the fort—sometimes three or four at a time—visitors enjoyed the amenities of a gold rush boom town, including several hotels.

"It was very sad when the last paddlewheeler left in the fall," Van Bibber reminisces, remembering the harsh, lonely winters of her youth. "It would be tooting its horn as it went around the corner," she adds, motioning upriver with her arm. "But in the spring, when they came back, we were very happy. We knew we were going to get fresh fruit."

Today, all that remains of Fort Selkirk is the schoolhouse, the church, and a few other buildings. There is a government campground, whose residents are usually canoeists making the two-week trip downriver from Whitehorse to Dawson City.

Danny Roberts was the last person to live permanently at Fort Selkirk. He and his family moved to Pelly Crossing in 1956, although he maintained a trapline near the fort until 1995. "There's a big pile of rocks where my house used to be," he told me, the lines on his face curled with laughter. Even after everyone else had left, Roberts remained, chopping wood and looking after the campground in the summer. He worked as a heritage interpreter there until illness forced him to stop. He died in 2000, at the age of seventy-six.

In the last twenty years, the Yukon Government has spent more than $2 million in research, archeology, and building restoration, and the site is now jointly managed by the government and the First Nation, which settled its land claim in 1998.

Today, in winter, Fort Selkirk sits alone, uninhabited, its hoar-frosted cabins surrounded by snowdrifts. In Pelly Crossing, when night falls, wood smoke hangs low in the sky as the temperature drops. The bannock and moose stew are warmed and waiting for the Quest mushers to arrive.

HUP!

At MCCABE CREEK, Joran Freeman decided to give the team one more shot. Pelly Crossing, the next checkpoint, was only fifty kilometres away, about a three-and-a-half hour run on a relatively straightforward trail, and he could scratch there if he had to. "Okay, guys," he said, as the team pulled out of the farmyard and along the long driveway.

The team barely moved. They stopped. They peed. They dumped. They looked back repeatedly, a sign of competitive apathy. After crossing the Klondike Highway, the leaders ignored his commands and turned the wrong way. Freeman had to stop the sled, wade through deep snow to the leaders, and drag them back to the trail. The sloppy pattern continued for another three kilometres or so.

Then Freeman decided he'd had enough.

"We've seen the low," he thought. "It's time for some high."

Freeman is not the sort of musher who jabbers constantly to his team during the race, or even says much at all. The fewer words he uses, the more receptive his dogs will be to his commands. But, faced with few other options, he decided to risk crying wolf. So he whistled, and shouted "Hup," his signal to the team to pick up the pace. It's a signal used sparingly by mushers; overuse it and the dogs will begin to ignore it, and when a musher really needs to whistle them up, near a finish line, they won't respond. It's like the turbo-boost in a race-car arcade game. You only get a couple to use, and when they're gone, they're gone.

Training a dog to listen to, and respond to, a musher's commands is a process that begins when it is only a few months old, a process that begins with merely getting the puppy used to the idea of running in a harness. All sled dogs will pull; that is their instinct, their purpose, in the way a border collie will herd or a Labrador retriever will fetch. (Most sled dogs, if you throw a stick for them, look at you blankly, if they pay any attention at all.)

As the puppy gets used to wearing a harness, mushers will gradually introduce it to running with a team, or alongside a team, wearing a harness but not actually attached to the gangline. Eventually, the dog, as it gets used to the idea, is put into a small team pulling a small sled, until it has learned basic commands.

Sled dogs are not, generally, pets, and so they are not taught to "sit," "stay," "come," "lie down," "hurry up," or any of the other commands that help a pet dog adapt to an urban lifestyle surrounded by humans.

Some people assume that, because they are not taught these things, they are wild, unruly, and nasty. This is not true. They are still dogs, and most dogs, by nature, are friendly, enjoy attention from humans, and derive great pleasure from pleasing their owners. Certainly, when a sled dog is brought inside a house, it might pee on the floor. And it will try to get up on the kitchen counter—that's where the food is, after all. But sled dogs are rarely inside houses.

These dogs learn a set of commands that are useful for their lifestyle. There is not much point in teaching a dog that spends the majority of its life outside a command to make it go to the bathroom. It goes when it pleases.

Instead, sled dogs are taught a command that urges them to turn left ("haw"), or right ("gee"), or to go straight ahead, speed up, or slow down. They are taught to ignore a team of dogs that they are passing within a few centimetres. They are taught to do a U-turn.

And whereas a person will teach a pet dog to sit using treats, sled dogs, when they are learning their commands, have much more appropriate instructors: their colleagues. A musher teaches a young sled dog the command to turn left by pairing it, in the team, with a leader who knows the commands well. When the musher calls "haw," the experienced leader will respond, pulling his junior counterpart with him. Soon the younger dog will learn, by repetition, what "haw" means, and will begin to turn on the command herself.

Like pet dogs, some sled dogs are more intelligent than others, and better at learning and remembering commands, at concentrating on the task at hand. They get to be leaders. Dogs that are less able to learn commands are placed back in the team, so they simply follow the dogs in front.

A typical sled dog team has two leaders in front, and the pair immediately behind them, called swing dogs, are often leaders-in-training. The rest of the dogs don't need to be experts at following commands. The pair of dogs closest to the sled, called the wheel dogs, tend to be the strongest on the team, because they are the dogs that physically turn the sled when it goes around a tight corner.

There is more, of course, to running dogs than simply ensuring that they learn their commands. Communication between musher and dogs is a subtle and evolved trust relationship. Dogs are, by nature, social animals, and, unlike people and cats, which have strong individualist traits, dogs need to know their place within their immediate world. There will always be a hierarchy among the dogs in the yard and on the team. The musher's role in this is complex: he has to make sure that he stays on the top of that hierarchy, making himself the alpha dog on the team. Along with this, the musher is chief coach, cheerleader, trainer, and disciplinarian. An experienced musher, who has spent hours and hours alone with his dogs, knows what they are capable of, and won't ask them to do something they can't do. Sled dogs are trained incrementally, by the musher setting goals the dogs can attain, challenging them a little more—to run a little faster, a little longer, each time—and each time returning home to the comfort of their houses, building a trust relationship.

A musher will address the dogs in the same even, friendly tone, even when circumstances seem dire. When a musher is being dragged by a snow hook caught in the sole of his boot, he must issue the "stop" command—"whoa"—in a calm, relaxed tone. Getting dogs to stop, especially when they are fresh, is a challenge for even the most experienced musher. "Whoa" is the least understood of all sled dog commands to begin with, and screaming the command at them loudly will confuse and excite them. When they get excited, they go faster.

Right at this point, Joran Freeman, on the verge of quitting, figured his dogs could stand a little excitement. So he hupped and whistled and gave them cheers of encouragement. And, slowly but steadily, the dogs responded.

Freeman knew most of his remaining dogs very well. There are advantages to travelling with eight dogs instead of fourteen. The sled is lighter, carrying less food and weight, and more manoeuvrable. A string of eight dogs stretches out only half the distance of fourteen. It's six fewer mouths to feed, and twenty-four fewer feet to put booties on when it's forty below.

The dogs and Freeman were spurred on by each other's enthusiasm, and, in very little time, they were charging down the trail like champions. He now had a team he could compete with.

Coming along the road, under the sparkling northern lights, Joran Freeman and his dogs were moving along so well that he thought he might just grab a few things in Pelly Crossing and continue straight on through. But then he let reason get the better of him. He decided to stop, rest, and see what the race leaders were doing.

When he got there, the first six mushers had left. He was still in seventeenth place. But after resting for only four hours, he left in twelfth, less than six hours behind David Sawatzky, who had also rested there. William Kleedehn, who had passed through, would have to take a long rest at Stepping Stone, only fifty kilometres down the trail.

The northern lights, as Freeman noticed, were swirling around the sky that Tuesday night. Even though they are a reasonably regular show in the northern night sky, people stop everywhere and watch. Occasionally, they change from their common white and green colour to a dancing magenta blaze. Drivers pull over to the side of the road to watch; excitement at seeing the aurora borealis, however common, never seems to fade.

The northern lights are perhaps among the most famous of the Arctic's attributes, but, really, it is the quality of light during the day that is the North's most distinctive trait. In the winter, twilight rules.

The sun spends very little time above the horizon between November and March: several hours a day, at best—usually in your eyes when you're trying to drive—and most of the light is incidental, reflected from a source below the horizon. The day is divided largely between the glow of the pre-dawn and a long evening embrace.

The southern Yukon and Alaskan winter night ends with the sky fading from black to a purple glow that hovers for an hour, gradually extinguishing the stars as it grows to pink and then to orange as the sun rides its oblique path towards the sky. In neither winter nor summer does the northern sun rise in the east or set in the west. In the winter, it kind of pops over the horizon somewhere to the south-southeast at the apex of an upside-down U-turn and then drops back off to the south-southwest. In the summer, it seems to rise in the south, float lazily around in a circle, and briefly drop back from whence it came before re-emerging in almost the same spot. For a precious several days, it doesn't go down at all.

When the sun has risen above the trees—where, in February, it stays for five or six hours a day—it casts the quality of light available in southern latitudes for but a few minutes, at sunrise and sunset, when the sun is just above the horizon, its rays refracted through a thicker swath of the earth's atmosphere. It's the light that film director Stanley Kubrick called "magic time," the warm, creamy glow that causes trees and snow and mountainsides to appear as though they are the source of the light and not merely reflecting it. The landscape looks as though rendered through pink-tinted polarized sunglasses.

The light gets briefly warmer as the sun dips back below the mountaintops, fading to orange, then pink again. Stars begin to shine again through a shadowy mauve canvas. An hour later, the black has returned, a blank slate.

Then, if the electromagnetic conditions are right, a thin wisp of greenish-white light starts to slither across a corner of the sky. It looks as though it could be a plume of smoke, or perhaps an errant cirrus cloud in an otherwise clear sky. Then another plume of light appears, and, within seconds, the sky is alive with a pale-green fire that swirls to and fro, expanding across the horizon one minute, shrinking to a thin stream in the middle of the sky the next. As the lights grow, they change in colour, from white to green to a purply magenta, often all in the same stream, so that the sky looks like a giant green curtain spread across a screen of stars, with a pulsing red hem.

The show can last minutes or hours, and go and come back. It can last all night, crawling away only as the pre-dawn light creeps onto the horizon.

If it's really cold, some people swear they can hear the lights hissing and crackling.

IT WAS ONE OF THOSE NIGHTS on the third night of the Yukon Quest. The clear skies of a pleasant day meant there was nothing to trap the sun's heat, and by the time it was pitch black, the temperature had dropped twenty degrees. It was pushing thirty-five below as the aurora borealis began to fire up.

The spectacular display of northern lights that night had an impact on nobody more than Sig Stormo, a Quest rookie from Alaska. He was travelling well behind the leaders and was still on his way to McCabe Creek when the display began.

Seven years before, Stormo, a slight, bearded fisherman, was a thirty-four-year-old single father with a twelve-year-old daughter, Jessica. They lived well out of town, on the Funny River, near the town of Soldotna, not far from Anchorage. Jessica was heading into that age when teenage girls get sullen, and Stormo was having trouble relating to her. He felt he was losing contact. She was getting into trouble at school and was in danger of failing her grade.

Stormo tried talking to Jessica, and he tried to be her friend. It didn't work. He was worried he'd lose her to that sullenness and depression.

His friend, Tim Osmar, with whom he had grown up in nearby Clam Gulch, had a suggestion: get her some dogs, and give her some responsibility.

Stormo went along with the idea, and he and Jessica began running dogs together.

"We started dogs," Stormo says, "and it just changed everybody's whole attitude." Jessica began sharing her life with the dogs, and sharing her life with her father. In the dogs, they found common ground, an activity that fostered an honest friendship and saw them become more like brother and sister than father and daughter. Her grades—and, more important, her moods and outlook—improved.

Jessica's interest in the dogs became a driving ambition. She competed twice in the Junior Iditarod, a 250-kilometre race run in two stages with a ten-hour camp in between. Her dream was to run a real long-distance race, like the Iditarod or the Quest, and she was steadily training, working towards that goal.

Eight months after she finished her second Junior Iditarod, when she was sixteen, she was driving home from school and lost control of her car. It swerved off the road, and she was killed.

Stormo didn't know what to do. Beside himself with grief, he barely took care of the dogs, much less himself. He couldn't bear to look at the dogs Jessica adored so much.

"I hardly fed them. She fed them and took care of them and combed them. For a long time they never got combed or petted or anything. I hate to say it, but it was sort of hard to go and see them. I'd see them, I'd see my daughter."

It took more than a year, but Stormo eventually found the strength to try to carry out his daughter's dream. Five of her dogs were in his team in this race.

When Jessica completed her second Junior Iditarod, she spoke, in her speech at the finishing banquet, about the thrill of being alone with her dogs under a sky swirling with northern lights. "Our big thing was the northern lights," Stormo remembers. "This is a lot of why I'm here, for her and me. Sure it's for me, and it's a lot of my own dream, too, and it's finding my own peace. I asked many times, *why, why,* and I don't know. Maybe someday I will know through this."

He would like to see her smile again, he said. And sitting at a table in the old curling rink at Pelly Crossing, Stormo, smiling himself, would say he believed he saw her that night.

But Stormo still had the Yukon River to contend with. It was just over ten kilometres of trail—barely a spoonful in a bucket—but it had the mushers talking, and worrying.

Stormo was running along the trail, on the river, when suddenly his team vanished before him over a drop nearly two metres high. Then, several metres farther along, he had to try to help the dogs get his sled up the other side of the crevasse-like gully, the dogs straining to get purchase on the ice. Then the same thing happened again, as the trail dropped off another ice chunk. Over and over, he found himself climbing over huge chunks of ice. It was like driving a dog team up and down a set of stadium bleachers. The best he could do when dropping off the ice chunks was to try to balance himself between the runners and hope he dropped straight down. Each time the sled hit the ice below, he felt its entire shape bend as it flexed to absorb the impact. Then, more often than not, there was a sharp turn at the bottom of the drop that spun the sled sideways, usually tipping it over. "When I say drop, I'm not talking a casual drop. It was out of the blue. You're going straight down and you're thinking, 'This is going to hurt.'

"We ran through trees before we got to the river, where you come down this big hill with four or five turns in the trail as it went between the trees. It was like a pinball machine in there, because you're bouncing off of trees. I got through that thinking, wow, you know, we made it.

"And then I get on the river."

Stormo careened off one chunk of ice that shattered one of the snowshoes tied to the inside wall of his sled. Another staved in his brush bow.

Getting around the corners, he had to jump off to one side and start running, frantically pushing against the sled to prevent it from tipping over. "There was ice the size of hay bales, sitting in the middle of the trail," he later recalled. "You could see cracks down clear to the water. I've seen a lot of things, but that was intense. Bam! I'm just bouncing off of stuff."

It got worse. Coming off one drop, the front of his sled hit the ice below, jamming the sled into a crack. The dogs, strung out ten metres in front of him, were going in several directions at once, the gangline zigzagging through the jumble ice. Stormo heard a loud bang and looked up to see that the razor-sharp ice had severed his gangline. The team was held together, literally, by one dog, whose neckline was attached to the front half of the gangline and whose tugline was holding on to the back half of the team.

Laying the sled on its side, he ran up with a spare piece of rope and tied the two sections together before the front dogs pulled the team—and the dog—apart.

Stormo wondered just what on earth he was doing in the middle of the Yukon River in the middle of nowhere and the middle of the night.

"I was all alone out there, and I guess you do a lot of soul-searching. I was just going through pure hell, and I look up, and here's the northern lights, and I'm going, 'You're laughing at me now, huh sis?' That's what kept my mind in it."

MEANWHILE, AT THE FRONT OF THE PACK, William Kleedehn had just demonstrated that, for the time being at least, he meant what he was saying about not hanging around, about wanting to race.

Pulling into the Pelly Crossing checkpoint—first, again—he set his snow hook but didn't park his team. He walked over to his drop bags, sorted through them for a minute, and grabbed some things, including one of his bales of straw. He came back to the sled and tied the bale of straw on top, putting the other things—

food, mainly—in the sled bag. Then, with a whistle, he was gone, having spent a grand total of eighteen minutes at the checkpoint.

All of teams that followed him in—David Sawatzky, Tim Osmar, John Schandelmeier, and Frank Turner, who all arrived within an hour and a half of Kleedehn—stopped to rest. Going straight through a checkpoint wasn't part of their race plan.

Next to the Coke machine in the lobby of the Pelly Crossing curling rink, John Schandelmeier was sleeping. For some reason, he had decided against using the area at the other end of the curling rink, a room reserved for mushers, and instead was curled up between the soft-drink dispenser and a table where several reporters were sitting.

A tall, bearded man walked through, wearing a lumberjacket and looking haggard. It wasn't the beard, or even the slouching gait, or the sloshing, half-drunk coffee in the Styrofoam cup. It was the eyes. They call it the thousand-mile stare, but you get it a lot sooner than that.

It's three days into the race when the lack of sleep really starts to catch up with the racers. Mushers get so tired, they will fall asleep standing up on the sled runners, or next to a clanging Coke machine. It affects reporters, too, around this stage. Mardy Derby, a CBC Radio reporter from Whitehorse, somehow thought it would be practical to try to dry out a pair of her underwear in a microwave oven. It didn't work.

The bearded man walked through the room and back outside, not bothering to acknowledge any of the other people in the room. He looked fearsome.

David Sawatzky was one of the most experienced mushers in the race, a nine-time veteran of the Quest, and, like Tim Osmar, an Iditarod crossover. He was also, along with Osmar, a favourite to win.

Born in southern Minnesota in 1952, Sawatzky married his high-school sweetheart, Jeanne, in 1971, the year they both graduated. They are still married, and she is the only dog handler he has ever had.

When they got married, he says, they had a dream of moving to Alaska one day. Three or four years after their wedding, several of their friends moved from Minnesota to Alaska to work on the Alyeska Pipeline, which moves oil from the rich fields of the Alaskan North Slope at Prudhoe Bay to Anchorage, where it can be loaded onto tankers and shipped around the world.

"We said we should go," he recalls, "but we didn't."

Instead, they stayed in Minnesota, where Sawatzky worked on his own as an interior decorator, doing drywall, painting, installing kitchen cabinets, and the like.

In 1981, during a recession in Minnesota, he and Jeanne moved two states westward, where he a got a job at an oil field in Montana. A year and a half later, he got laid off.

"Well, we've always wanted to go to Alaska," Jeanne told him. "Let's go to Alaska."

"You're crazy," he replied.

Three weeks later, they were on their way. It was 1983, the summer before the first Yukon Quest began.

They wound up in Healy, a small, sleepy town on the northern edge of Denali National Park. Sawatzky got a job at the coal mine there. Eighteen years later, he's the foreman, and a senior heavy-equipment operator, with one of the better-paying jobs in the state.

One of their friends in Healy had twenty sled dogs, and, from time to time, Sawatzky would go out mushing with him. Then he started borrowing the dogs, and the obsession grew.

"This is crazy," he remembers thinking one day after he'd borrowed his friend's dog team for the umpteenth time. "We should get our own dogs."

So he did, mostly cast-off trapline dogs, big, slow, and strong mutts, heavier and woolier than the dogs used for racing. Soon they had twelve dogs of their own.

In 1986, he went to watch the start of the Yukon Quest in Fairbanks, which is a two-hour drive to the north. Another nearby friend, who was running the race, had said he was going to sell all his dogs at the end of the Quest. "I told him to call when he got back to Fairbanks."

He called, and, $2,700 later, Sawatzky had nine racing sled dogs and a sled. These days, he points out, mushers easily pay that much for a single dog. "We figured we would play around with those dogs for a couple of years, running some shorter, mid-distance races, and then maybe the Yukon Quest."

The following year, Sawatzky competed in the Quest. So much for the shorter, mid-distance races. Not surprisingly, he had no idea what he was in for. "That was a real eye-opener for me," he admits. "I'd never been out on a trail like that for an extended period of time. I'd done some camping trips, but never just going off on a race like this, not knowing at all where you're going."

Still, Sawatzky had enough fun that he came back the following year, but he scratched at the 500-kilometre mark when his team picked up a virus. In 1989 he was sixteenth, eighth in 1990, fourth in 1991, fifth in 1992, and third in 1993. He was convinced that 1994 was his year until he got to Angel Creek, the first checkpoint in the race that started that year in Fairbanks, and accidentally drove a hunting knife through his finger. Rick Swenson, the only musher to have won the Iditarod five times, offered him $10,000 for his leader. He declined.

However, by that point, he'd had enough of the Quest. He swore he'd never run the frustrating race again.

He decided to try his luck on the Iditarod, which offered a $350,000 purse compared with the Quest's meagre $50,000. His first year, he was rookie of the year, coming fifteenth, and in following years he placed well, although he never came close to winning.

So this year, his resolution notwithstanding, he had come back to the more physical, but less competitive, purist's race. And he'd come to win.

David Sawatzky is a big guy, about six-foot four, and he doesn't seem to believe in space-age insulating fabrics. Even in forty-below temperatures, he wears only a lumberjacket and a pair of Carharrt overalls. He looks mean, talks gruffly, and appears older and more crotchety than his fifty years would suggest. He scares the media, who back away, which is just fine with him.

The bluster, however, is all show. There are few mushers, it turns out, who are better gentlemen. Sawatzky is a gracious competitor, friendly, and, what's more, his wife, Jeanne, is lovely. They finish each other's sentences. They live north of Denali National Park on property they bought in 2000 for their seventy-odd dogs. In the interests of neighbourhood relations—that is, neighbours' sleep—they left Healy.

Sawatzky had had a horrible training season, like most mushers in the southern half of Alaska. There had been little snow, and the largest number of dogs he'd managed to hook up to a sled was six. Any more risked a loss of control on nearly bare ground and near rivers and lakes scarcely frozen.

Still, with a good team and the competitive experience of numerous Quests, plus the exposure to the ruthless racing that typifies the Iditarod, he considered himself a contender for the top three. Winning, he said, is a "primary" goal.

Sawatzky took fifteen dogs to Whitehorse for the start of the race. He was sure of thirteen of them, but had to decide between two to fill the final spot: Jessie, a four-year-old male who Sawatzky wasn't sure would make it all the way, and Misty, a leader, one of four females on his team, who had just been in heat but was past it.

Or so he thought. Turned out that Misty, upon arriving in Whitehorse, came back into heat.

Mushers rarely spay or neuter their dogs; it wouldn't do much for their breeding programs. However, females in heat can be dangerous to a dog team, making the males ornery, aggressive, and unable to focus on running the race. But with careful attention, they can be kept out of harm's way, and, if the estrus recurrence is temporary (which it should be) it isn't much of a problem. Moreover, with three other females, all of whom had been out of heat for nearly a week, it would be possible for Sawatzky to position her far enough away from the teenaged boys on the team.

Misty, Sawatzky was sure, would finish the race. Jessie, he was equally sure, would not. He told Jeanne he'd be surprised if the dog made it as far as Dawson, being prone to injury. The day before the race started, he decided to take Misty.

This proved to be a bad decision.

By the end of the third day on the trail, Misty brought Maimie, Blackie, and Tipper, the other females in the team, into the same powder room.

One dog in heat is a manageable problem. Two dogs in heat is a real challenge. Three dogs is a nightmare. Four dogs, well, you might as well sit back and let the orgy begin, because you're not doing much else.

Mating dogs are a caricature of themselves. In the 2000 Quest, as a handler for Frank Turner, I watched Frank work on his sled, clearing my throat as loudly as I could (because handlers aren't allowed to offer any assistance at all) as Latte casually leaned over the gangline on the third day of the race and embraced Brandy, the only dog on the team in heat.

If the musher catches dogs in the foreplay stage, he or she can get them apart. He can tie the female off the back of the sled when he's camped so the males can't get at her. But mushers get tired, and they get forgetful. Or, in this case, they get angry at their handler, who had promised, but failed, to bring him from Toronto a new pair of Gore-Tex pants to replace the ones he was wearing. Those would be the pants with the broken side zippers, the ones that he was forced to pull up from around his knees every few minutes while trying to drive his dog team.

Frank missed the foreplay while swearing at me. When he did see, it was too late. Amorous intent had turned into intense passion. It is potentially physically harmful to the female—not to mention impolite—to pry mating dogs apart. And, after all, it was Valentine's Day.

The mating process can take anywhere from twenty minutes to an hour, a long time for the dogs to stand there, embracing, looking around with blank expressions on their faces. They don't always stand in a mounted position, either. Thanks to obvious flexibility, they seem to be able to stand back to back or side to side, the same nonchalant look on their faces.

At the end of it all, the male withdraws and has to get away before the female eats him alive. In this case, Brandy didn't stop snarling at Latte for at least a week.

It's not that you would have noticed that Sawatzky had four dogs in heat. He managed it better than Bruce Milne, a musher from Two Rivers, Alaska, who took twenty-four hours to cover sixty kilometres in the Quest because his female in heat was mated six times. I passed him on the Pelly Farm Road, sitting, again, waiting for the process to finish. "To be frank," he said, "I've had enough of sitting around watching dogs fuck."

No, Sawatzky was holding his own at the front of the pack: third out of Braeburn, second out of Carmacks, second out of Pelly Crossing. It was a testament to his skill as a driver.

THE TRAIL FROM PELLY CROSSING to Dawson City is the longest section between checkpoints on any sled dog race in the world. Mushers must carry enough food and supplies for 326 kilometres of rugged, hilly, cold, wet, moose-infested trail. It takes even the fastest teams more than two complete days, and slow teams may take much longer.

It began, this year, along the road to the Pelly Farm, a working farm some sixty kilometres west of Pelly Crossing, near where the Pelly River flows into the Yukon. Normally, the trail would go along the Pelly River itself, but this year ice conditions on the river were too challenging even for the Canadian Rangers to attempt.

Frank Turner's dogs waiting
to be unloaded from his truck
at the start of the race.

Handlers hold John Schandlemeier's sled back at the start line.

David Sawatzky's team launches off the start of the
Yukon Quest in downtown Whitehorse.

Steve Watson, a tourist
attraction in his own right,
holds up one of his
mammoth cinnamon buns
behind the counter at
Braeburn Lodge.

Jerry Louden and his dogs cross the
Klondike Highway at Braeburn Lodge.

Jim Hendrick's team
approaches McCabe Creek
on the Yukon River.

David Sawatzky snoozes on a work bench
at Jerry Kruse's farm at McCabe Creek.

A team turns off the
Yukon River onto
McCabe Creek.

Bill Pinkham philosophizes at
Stepping Stone.

David Sawatzky arrives
in Dawson City with
Jack in the sled bag.

Joran Freeman
packs his sled.

Inside the dog tent at Camp Turner in Dawson City.

Sebastian Jones's and Shelley Brown's cabin at Fortymile.

Jumble ice near the junction of the Fortymile and Yukon Rivers.

Frank Turner sleeps
on the pool table at
O'Brien Creek Lodge.

CBC reporter Mardy Derby tries to stay awake inside the one-room
schoolhouse that serves as the Eagle Checkpoint; the blackboard
becomes an unofficial race progress chart.

Dropped dogs at Slaven's cabin wait for takeoff.

Jerry Louden pushes his sled as he nears the top of Eagle Summit.

Andrew Lesh shares a joke while cooking dinner for his dogs.

Tim Osmar cracks open a beer after crossing the
finish line at nearly four in the morning.

William Kleedehn chats with
Doug Harris, the race marshal,
at the finish line.

After about fifty kilometres, the trail crosses the Pelly and travels to a peninsula that juts out into the confluence of the Pelly and the Yukon, across the Yukon from Fort Selkirk. There is a camp there, with several cabins, called Stepping Stone.

Owned by Carol and Jim Tredger, Stepping Stone, although on a much smaller scale than Fort Selkirk, is itself a storied, and very rarely visited, Yukon landmark, a fifty-year-old camp that served as one of the first bases of ecotourism in the world.

The area around Stepping Stone is one of the more biologically fertile regions of the territory. Moose are plentiful, and wolves are often heard howling at night.

At just after 5:00 a.m., Joran Freeman pulled the hook on Pelly Crossing and dropped down to cross the Pelly River under the Klondike Highway. He was tired—he hadn't really got any sleep in the four hours he'd spent there—but elated: for the first time in the race, he had left a checkpoint with the same number of dogs he arrived with.

The trail along the Pelly Farm Road, a seldom-used dirt side road that parallels the Pelly River for about forty kilometres, is wide, and, at night, usually dull. Many mushers find it is one of the most difficult sections of trail to stay awake on.

The spark that had ignited Freeman's run into Pelly Crossing—and stopped him from scratching there—somehow went out along the Pelly Farm Road. The team, although intact, was plodding along slowly, with Cim Smyth's team.

Expected by many to be a frontrunner, Smyth, a young musher from Big Lake, Alaska, had had numerous problems so far in the race, and making sure his dogs had commensurate attention had left him well behind the leaders.

A quiet competitor, Smyth, at twenty-four, was the rookie of the year in 2000, his first Quest. He finished seventh, despite having Crohn's disease, an often debilitating inflammation that affects the digestive tract. A winner of the Junior Iditarod, he was the Iditarod rookie of the year in 1996, when he was only twenty.

(His father, Bud Smyth, his handler in this year's race, is an Iditarod legend who once showed up at the start of the race with a system to carry eight dogs in cages on a sled as spares; by rotating dogs, he reasoned, he would never have to stop. He also had a stove that could prepare food while on the move. When race officials saw the rig, however, they wouldn't allow it.)

Although Freeman knew Smyth was having a tough race, with several of his dogs ill and some suffering injuries from stepping in cracks on the jumble ice, he thought Smyth would be a good travelling companion. So they continued along, on the twisty, hilly road.

Just before it reaches the Pelly Farm, the trail veers onto the rumbling, frozen river and crosses it, threading through a series of wooded islands and outcrops. The trail is narrow, bumpy, and distracting: nailed to trees every several hundred metres are hand-written advertisements that call to mushers like sirens after four days of gorp, PowerBars, and whatever other trail food they have been shoving down their throats. "Nachos!" reads one. "Hot Pizza!" promises another. And they continue, for several kilometres, until the trail turns suddenly, climbs a steep hill, and is romantically illuminated by candles placed, Martha Stewart–style, in translucent bags guiding the way to a squat, dark cabin with smoke above, hanging still in the frigid air: Stepping Stone.

Freeman had stopped to snack his dogs at dawn, just before seeing the first sign. It was now cold, pushing thirty below, and the warm cabin was tempting. But he also knew that the trail rose as it headed north from Stepping Stone, and that, with the warmer, higher air, the dogs would rest better. He decided to press on for a couple more hours. The dogs weren't eating that well anyway, and perhaps they would as the day grew warmer.

Mushers try to get into a rhythm of running the dogs when the weather is cooler and resting when it is warmer; the dogs perform better when the temperature is below minus twenty; if it gets above minus ten, especially if it is sunny, they can start to overheat.

Generally, this means mushers will try to avoid running during the heat of the afternoon, when the dogs will sleep better because it will require less energy to keep warm. "Sleep warm, run cold," is the way one musher describes it.

FRANK TURNER WAS AT STEPPING STONE when Freeman passed by.

He had arrived there in the middle of the night, having left Pelly Crossing to the encouragement of his own cheering section of children and elders. The former native band manager there, Turner is the most popular musher to pass through on the Yukon Quest. Frequently, there is a banner strung between trees urging him on. This year, they rang the town's fire-alarm bells for a full ten minutes when he arrived, to let everyone know that Frank was in town. While he likes and appreciates the attention, he often finds it difficult to sleep there.

I had come out hoping to see how Frank was doing. Following the race leaders, I hadn't yet had much chance to speak to him. I had made the two-and-a-half-hour trip from Pelly Crossing by snow machine, with Mark Lindstrom, one of the race officials. We arrived to the Tredgers' warmth.

After eating some of the advertised pizza and chatting for a while, I lay down on the floor behind an old piano to get some sleep.

I woke up, a couple of hours later, shivering. The floor of a not terribly well-insulated cabin is not the best place to curl up when it's thirty below.

Coming back to the wide, circular table lit with candles, I noticed that John Schandelmeier and Frank Turner were involved in a deep discussion. Both of them had arrived while I was asleep.

Schandelmeier has run the Quest nearly as often as Turner has, and is one of only two people to win the race twice. A small, wiry man with a bushy moustache, he's a trapper in Paxson, Alaska, not far from Denali National Park. He is known as one of the best dog men around, and he gives his animals excellent care. In his team this year is a once-feral dog that was accidentally caught in one of his traps; he nursed it back to health, and now it's running for him. He has a soft, gentle sense of humour and mischief. He's also tough as nails.

This year, he's trying out an innovation. Schandelmeier has lousy eyesight, but he can't wear his glasses on the trail because they would constantly fog up under the warmth of his hood. So, in this race, he's taken to wearing a pair of orange-lensed ski goggles over his face, under which he can wear his regular glasses.

It makes for an interesting, if a little strange, sight as he pulls into checkpoints. Known particularly for his frugality—he's worn the same beaten up green army surplus parka for years, and his sled is homemade, with cut-up highway signs reinforcing the stanchions—the sight of him rolling into a checkpoint with a pair of ultra-modern, tinted ski goggles on is mildly incongruous.

Hence the debate. Turner, who deals with the same problem, now wears tiny, steel-rimmed circular glasses when he's on the trail, his theory being that the smaller glass surface gets better air circulation around it and suffers less fogginess.

It also makes him look funny, though, in a different way. Instead of a musher, he looks, with his rangy, Hasidic beard, like a rabbinical scholar trotting along the trail.

Schandelmeier and Turner were trying to convince each other of the merits of their systems. (Later that morning, Carrie Farr would arrive and take her contact lenses out for a soak. These are perhaps the best idea for trail eyewear, but they come with a risk. In 1998, Keizo Funatzu, a Japanese musher in the race, arrived at a checkpoint with one eye bloodied and mostly shut. One of his contact lenses had frozen and shattered while on his eye.)

The conversation was jovial, as dawn was breaking. Finishing their pizza, Schandelmeier and Turner went to the back of the cabin to get some sleep. I put my parka on and returned to my spot on the floor.

INTO THE WHITE SILENCE

WHEN I WOKE UP and walked outside, it was an overcast, bitterly cold morning. Jim Tredger was standing just outside the cabin, where the bag-covered candles sat extinguished. He was looking worried.

"I was coming to get you," he said. "You should talk to Frank. He's going to scratch."

I put my parka back on and walked down towards the river, where Frank was standing with his team. The dogs looked terrible.

Decaf, at the front of the string, was shivering. So was Tank. The rest of the team were curled up, not moving.

"Do you have your cellphone?" Frank was standing dejectedly at the sled. "I need to call Anne and tell her to come back to Pelly Crossing and pick me up."

"Why?"

"Look at these guys. They're done. They won't eat. They won't get up. It's a long way to Dawson from here."

The team did look depressed. In an oversight, the night before he hadn't laid out the blue foam camping mats he carried with him in the sled. The dogs had been lying on bare snow and ice, and there were body-shaped depressions where their heat had melted the snow underneath them.

"My cellphone doesn't work out here," I told him. The Yukon has mobile-phone coverage only around Whitehorse.

"Come on, Frank," I said. "Don't quit. These guys love you. They'll be fine. Everybody gets down sometimes, and they're cold. They'll go."

I felt silly, trying to dispense encouragement and advice to the most experienced Yukon Quest musher around. I expected him to get annoyed with me, to tell me that I didn't know what I was talking about, which was pretty much true. I did know, however, that if he scratched, he would regret it later.

"I don't know," Frank mumbled, and he walked back to the cabin.

I stayed out by the dogs, who looked at me, plaintively. Latte, who usually jumped up to greet me, swished his tail anemically.

Frank came back. "Have you tried the fish?" I asked, referring to the salmon chunks he'd been given by a Whitehorse fish hatchery. I figured he would have.

"No," he replied, shaking his head.

"Why don't you?" I said. I'd never seen him like this, not the year before, when I was handling for him on the race, or this winter, living in his house.

He shrugged, tore open a Ziploc bag full of frozen, apple-sized chunks of raw salmon, and handed them out. Some dogs took the pieces in their mouths, then dropped them, unchewed, on the snow; others just looked dismissively at the fish as he put the frosted, pink chunks down in front of them.

He shook his head and walked away again, not noticing that Tank, the fussiest eater on the team, had begun to nibble on his piece of fish. Slowly, the other dogs began chewing too. Within a minute, all eleven dogs on the team had eaten their treats. Decaf and Tank stood up, shaking themselves off. They looked at me, as if to say, "Well, we're up now. Let's not hang around."

I ran back up to the cabin door, where Frank was talking to Jim Tredger. "Frank," I said, breathlessly, "there are some guys down there waiting for you. They want to go."

Fifteen minutes later, when the sled was loaded up, the team roared over the riverbank and shot off up the trail to Dawson City.

Stepping Stone is about 500 kilometres into the race. Somewhere around that 500-kilometre mark, mushers and their dogs run into what is colloquially called "the wall." It's brought up every year in the rookies' meeting before the race starts. At 500 kilometres, the dogs are getting tired. Their feet are sore. They're sick of this stuff, and they want to sleep. They don't want to eat. It's not a physical barrier; it's psychological. And it's the musher's job to nurse them through it. It means switching leaders, finding one dog who wants to run.

After dogs get past that point in the race, their metabolism has adjusted to the rigours of the run-and-rest cycle, or, as the mushers say, they've become trail-hardened. Their feet get used to the snow and ice. For the most part, dogs that make it past the 500-kilometre mark will finish the race.

Bill Steyer's dogs gave up just north of Stepping Stone. But he rested for twenty-four hours and then kept going. Although that break cost him a position near the front of the pack, his was one of the fastest teams between nearly all the checkpoints for the rest of the race.

It's the same for the musher, too. Sleep deprivation is settling in, it's cold, and every problem is magnified.

"The challenge for me in this race is usually myself. We've been through the cold temperatures, the overflow, Eagle Summit. The really big variable in the race is usually myself, and the way I manage my own emotions," Turner said later of his experience at Stepping Stone. "I can sometimes get on a bit of a roller coaster."

Turner knew, coming into the race, that this was a rebuilding year for him: he had several young dogs, and, gradually, the veterans on his 1995 record pace–setting team were retiring. He had decided he wasn't going to push the envelope, and because he knew he wasn't likely to win, he would use this race as a chance for the younger dogs to get the experience they needed for future races, where he could be more competitive. He knew there would be moments when the dogs would find it difficult; he hadn't counted on the drive of his own competitive urge. "I found it kind of hard to balance my desire to race with my plan not to race, and it created some inner tension for me. I wasn't having a good time. It was a real internal struggle. You look at the dogs, and the glass— is it half full or half empty? Well, everything was half empty for me at that point. I should know by now that the dogs usually are going to rise to the occasion. I've never had a dog team in the Quest that's quit on me or really even come close to quitting on me."

From Stepping Stone the trail turns onto a mining road, called a "cat" road after the Caterpillar bulldozers used to move earth at mine sites. Mushers follow this for about 110 kilometres, climbing and dropping repeatedly through woods, with the road often covered by wet or glaciated overflow at the bottoms of hills. Eventually, the trail reaches the Stewart River, another major tributary of the Yukon, and there, the Canadian Rangers set up a camp at Scroggie Creek where a veterinarian is flown in, as well as enough steak for every musher in the race.

The Scroggie Creek camp is little more than a cramped, four-metre by four-metre cabin that, before the Rangers come out and insulate it, has four-centimetre gaps between the logs. Behind the cabin is a heavy white canvas tent about three metres wide and five metres deep with no floor (save a blue tarpaulin spread out over the snow), held up by a frame of hand-hewn spruce trunks cut from the nearby forest, tied neatly together with yellow nylon rope. A piece of scrap plywood is tied, with similar rope, to one of the trunks. "Vet," it says in scrawled letters, though it might as well say, *à la* Charlie Brown, "The Doctor Is In."

Straw bales are piled at the side of the tent, but not for general use by mushers. These are what pass for veterinary hospital beds. Near the tent, sheltered from the wind in a grove of trees, is the infirmary: a chain strung out, to which the dropped dogs are attached, to recuperate on the straw while waiting for their flight to Dawson City. It's a bargain: fifty dollars a dog, postpaid, and the dog is taken to the next checkpoint with road access, and the arms of a waiting handler. Or, in the case of Dawson City, to the animal shelter, where the handler can go and pick the dog up.

Getting a dog on a plane is no easy task, particularly if it doesn't really want to go. Most sled dogs, to be sure, are docile creatures, used to being handled by different people. But some dogs are cranky, tired, and, if they have a sore shoulder, resistant to human contact.

To go in a plane, most dogs are put into burlap or canvas bags that cover their legs and leave just their heads exposed, which prevents them from moving around in a small plane and potentially creating havoc. One pilot recalls two dogs who actually got in a fight while being flown to a checkpoint. "They were barking, and snapping, and I couldn't reach back to pull them away from each other." So he let gravity—or lack thereof—do it for him, dropping into a steep dive. The dogs were so startled by the effect of the dive that they forgot about antagonizing each other and were quiet for the rest of the trip.

AFTER STOPPING TO CONFER with Frank Turner about a sick dog, Cim Smyth carried on past Stepping Stone, with Freeman, and then Turner, right behind. Smyth stopped to camp, but Freeman's dogs were moving well, and he didn't want to lose the momentum. Again, as the sun rose to its meagre zenith, Freeman felt as though he'd been given a new lease to race. Like a marathon runner, he got into a pick-off mode, spotting teams ahead that were labouring on the hills terraced by the Scroggie Creek Road.

ONE HUNDRED KILOMETRES AHEAD of Freeman, David Sawatzky had moved into the lead of the Yukon Quest. He was alternating with Tim Osmar, having already passed William Kleedehn, who was resting his dogs at Stepping Stone.

Somewhere between Stepping Stone and Scroggie Creek, however, things started to get a little difficult for Sawatzky, and the pressure of four days' worth of canine testosterone was building. The males stopped eating, more interested in growling at each other and jockeying for position among the females.

Each time he stopped to camp, they wouldn't lie down. Or they would, and then they would get up every five minutes to bark or growl. They were getting thin and tired.

The trail to the camp seemed to be taking the team forever. After going through Stepping Stone, Sawatzky and Osmar camped a little way up a nearby hill. Then, they calculated, a seven-hour trip to Scroggie Creek.

Seven hours came and went, but no sign of the camp. Sawatzky and Osmar stopped and looked around. "God, I remember this territory here but it just isn't happening," Sawatzky thought.

A musher appeared from around a bend in the trail. It was Frank Turner. "I feel like I'm on a treadmill," he said as he went by. "I'm going and going and I'm never going to get there."

The temperature was thirty-five degrees below zero, and the dogs were tired. Sawatzky and Osmar decided to camp, and they built a big campfire, which was soon roaring warm. Hugh Neff came by, shivering, but he was determined to press on. "We tried to get him to stop," Sawatzky recalls, "but he was so. . . ." His voice trailed off without finishing the sentence. Andrew Lesh joined them, and, eventually, just as Osmar and Sawatzky were getting ready to leave (Lesh was still snoring, having overslept by two hours), Joran Freeman passed by.

Carrying on just a couple of kilometres, Freeman arrived at the tiny, sweating Scroggie Creek cabin in fourth place, although he knew that would change as those just behind him moved on. He had never really expected to see the leaders again.

During the longer sections of the race, it is virtually impossible to divine which team is winning, because they stop to camp at different places, at different times, and for varying periods of time. Only the mushers know for sure where they stand. Frank Turner, the first musher through Scroggie Creek, was certainly not leading the race. He was, in fact, about six hours behind the leaders, who would later pass him when he stopped to camp several kilometres past the cabin.

When he arrived at Scroggie Creek, Freeman knew he had made up some serious time and had passed numerous teams. He knew, at least, that he was keeping pace with the leaders, if not going faster. At McCabe Creek he'd been nine hours behind the leaders. Sixty kilometres past Stepping Stone, he had made up three hours. The leaders were still running at least thirteen dogs. Freeman, with his eight dogs, was, it seemed, on fire. His dogs were running in step; instead of the jumbled patter of tens of feet haphazardly striking the ground, his dogs were trotting in a single, perfect percussion, like a marching brigade. It was music to his ears.

Although Freeman was obviously at a dog-power disadvantage, any musher will tell you that a well-performing, in-tune eight-dog team—carrying less weight in food and supplies—can match a less organized team with more dogs.

After their six hours' rest, Sawatzky and Osmar left Andrew Lesh sleeping and carried on towards Dawson. Sawatzky's dogs hadn't slept much, though, what with the growling and the barking, and they hadn't eaten much either. It was going to take a lot of careful attention and work in Dawson City to get them back into top form. Sawatzky wasn't sure if he could.

He was travelling about half an hour ahead of Tim Osmar, who had stopped to snack his dogs. And he was coming into the Black Hills, a succession of creek valleys framed by small but annoying mounds covered with dwarf willow and aspen.

Preoccupied by his thoughts about what he had to do in Dawson, Sawatzky let his attention to the trail before him slip.

As he came to the bottom of a hill and moved across the glaciated creek, his sled rode up on the ice, and, sliding on top of the shine with no snow under the runners, it began to slip sideways, farther down. The dogs, feeling the sled lurch, turned in the same direction.

Sawatzky slipped off the runners and fell awkwardly, landing between them with his butt in the ice, his legs crossed, yoga-style. As the sled dragged sideways, Sawatzky twisted his body so he could see where the out-of-control sled was going. Suddenly, the glacier ended in a sharp, short drop-off. As the sled fell over the drop, his right leg slipped underneath the runner. His left leg and the rest of his body were on top of the runner when it hit the ice below.

The combined weight of David Sawatzky and the contents of his sled was about 180 kilograms. It all landed neatly on his right ankle.

He heard—and felt—a snap. He screamed. "Son of a bitch!" he shouted. "I broke my fucking leg."

He managed to shove the sled away, and the startled, stopped dogs, looking back, stood there anxiously.

He was still a good 120 kilometres from Dawson City. And he hadn't packed any painkillers to compensate for the two chips of bone that had shattered from his right ankle, or to ease the sprain he had suffered at the same time in his left.

He taped the ankles with duct tape, and, with some more colourful language, relinquished the lead to Tim Osmar, who had pulled up behind him.

KLONDIKE

LIKE A MONOLITH, King Solomon's Dome looms over the Klondike goldfields. From its gentle slopes flow most of the creeks that spawned the greatest gold rush the world has ever seen. It earned its name from miners searching its sides for the mother-lode, looking for an El Dorado reminiscent of King Solomon's lost mines. At its top, 1,200 metres above sea level, mushers find a commanding view of the goldfields and the stubbly, scrubby ridges that repeat themselves until they merge with the sky.

This marks the highest point on the Quest trail, and, coming from Fairbanks, one of its more frustrating climbs, more than four hours of switchbacks along a narrow road that has a steep wall of mountain on one side and a drop into oblivion on the other. Approaching the ascent from Whitehorse, the rise is more gradual. Mushers, having already gained altitude in the Black Hills and from terracing around Eureka Dome, must now prepare for the dangerous descent to Bonanza Creek, where, in 1896, the Klondike gold rush began. From the top of King Solomon's Dome it is just over fifty-three kilometres to the visitor reception centre in Dawson City, the site of a much-needed thirty-six-hour rest, halfway to Fairbanks.

After more than two hours of switchbacks on the descent, the trail hits a wider road and passes Gold Dredge Number Four, now a museum, on Bonanza Creek.

On August 16, 1896, George Carmack, Skookum Jim, and Tagish Charlie—a white man and two natives—were prospecting on Rabbit Creek, at the foot of King Solomon's Dome. The record is blurry: Jim said Carmack was sleeping under a tree, Carmack said he was not, when a thumb-sized piece of solid gold was found sticking out from bedrock at the side of the creek. As Canadian popular historian Pierre Berton, himself a local boy, described it in *Klondike:*

> . . . the gold was there, lying thick between the flaky slabs of rock like cheese in a sandwich. A single panful yielded a quarter of an ounce . . . this was an incredible find. Carmack flung down the pan and let out a war whoop, and the three men began to perform a wild dance around it—sort of a combination Scottish hornpipe, Indian fox trot, syncopated Irish jig, and Siwash hula.

The following day, after a night spent dreaming of how to spend their riches, the trio staked their claims on Rabbit Creek. August 17, Discovery Day, is a statutory holiday in the Yukon.

That first pan was worth about four dollars, at a time when a dime's worth was considered a good find. Within five days,

Rabbit Creek was renamed Bonanza, and the entire twenty-two-kilometre-long creek had been staked by the end of the month.

A neighbouring, nameless creek soon put Bonanza to shame. Eventually named Eldorado by a literary wit, by the end of the season it would be yielding single pans worth a rumoured $1,000—a king's ransom a century ago.

A wedge-shaped sliver, twenty-metres wide at the thick end, of Bonanza Creek, where the Eldorado flows into it, became the single most valuable piece of real estate ever discovered. Within eight hours, the owner of the claim, Dick Lowe, had pulled out $46,000 worth of gold, and it ended up yielding half a million dollars. It was estimated that at least that much was stolen from the claim as well.

One man, Joe Ladue, who was regarded by many as somewhat of a scam artist, decided to forgo the gold, and instead registered a townsite claim to the swampy flats at the confluence of the Yukon and Klondike rivers, the only place nearby suitable for a settlement.

He built a cabin, which served as a saloon, and a sawmill and a warehouse. He named his mining camp after George M. Dawson, a Canadian government geologist.

By January, there were five houses in Dawson City, and a smattering of ragged, dirty white canvas tents. The following year, he was selling lots at $5,000 apiece. Within two years, it would be the largest city in North America west of Winnipeg and north of San Francisco.

News of the strike was difficult to get out, and, when word of a massive gold find did spread across North America, it was greeted with skepticism. Bureaucrats in Ottawa were unimpressed. It was only the following summer, when two steamers, the *Excelsior* and the *Portland,* arrived carrying three tons of gold between them and the first generation of the Klondike nouveaux riches, that the world took notice. The *Excelsior* arrived first, in San Francisco, and, when word of its cargo got out, more than 5,000 gold-fevered people went to Schwabacher's Dock in Seattle to greet the *Portland,* which arrived two days later.

In the next two years, more than 40,000 men, women, and children would scale the Chilkoot Pass, after enduring the larcenous burg of Skagway, Alaska, to cross the Coast Mountains from the Alaska Panhandle to Bennett Lake, in the headwaters of the Yukon River. There, they would build a boat and float, paddle, or pole their way down the Yukon to Dawson. Like the dot-com crazes and quick market gains of today, however, once everybody knows about a "gold mine," it's too late. The vast majority of the Klondike stampeders left the area destitute, many worse off than when they struggled over the fifty-three-kilometre-long Chilkoot Trail.

TIM OSMAR LED DAVID SAWATZKY over Eureka Dome, and they stopped near the top to rest the dogs.

William Kleedehn was also camped nearby. Sawatzky and Osmar had finally caught him, not so much by chasing, but by patiently following their own run-and-rest schedules. They had all arrived together at the last resting area before the run into Dawson.

Osmar left first, and Sawatzky, his ankles growing in dimension and increasingly painful, followed him. Kleedehn left third.

Kleedehn had broken his run from McCabe Creek to Dawson into a series of four 120-kilometre runs, instead of the usual five 95-kilometre runs. When run equals rest, in theory, both systems should cover the distance in roughly the same amount of time. However, the musher doing the longer runs saves time by having to set up and dismantle one less camp. On a longer run, though, a team might travel more slowly, and this early in the race there is a risk of tiring a team out too soon.

In a 1,600-kilometre race, most mushers start out with shorter runs, to get their teams past "the wall" and to get them used to the race. As the dogs' metabolism changes into race mode, mushers gradually introduce longer runs. Early on, most runs are no longer than 90 or 100 kilometres. On the last leg, a competitive team will usually run 160 kilometres non-stop.

Running behind Sawatzky, Kleedehn, his foot on the brake to keep his team slowed, could see the other musher was having problems. He waited several times while Sawatzky changed leaders around.

This was fine, Kleedehn thought, because one of his own leaders, Chase, was limping slightly. He wanted to hold the team back to see whether Chase's limp would develop into something more serious, or whether it was just a soreness that would go away once he got warmed up and running.

Chase has his name for a reason. As a leader, he gets very excited when he's allowed to pursue other teams. Running behind Sawatzky, he perked right up, seeing another dog team he wanted to catch. Within an hour, the limp was gone.

Easing off the brake, Kleedehn caught the struggling Sawatzky almost immediately, passed him, and left him behind.

Osmar was still ahead, but Kleedehn had no idea how far. An hour or so later, as he began climbing King Solomon's Dome, he caught the glint of Osmar's headlamp several switchbacks ahead.

Chase perked up again. The race was on.

Kleedehn is perhaps at his biggest disadvantage climbing hills. He can run, after a fashion, but he cannot sprint. And, of course, he must keep one hand on the handlebar at all times, lest the team get away from him. "If I lose that handlebar, the sled is gone," he says, bluntly. This is generally true for most mushers, although most are able to lunge or chase after a runaway sled in a way that Kleedehn cannot.

His solution is to carry two ski poles. He ties a piece of rope around his waist, attached to the sled with a snap. Then he balances on the runners, pushing with both poles at the same time like a cross-country skier trying to throw himself across a finish line. It ensures that he remains connected to the sled without having to hold on.

Most of the time, he just uses one pole; that way, he can keep one hand on the sled and steer it around corners. The trail is rarely level and smooth enough that he can use both poles. He goes to the gym, year-round, to practise and to overcome his disability. "I'm a really fit man. I can pole like you wouldn't believe it," he says, and, looking at him, there's little doubt. "Sometimes with the dogs I can push the sled so the gangline is loose all the way," he adds, laughing.

It's the closest thing the Quest has to a lap bonus: the first team to arrive in Dawson City gets four ounces of gold in a poke, the sole condition being that they have to finish the rest of the race— a rule imposed to prevent mushers from burning their dogs out in order to win the gold. The gift of a local jeweller, who usually allows the musher to come and select the nuggets himself or herself, it is a tease worth about $1,000 on current markets.

With this prize in mind, Tim Osmar urged his team to go a little faster for the first time in the race. Osmar has one of Alaska's finest mushing pedigrees. His father was a successful musher, and, between them, they have a kennel of 120 dogs, enough to create two separate teams: one for the Quest, and one for the Iditarod. He hadn't even used his best leader, saving him for the end of the race, should he be in a close run to the finish. Which, the way the race was going so far, he almost certainly would be. Kilo for kilo, he had the best team in the race. He had no females in heat. He hadn't had a single injury or foot problem. He'd dropped one dog, with a sore shoulder, but was still running strong. So far, his race had been about as perfect as it could get.

As he began the descent from the top of King Solomon's Dome, he knew Kleedehn was chasing him and gaining. On Bonanza Creek Road, a scant twenty kilometres from Dawson City, he could, when he turned off his headlamp and glanced back, see the flash of Kleedehn's light from time to time on a straight stretch.

He whistled quietly to his dogs, who unhesitatingly increased their pace.

He reached the Klondike Highway, glowing under the haze of the orange lights of the town. The trail dropped down onto the Klondike River after passing by a gas station and running through the parking lot of a hotel.

He heard the town's volunteer fire department alarm start to wail. He'd been spotted, and people were gathering downtown at the checkpoint to greet the first team to make it halfway to Fairbanks.

As he neared the Yukon River, the trail turned up onto a dike that runs the length of the town's riverfront. Less than a kilometre to go, and he could see Kleedehn bearing down on him, only a few hundred metres back. He was gaining, his dogs loping, their tongues lolling out as they concentrated on the pursuit.

Kleedehn ran out of real estate, though.

At 11:17 p.m., Thursday, Osmar turned smartly off the dike and smiled, his gold tooth gleaming, as he cruised the last hundred metres to the banner, where a couple of hundred people thronged, cheering loudly, camera flashes going off everywhere. He lifted his sled up on one runner and leaned over to set the snow hook.

"Welcome to Dawson," the checker said. "What's your bib number?"

Osmar, still smiling through his ice-encrusted beard, gave his number. "Thank you," he said. "It's real nice to be here."

He was still there when Kleedehn barrelled around the corner and stopped. Chase, in lead, was panting a metre behind Osmar's sled runners. Less than two minutes separated the teams.

When David Sawatzky pulled into Dawson City, nearly an hour later, his ankles were the size of oranges. After checking in, he went straight to the nursing station—there is no hospital in Dawson City—and sought help.

While coming over King Solomon's Dome, Jack, a three-year-old dog Sawatzky raised from a puppy, had begun vomiting, probably from some kind of bacterial infection he'd picked up. Despite being barely able to steer the sled—much less walk—he'd picked Jack up and carried him back to the basket, where the dog rode the rest of the way into Dawson City.

By the time Sawatzky arrived, his dogs had missed three meals in weather that hadn't seen the warmer side of thirty-five degrees below zero. They looked skinny and tired as they came around the corner in front of the visitor reception centre.

His wife Jeanne and Sara, his eleven-year-old daughter, were there to meet him, and Sawatzky's tired, strained face lit up with delight. Awkwardly, in the sharp glow of the floodlights, Sara got on the runners in front of her father, and, between them, they drove the dogs across the river to the campground. Jack, a handsome dog with German shepherd markings and brown eyes, peered out over the sled bag.

BACK AT SCROGGIE CREEK, Bill Pinkham was hungry. He had stopped to snack his dogs on the trail in when a team came up behind him. Instead of stopping, or simply passing him, the lead dogs had lurched up beside his sled and, seeing an open bag containing Pinkham's personal food, attacked it, tearing the bag to shreds and consuming everything he had to eat for the next 200 kilometres.

The dogs belonged to Kyla Boivin, an eighteen-year-old musher from Dawson City who was running her first long-distance race. "Sorry," she said, sheepishly. "I have a bit of a hard time controlling them sometimes."

Pinkham graciously told her not to worry. He could have filed a complaint, and Boivin could have been penalized, but it seemed an honest accident, and he did have a little more food. His mother, to help, had sent him hundreds of bags of precooked bacon strips, which he hadn't yet touched. A bunch of them were in the bottom of his bag, and they would form the basis of his diet for the next several days.

Feeding his dogs at Scroggie Creek, he was philosophical about the attack. "At least they didn't get into my dog food," he said, offering me a slice of frozen bacon. "Try it, it's really good." Then, louder, he shouted across the dog yard, "Hey, anybody want some bacon? I've got tons of it!"

Where Boivin's dogs were concerned, however, Joran Freeman was not so lucky as Pinkham. When she arrived at Scroggie Creek, Boivin's dogs yanked her across the yard, and tore into Freeman's open sled basket. Freeman, who was off getting some water, couldn't get there in time to stop her dogs from eating his dogs' food.

"They were in a pirhana-like frenzy," Freeman later said. "She pulled up, and the dogs saw a white bag, and they ran over there and it was a huge pileup of dogs, just ripping though all of this food. They ate it all within seconds."

Boivin felt horrible, he saw, and she offered him some of her own food, as much as she could spare. But it was nowhere near enough. Freeman would have to run the last 160 kilometres into Dawson with hardly any food for his dogs. He might have asked her for more food; it was, after all, her mistake. However, the code of the trail seemed to take a back seat to chivalry in this case. Boivin, pretty and exuberant with a tough-talking exterior and a noticeable nose ring, was about the only musher in the race who could have got away with it.

Freeman left Scroggie Creek determined to maintain his pace. On the Black Hills, he worked almost as hard as the dogs, jumping off the sled at the bottom of each hill and running between the runners, pushing the sled to ease the strain on the animals. He felt, for the first time in the race, that he was part of the team, not merely its director or cheerleader, and that he had as much a responsibility as any of the dogs to carry his share of the load. In hilly sections, a bigger dog team usually means faster progress. One of the fittest mushers in the race, Freeman promised himself he would make up for his lack of dogs through his own exertion.

Joran Freeman had left McCabe Creek on Tuesday with only eight misbehaving dogs, despondent, in eighteenth place, nine hours behind the leaders. Late Thursday night, 400 kilometres later, he arrived in Dawson City tired, cold, but smiling. With only eight dogs, he had posted the fastest time over the Black Hills, Eureka, and King Solomon's Dome.

He was in fifth place, a mere four hours off the pace.

After the performance of his team, Freeman didn't find himself terribly surprised at his placing. Race officials, however, who had been expecting Frank Turner or John Schandelmeier, were clearly shocked. And Freeman soon learned that a euphoric run on the trail matters only to the musher. Veterinarians are more interested, quite correctly, in the physical health of a dog team that has just run faster than teams almost twice as large over the longest section of hilly terrain on the trail.

Freeman's first problem was finding his handler, who seemed to have vanished. He had hired Ingebritt Schlossen shortly before leaving Fairbanks. A former Quest entrant, who had scratched in 1998, she connected well with the dogs.

When Freeman arrived in Dawson City, where the handler plays the most important role, Schlossen was nowhere to be found. She wasn't at the checkpoint or the house where they had been billeted. She wasn't over at the campground where the dogs would be. People fanned out looking for her, calling her name.

Exhausted, Freeman waited and waited. While most handlers wait, doze, play cards, and chat at the checkpoint so they are available when their musher arrives, Schlossen, finally arriving at the checkpoint, said she had been sleeping in the truck. She seemed annoyed that nobody had come to wake her up.

After Freeman had taken the team to the campground and bedded the dogs in their tent, several veterinarians examined them closely. Some dogs were looking gaunt and had obviously lost weight during the second quarter of the race. Some of his dogs' feet had suffered abrasions, which suggested he hadn't been using booties when he should have, or properly applying foot cream when they were stopped. The abrasions are called "raspberries," because of the appearance of the irritated skin.

Although he felt confident that the team, overall, was in fine shape, the vets kept coming back. Together, they worked out a way for Freeman to get weight back on and feet healed.

"I knew I was in a real touchy situation. I was a rookie, and I knew that they probably thought that I was blowing out my team. I understood what they were talking about, but I was real confident in myself and in my dog-mushing ability. I knew that it was just a matter of explaining to them and relating to them what was going on in my mind, and how I was going to rectify that situation," he said later.

Because the first section of the race had been relatively warm, Freeman hadn't been snacking his dogs as often as he might, as a strategy to keep their appetites up. Plus, he didn't have much food, thanks to Kyla Boivin's ravenous animals.

One hour and forty-five minutes after Freeman arrived, Hugh Neff pulled in, seventh, and ecstatic at placing ahead of people like Frank Turner, who was one of his heroes. "What's the secret to doing well without big kennel and bucks? Desire and destiny. I put about $2,500 into the race. Some teams spend $40,000," he pronounced triumphantly.

However, his dogs looked mangy and tired, and some were favouring their feet. Altogether, they appeared much worse than Freeman's.

He had no handler, but, fortunately, another musher's handler had helped to set up his camp. Neff spent his first night sleeping on a table in the veterinarian's cabin; the second night he spent in the back of a church, where the priest, who was going out of town, had offered him a room and food. There was also a liquor cabinet, Neff noted. (He helped himself to three beers, he said, which, when word got out, prompted a flood of calls from annoyed parishioners.)

The day after Neff arrived, Joe May, a former Quest and Iditarod champion who was a race official in this year's Quest, approached him. Known for his gruff, straightforward demeanour, May pointed out a cut on the foot of Gracie, one of his fastest dogs. "I don't like the look of your team at all," he said.

Neff stomped off, furious. He disagreed with May about his team, and the cut in the dog's foot, he thought, was only a centimetre wide and not terribly serious.

Most mushers would drop such a dog without question, but Neff was annoyed at the suggestion. She had been running fine, he said later, resenting that a race judge could look at his team and pass judgment so quickly. "After all," he added, "we are in seventh place."

AT THE TURN OF THE TWENTIETH CENTURY, Dawson City was one of the most expensive places in the world to live. The simple law of supply and demand drove the price of scarce eggs to a dollar each. Salt was worth its weight in gold. Five minutes' bath in a wooden laundry tub cost a buck and a half. Dance-hall girls were making $100 a night, and much more if they left with a miner to provide "extra" services. The only thing in large supply, it seemed, was gold.

In one of the stranger stories from the Klondike, there was even a hockey team, which in 1905 challenged the Ottawa Silver Seven in a brave effort that showcased the tenacity and determination of the locals. At the turn of the twentieth century, any team that could demonstrate its worthiness to a governing body could mount a challenge for the Stanley Cup, the Holy Grail of North American hockey. The Dawson City Nuggets managed, through a promoter, to convince the powers that be that they were worthy of the attempt.

So, on December 21, 1904, the Nuggets set out by dog team to travel the 600-kilometre-long Dawson Overland Trail to Whitehorse. Some were riding bicycles, and others walked. It took them eight days, roughly twice as long as it takes the top Yukon Quest teams.

From Whitehorse, they took the White Pass and Yukon Route train over the Coast Mountains to Skagway, Alaska, where they embarked on a steamer bound for Seattle. (They'd been hoping to catch a boat for Vancouver, but the train arrived late.)

From Seattle, they took a train to Vancouver, and, from there, they traversed some 5,000 kilometres across Canada by train to Ottawa, in the smoking car.

Twenty-three days after leaving Dawson City—and after picking a player up in Winnipeg to replace someone who had become ill—they arrived in the capital. They hadn't had any physical exercise since they'd left, much less laced on a pair of skates. They arrived a scant thirty-six hours before their first game, a sold-out affair against the Stanley Cup champions on January 13.

In those days, hockey was played with a goalie and six skaters, and there were no substitutes. The train-lagged, out-of-shape Nuggets figured they would be in for a test.

They lost the first game in a best-of-three series 9-3—not a bad result, they thought, given their lack of exercise. The resulting hubris, however, meant that, instead of doing some practice drills in the two days before the next game, they hung out—and got hungover—at Casey's Bar.

They took to the ice in game two reeking of bravado and booze. They lost 23-2, which stands today as the most embarrassing defeat ever handed a team in Stanley Cup history.

Jump ahead ninety-two years to 1997. That year, the Dawson City men's old-timers' team decided that they would recreate the trip as a fundraising effort for sports facilities in the town. Instead of the Ottawa Silver Seven, they would play the Ottawa Senators' Alumni, ex–National Hockey League players living in the Ottawa area. Some had played for the Senators, who had recently been admitted to an expanded league. Others had played for other NHL teams, but had retired to the Ottawa Valley.

Like the Nuggets of old, the players travelled to Whitehorse with dog teams, although the bicycles were replaced by snow machines to carry gear. They caught a bus to Skagway—the narrow-gauge railway train, now a tourist attraction, no longer runs in the winter—and caught a ferry to Vancouver. They took the train to Ottawa, stopping in most cities for promotional events (one of which included driving a sled dog team into Wayne Gretzky's restaurant in downtown Toronto). They also picked up a player in Winnipeg, a fellow selected through a radio station contest.

In Ottawa, as a mark of respect to the original Nuggets, they too drank a great deal, although they also went to see a Phil Collins matinee concert (they were old-timers, after all).

The big game—and this time there was only one game—was at the Corel Centre, and 8,000 tickets were sold.

The Dawsonites played with bravado, and the crowd was clearly cheering for the visiting team. It didn't help much, though. The final score was 18-0 for the Senators.

And history repeated itself again, in a town where exploitation and a take-all-you-can-before-you-leave attitude has long prevailed, when Hollywood researchers began interviewing the players on the 1997 Nuggets shortly after they returned from Ottawa. The players, a decent lot, willingly obliged. A year or so later, to the surprise of the Nuggets, the movie *Mystery, Alaska* came out, about a ragtag team of Alaskans who challenge the New York Rangers to a game.

Don't bother to see it.

GOLD MINING IS STILL BIG BUSINESS in Dawson City. As drivers travel along the Bonanza Creek Road today, mine tailings dominate the landscape, long, tube-shaped piles of gravel that, from the air and covered with snow, look like giant, sleeping caterpillars. They are hideous, the result of siftings and reshiftings every time some new technology comes out that can squeeze a few more ounces from the tired rocks.

There aren't as many small-time prospectors these days as there are larger, placer operations, using jets of water to erase hillsides which are then sifted for gold. A large-scale gold mine operates east of Dawson, providing year-round employment in a place where most of the jobs are seasonal. Today, fewer than a thousand souls live in Dawson year-round, a number that swells to more than double between May and August.

In summer, tourism is the town's bonanza, and legions of aging Americans travel through in motorhomes to try their hand at panning gold, or to gamble and watch cancan dancers at Diamond Tooth Gertie's, the oldest legal casino in Canada. There are about the same number of students, who descend on the town from all parts of Canada to work as bartenders, hotel housekeepers, and blackjack dealers. The ones who arrive early find a room to rent; the rest end up living in a tent village that springs up every year across the Yukon River, with poor sanitation and no running water. It's an eerie recollection of the town's infamous past. The worst of the summer residents buy or get dogs, and then, when they pack up to leave in the fall, abandon them to the dirt streets. Every year, canine control officers are forced to kill dozens of loose and uncontrolled dogs.

Nearly every business in Dawson has some reference to the Klondike gold rush in its name: the Eldorado Hotel, Klondike Kate's, the Jack London Saloon, Bonanza Aviation, Maximilian's Gold Emporium.

Dawson has a strict building code that forces downtown property owners to build and renovate to the style of 1898. Some of the buildings from the era are still standing, though many are just façades propped up by scaffolds. There are no paved roads in

Dawson—which nobody notices in winter, of course—and all of the buildings and wooden sidewalks are built a metre or so above ground, on stilts or pontoons, to clear the shifty permafrost below.

You can stay in a restored brothel called Bombay Peggy's, and, in the summer, you can listen to Tom Byrne, who recites poetry outside Robert Service's cabin, dressed as the Bard of the Yukon. You can even recite the first few stanzas of "The Spell of the Yukon" on one street corner yourself, if you look up. It's printed in large, elegant type on the side of a building. You can see where Jack London lived, gathering the tales that would inspire *The Call of the Wild* and *White Fang*. You can even get a pretty good caffe latte at the River West Café, which is on the east side of the river.

Every August, the town fills up for the Dawson City Music Festival, which brings in new and old acts, mostly from Canada but also from around the world. Bruce Cockburn has played there twice. So have the Barenaked Ladies. The organizers have a knack for picking up-and-coming bands, and, even for established musicians, it's a chance to see a part of the world not known for its pop culture. Tents take over the town, pitched almost anywhere there's a flat surface. It's the only weekend of the year local residents bother to lock their doors.

If you want to hang out with the locals, there's really only one place, winter or summer: the Westminster Hotel, also known as the The Pit or The Pink Palace (because of its distinctive exterior paint job), where the house band, the Pointer Brothers, have been playing so long that the painted sign promoting them on the side of the building is faded and chipped. If you're lucky, you'll hit a night when Willie Gordon, Dawson's fiddler laureate, is playing with them. Inside, it is a smoky, smelly mess reeking of character.

For several months each year—a period of time that seems to grow annually—it is impossible to get across to the other side of the Yukon River. Either the ice is not sufficiently frozen, or it's not sufficiently thawed, depending on what time of year you hit it.

(There's a joke about the weather there: it's nine months of winter and three months of bad dogsledding.)

During the summer, the campground across the river is nearly always full. In the winter, it is used only once, when the teams from the Quest pull in for their thirty-six-hour layover. Vehicles drive across the ice, on which a roadway has been cleared of snow.

Dawson City is unique on the Quest trail because it is the one place where the mushers get a break, and the handlers step in. Mushers slip away to a land of massages, queen-sized beds, and fine dining, while the handlers sleep outside in a tent, feeding and walking dogs to a prescribed schedule, spending their time under the blue haze of a tarpaulin with the dogs as the animals convalesce on a bank of straw, getting all sorts of holistic pills and ointments.

Frank Turner, who arrived in Dawson in sixth place, clearly has the best campsite setup each year. There is a tent for the dogs, who rest collectively on eight bales of straw. And in case that isn't a thick enough buffer, the mattress is protected from the snow by a layer of blue foam (the same stuff he forgot to use at Stepping Stone). Off to the side, there is a meds tent exclusively for Turner's dogs, and, below, there is another tent for the various foods: fish, heart, tongue, turkey skin, fat, and bison testicles, known colloquially as prairie oysters. If the dogs really aren't eating, there is, at the back of the tent, a crate of that most decadent of luxuries: tinned cat food.

The whole place looks something like a M*A*S*H unit after a snowstorm. It is run by Anne with military precision: handlers are given a binder detailing their responsibilities, minute by minute, for the thirty-six hours.

Here is how the Camp Turner system works.

Two days before any of the teams begin to arrive in Dawson, several of Turner's friends arrive and set up the camp, making sure the site is shovelled clear of snow and the tents are erected properly.

Half an hour before Turner's estimated arrival, which is drawn from his running times in previous years and from sporadic reports from the trail, food is soaked in warm water in an insulated container so it will be ready to eat when the team gets there. When the team arrives, it is moved off to one side, where the dogs are given their food. Every available snack and trick of the trade is used to make sure that every dog eats. "Stand on your head, if necessary," Anne's instructions read.

While the other handlers are feeding the dogs, Anne talks to Frank, taking notes on injuries and sore spots. Once the dogs have eaten, Frank, sometimes with Anne on the sled, drives over to the designated spot on the campground. The handlers drive the kilometre or so across the river by car.

Frank is whisked away for a meal and bed.

Once the dogs are bedded down in the straw, their feet are examined closely for cracks and sores, and then, if necessary, healing ointment or antibiotic cream is rubbed into their pads. Their chests are checked for redness that might result from the harness rubbing if it hasn't been fitted properly. Joints are manipulated for soreness, and then rubbed and treated.

There is a veterinary cabin at the campground that is staffed twenty-four hours a day, and any dog requiring attention receives it almost immediately. Wrist wraps—neoprene sheaths that take pressure off joints and work the same way a tensor bandage does—are applied where necessary.

As a last measure, the dogs are all cuddled generously. Then, an hour after they arrive at the campground, they are left to rest, and the handlers' job is to guard them, ensuring they get an uninterrupted sleep.

Ten hours later, they are fed again, walked a few hundred metres, and checked once more. Eighteen hours after the team's arrival, they are fed and walked again. Ditto at hour twenty-six.

It's not as simple as it sounds. Dogs, which tend to lose their appetites when they are stressed, don't always want to eat.

Obviously, however, when they are burning up the equivalent of fifty cheeseburgers a day, they have to consume food.

When I was handling for Turner in the 2000 Quest, I was charged with the responsibility of getting Brandy, the dog in heat that had mated with Latte, to eat. She was refusing pretty much everything except the bison testicles, which, after a week of near-constant harassment from her teammates, she snapped up in defiance. Potentially more serious, however, was the fact that she wasn't drinking either. Sled dogs generally won't drink straight water like a house dog, because they are used to it being mixed with food (a method that saves both time and the weight of carrying extra bowls). Water has to be disguised as broth or mixed into a slop with kibble. Fish and some meats contain a lot of water, too.

But Brandy was having none of it. After six hours of trying every combination of food and water possible in her bowl, only to be rebuffed, I stuck my bare hand in a messy slop of kibble, fish, and gravy, held it up to my nose, and sniffed it. "It looks good to me, Brandy," I said, smiling at her and extending my slop-filled palm to her nose.

She looked up at me, her eyes moist. She slowly bowed her head and began licking my hand, finishing all the food and broth.

She looked up, plaintively. I scooped my hand in again, and again she ate from it. For half an hour, one tablespoon at a time, I gave her food from my hand.

It turned out all she wanted was a little bit of personal service, a little special attention. It brought tears to my sleep-deprived eyes.

Two to four hours before the team's scheduled departure from Dawson, the dogs are given a light meal, walked again, and Frank returns to make his final preparations.

Of course, Turner's system only works if, like him, you have the army of volunteers and friends to make it happen. At one point, for example, six people stood around watching a dog defecate, to examine the firmness of the steaming product. While some people are looking after the dogs, others are repairing his sled and making sure all his equipment is in top working order.

Frank shows up at the campground from time to time, does media interviews, and hosts a dinner for all his handlers and volunteers at the El Dorado Hotel.

To show exactly how far treatment of the sled dog has come from the stick-and-whip driving days of Jack London, Frank Turner even arranges for each of his dogs—and himself—to get a massage from a naturopath. Christina Hobe, a Whitehorse practitioner who splits her time between dogs and people, comes to the campground and massages the dogs, straightening their spines and applying acupressure. Acupuncture is forbidden—as is any treatment that breaks the skin of the dog—but other holistic practices are becoming more common and are encouraged.

Other mushers employ similar New Age tactics.

Andrew Lesh, who also employs Hobe at the Dawson checkpoint—and provides a massage for his handlers, as well—uses Moxa sticks, a Chinese, cigar-like herbal therapy that helps the dogs rest more efficiently when the sticks are ignited and held close to the backs of the their knees. "You begin to see their eyes start to droop as soon as you put the stick there," he quips.

Other teams, lacking the resources of a Frank Turner, have more rudimentary systems, with only one or two handlers to do all the work. John Schandelmeier, for example, tends to sleep with his dogs, eschewing the comforts of a nice meal and a warm bed. But most mushers—tough, wilderness bush people though they are—are craving those creature comforts, like showers, that most of us don't think twice about. Then again, most downwind people don't run for cover when we step onto a street, either.

Even William Kleedehn, dubbed "the toughest man in the Yukon" by the *Fairbanks Daily News-Miner,* accepted a massage in Dawson City. Grudgingly, to be fair; it had been arranged for him by a friend as a gift. "A massage, what kind of bullshit is this?" he told me later with typical candour. "If they would have had a brothel right now, I would have gone there first."

The race is often as brutal for the mushers as for the dogs. Consider what happens to a musher's hands on the trail.

During the course of the race, a musher might change the booties the dogs wear to protect their feet from ice and snow several times a day. Every time they stop, up to fifty-six Velcro straps are undone. When they start again, fifty-six Velcro straps are done up again. Of course, the booties fly off on the trail, too, and have to be changed every time the dogs run through water. By the time he reaches Fairbanks at the end of the race, a musher will have changed between 2,000 and 3,000 booties. Always outside, always without gloves, and often in temperatures of minus forty or colder. The result is a manicurist's nightmare.

Mushers have actually dropped out of the race because their hands are in so much pain. It's not just replacing the booties. The ointment all mushers rub into their dogs' feet also causes problems. It contains a desiccant to dry up wounds on dogs' pads, and it causes human hands to dry out and crack, like badly chapped lips. Anne Tayler told me once that Frank's hands, scarred from frostbite and exposure, are like sandpaper to the touch.

"Sometimes, at home, he comes over and offers to rub my back," she says, "but I try to think of a reason why he shouldn't, because I want to keep my skin."

BILL PINKHAM ARRIVED IN DAWSON in seventeenth place, at 8:20 p.m. Friday, nearly a day after the leaders. He wanted a drink. Scotch. Glenlivet, preferably.

After looking after the dogs, before he had a shower or went to his billet's home, he headed over to Diamond Tooth Gertie's, the casino, which during the winter opens just for special events like the Quest.

There, we had a few drinks, chatted about the race, and enjoyed the cancan show on stage. Pinkham, ever loquacious—sleep deprivation affects people in different ways—began talking to an attractive French woman at the next table.

Around midnight, I and several other journalists there departed, leaving Pinkham to flirt.

The following morning, I saw him at a mushers' meeting. His eyes were all puffy, his hair was pointing everywhere, and he looked considerably worse than he had when he'd arrived after 800 kilometres on the trail.

"Don't tell anyone," he whispered to me conspiratorially, a silly grin on his face, "but I haven't been to bed yet."

Following another invitation to go dancing that night as well, the possibility existed that Pinkham might actually get less sleep in Dawson City than he had on the trail. At dinner, Ray Gordon, his handler, a septuagenarian ex-marine and a pretty good musher in his day, looked at the woman, then looked at Pinkham. "Bill," he said, "it's your race, but I suggest you get some sleep tonight."

By the time he left Dawson City, he'd managed six hours.

WHILE HER HUSBAND RESTED his shattered ankles, which had been wrapped in tensor bandages by a nurse, Jeanne Sawatzky worked miracles at the campground on their dogs, getting them to eat and replace the weight they had lost.

Sawatzky's would be the third team to leave, after William Kleedehn's and Tim Osmar's.

The staggered start in Whitehorse is made up in Dawson, and, because Kleedehn left sixteen minutes after Osmar from Whitehorse, he was allowed to leave fourteen minutes before him from Dawson, the time difference minus the two minutes he arrived after Osmar. (This led some to argue that Kleedehn's had been the fastest team to reach Dawson, and that he deserved the gold. However, the rules dictate that the gold goes to the first team to arrive in the town, regardless of the starting order.)

All three of them were leaving within an hour of each other, beginning at 11:37 a.m. Andrew Lesh would leave an hour and twenty minutes after Sawatzky, at 1:50 p.m., and Joran Freeman would leave at 2:38 p.m. Hugh Neff, leaving in seventh place, was due out at 4:45, and, two mushers later, Frank Turner would leave at 6:25 p.m.

EARLY IN THE MORNING, the day after the leaders had left Dawson, Sig Stormo, running the race in memory of his daughter, was making his way towards the checkpoint. At five minutes to five, he signed in, tired and cold.

Of all the hours spent awake, or trying to stay awake, on a dog sled, it's the time just before dawn that seems to be the hardest. Staying up late into the night is not terribly difficult, and, once the sun comes up, some sort of metabolic regeneration seems to occur and energy is found. Frank Turner knows it; he forces himself to hang in before that second, solar wind arrives.

Time, at least that recorded on a clock, is an alien sensation during an event like the Quest.

For a musher on the trail, the day is not divided into morning, noon, and night. There are no breakfasts or dinners. Even the distinction between darkness and sunlight becomes important only in terms of finding an optimal temperature at which the dogs can run. It all comes down to a constant examination of the dogs' gait, movement, waste expulsion, demeanour, and appetite. The passage of hours is marked only in terms of run and rest, which should be split evenly. "Very quickly our normal reference points fly out the window," Turner explains. "At the beginning of the race, you just want to start it. Then it just becomes a blur; the feeling of time, it's just a memory. It's just the immediacy of the moment. There is a future, but the intensity is on the moment. It's all strung together, all these intense moments. There's no relief."

Stormo, arriving during that dark period, just wanted to get his dogs down so he could eat and sleep himself. He took his team across the river to the campground, and, with his handler, the dogs were bedded down and looked after.

He was thirsty. He asked his handler if there was anything around he could drink. The handler, who had also been up all night, absently pointed to a bottle of Sunny Delight, the American orange drink.

Stormo unscrewed the cap and took several gulps. There was a brief pause. Suddenly, Stormo gave out a horrible, screeching sound, an agonizing, heart-stopping scream, and fell to his knees.

It wasn't Sunny Delight in the bottle. It was methanol, the fuel mushers use in their cook stoves because it burns well and never freezes. The temperature was thirty degrees below zero, and the fuel had been stored outside.

Stormo collapsed to the ground, unconscious and barely able to breathe. The alcohol in the fuel, at minus thirty, tore apart the flesh on his throat and was now doing the same thing to his stomach lining.

Mark Lindstrom, a race official, was standing nearby and saw what happened. He got Stormo into a Quest truck and drove as fast as he could across the ice bridge on the Yukon River and across town to the nursing station.

Besides burning the stomach and esophageal linings, methanol causes blindness. And, if not treated immediately, it is fatal. A person who swallows it must have his stomach pumped as soon as possible, along with being tube-fed charcoal to absorb the alcohol.

Stormo's condition was too serious to be treated at the nursing centre; he would have to be medevaced to Whitehorse by plane.

If he had made that mistake alone on the trail, he would have been dead. Even now, he was far from out of the woods. With one simple act, his wits badgered by sleep deprivation, Stormo had nearly killed himself. His quest to honour his daughter was over, and he was fighting for his own life.

A couple of hours later, as the journalists were preparing to board a plane to Eagle, the next checkpoint, accessible only by air or the Yukon River, another plane was landing at the tiny Dawson City airport, which can be used only during daylight hours because it has no runway lights.

As the plane taxied in, a stretcher was wheeled out towards it. On it was Sig Stormo.

Libby Casey, a radio reporter from Fairbanks who had interviewed him several times before and during the race, walked over and stood beside him as he was loaded onto the small plane bound for Whitehorse. She sat with him as he was waiting to take off.

His face was red and puffy. His hands were swollen.

His glassy eyes were filled with tears. He looked at Libby and clutched her hand. "I'm so sorry," he said, his voice barely a croak. "I've failed. I've failed. I've let everybody down."

JACK

AFTER MUSHERS END THEIR LAYOVER and head out of the camp-ground, they travel roughly 100 kilometres to Fortymile, a collec-tion of cabins where the Fortymile River empties into the Yukon. It's not forty miles from Dawson City, as one might expect, and more than one journalist has been caught wondering why it takes teams seven hours to get there when they run at ten miles an hour.

The name Fortymile refers to the distance from Fort Reliance, a trading post upriver. Apart from several small portages around open water or impassable jumble ice, the trail between Dawson City and Fortymile is entirely on the Yukon River. There are numerous overflow sections, where creeks flow into the river, and several cabins along the way.

This year, the jumble ice was so bad that Sebastian Jones, who lives with his spouse, Shelley Brown, at Fortymile, actually cut an archway through two joined blocks of ice to grant access to the settlement.

When David Sawatzky came to the Dawson City campground ready to leave, the dogs, while still ornery, had regained their weight. Even Jack jumped around, ready to go. He had made it halfway and he was ready to take on the second half of the race.

Sawatzky had accomplished something most mushers aspire to but few achieve: halfway to Fairbanks, he had a full fourteen dogs in harness, a feat requiring excellent dog care, particularly given the conditions of the trail and the added stress of running with females in heat. Only one other musher in the race, John Schandelmeier, was running with a full team.

An hour outside of Dawson City the dogs were running well, and, although there were massive pieces of ice scattered everywhere, the trail from Dawson to Fortymile was well made and had been smoothed by dog teams belonging to cabin-dwellers along the river, who use the trail regularly to travel to Dawson. There were still treacherous sections of uneven trail and metre-high drop-offs, but these had become, for better or worse, normal mushing conditions on this Quest.

After five hours, Sawatzky and his dogs were approaching Cassiar Creek, the home of Quest musher Cor Guimond. An hour earlier, William Kleedehn had wiped out just outside the trapper's cabin trying to get out of the way of an approaching recreational dog team. The musher had a loose dog, and Kleedehn's team chased after it. He crashed when he fell into a hole on the side of the trail while trying to get his team under control.

It was after nightfall when Sawatzky approached the spot. Even with a headlamp, he could see only several metres in front of him, but it was enough for him to know that it was a challenging section of trail: it turned suddenly to the left and went up a several-metre-high embankment, just high enough that Sawatzky could see the hole at the top that Kleedehn had fallen into. He didn't think that the trail should have turned in that direction, but there was no way it could have gone through the large boulder in front of him. So he called out, "Haw," and the dogs obediently turned to the left and broke into a lope up the hill; they generally like to get through difficult trail sections as quickly as possible.

The trail dipped a little more just before it rose, so that Sawatzky and his sled were directly below the string of dogs as they went up the mound, and the leaders had reached the top before Sawatzky had started pushing the sled up.

The sled lurched as it climbed, and Sawatzky pushed it forward. As he came over the crest, he saw that Jack had stumbled and fallen into the hole. The dogs, still loping, dragged him out by his neckline and tried to continue down the trail.

Frantically trying to get the excited dogs to stop, Sawatzky repeatedly attempted to jam the snow hook down into the ice. After several tries, he got purchase, and the team stopped. He limped off the runners, lurching forward to get to Jack, and, just as he reached the prone dog, the team pulled the hook out and lurched forward once more. They almost got past him before he was able to dive onto the runners, shouting in pain.

He jammed the hook into the shallow layer of snow, stomping on it with the foot that was merely sprained, not broken.

Sawatzky made his way down the gangline a second time, got to Jack once again, and fell to his knees beside him. He'd had Jack since the dog was four months old, after getting him from a friend and fellow musher.

As he got close to Jack and shone his headlight on the dog's face, he felt his heart sink. Jack, lying prone in the snow, had stopped breathing.

Rolling Jack onto his right side, Sawatzky tried artificial respiration: he straightened the dog's neck and opened his mouth, pulling the tongue out to make sure there were no obstructions. Gently, he closed his mouth, wrapped his hand around the dog's snout, and put his own mouth over his nose. He exhaled down Jack's nostrils, slow, long breaths, five times. No reaction.

Removing his glove and holding his finger on the inside of Jack's thigh, just above his knee, he felt for a pulse. Nothing. Still with Jack on his right side, Sawatzky put his hands on the wide part of his chest, near his front legs, one on top of the other. He began compressions, fifteen of them, quickly, pushing down about three centimetres each time. He went back to Jack's nose and gave him two breaths. Checked for a pulse. Nothing.

He repeated this several times, the lump growing in his throat. No response. Jack was dead.

Sawatzky leaned back, still kneeling, and looked at the black sky. He felt sick. The rest of the dogs continued to growl at each other, still after the females. Sawatzky silenced them with a growl of his own.

After several minutes, he unclipped Jack's neckline from his collar and from the gangline, putting it in his pocket. Unhooking his tugline, he clipped the empty end into a spare loop on the gangline.

Straining on his ankles, he cradled the dead dog in his forearms and struggled, half kneeling, half walking, back to his sled. He laid Jack inside, covering him over with the flap on the sled bag.

With nothing more to do but carry on in the silence, he pulled the hook up, and the dogs began to trot towards Fortymile, thirty kilometres away.

LESS THAN ONE PERCENT OF SLED DOGS DIE while training or racing, a statistic that compares favourably with pretty much every other animal or human sport. Proportionately, many more people die cross-country skiing than dogs die in harness.

But it does happen—over the years, an average of about one dog has died per Yukon Quest. The cause of death, however, is rarely something within the musher's control. It is almost always a pre-existing, undiagnosable condition.

The most common cause of death on the the trail is called sled dog myopathy or, more technically, exertional rabdomyalisis. Like tying-up syndrome in horses, its origin is enigmatic. A dog will start to wobble while running; after wobbling for several seconds, it will collapse; and, within the few seconds it takes a musher to stop and anchor the sled and get to the dog, it is usually dead. Sled dog myopathy is unpredictable, and there is no known way to prevent it.

There are several theories about the syndrome, none of which has been proven conclusively. It appears to have its root in muscle damage caused by prolonged exercise, but how the muscles are damaged is much less clear.

One theory blames free radicals, the by-products of oxygen metabolism created when dogs (and people) breathe, which, unchecked, can break down cell molecules. The harder you're working—and, hence, breathing more frequently—the more free radicals you create. Normally, our tissue cells contain vitamin E, vitamin C, and beta carotene, which are antioxidants that quench the free radicals before they can do prolonged damage to molecules in the cell. If antioxidant levels fall too low, however, muscle cells throughout the body begin to break down. Myopathy occurs when a critical mass of damage is done at the cellular level; the body loses its ability to function properly and effectively shuts down.

Another theory suggests that dogs with a specific genetic weakness are simply running out of energy, and, at some imperceptible point, they lack sufficient energy to maintain normal cellular function while they're working. The ability of individual cells to function normally, importing energy and exporting waste across their membranes, becomes compromised, and the cell's ability to hold things inside that need to stay inside—and keep things outside that need to stay outside—breaks down, resulting in an improper balance of chemicals in individual cells. This damages and eventually kills the cells.

The problem is, once a muscle cell is damaged badly enough, it leaks potassium—of which there is normally a significant quantity within cells, but not in intercellular fluid or blood. If too much potassium escapes from too many muscle cells, it will suddenly interrupt the electrochemical signalling essential to heart functions and cause cardiac arrest—not unlike the lethal injections of potassium chloride administered as the final step in a state execution.

In seconds the dog literally tips over, and it's gone.

In rare cases, a dog can be revived through cardiopulmonary resuscitation, although some vets feel that, given the shape of a dog's chest and the distance from its rib cage to its heart, it's a fruitless task.

Sometimes the musher might have time to stop the wobbling and rescue the dog, put it in the basket, and carry it to the next checkpoint, where it can be retired to the handler and veterinary care. Often, however, the collapse happens with no warning at all. Long-distance sled dogs, through selective breeding, are naturally very tough and love to run so much that they won't show signs of myopathy until they are in real trouble.

Fortunately, dog deaths like that are very rare, and most mushers know their dogs so well that even the slightest change in their gait or demeanour signals trouble to them. However, add disease or infection—always possible, given the number of dogs in close quarters—and the issue becomes more complicated. Dogs might already have difficulty maintaining their metabolism because they are stressed, and might behave differently than when they are at home in the dog yard. This makes it harder for mushers to see that a dog is in any kind of mortal trouble.

As it turned out, a necropsy performed at the University of Alaska in Fairbanks (where any dog that dies in harness is sent for study) determined that Jack did not die from myopathy. Rather, the dog had, at some time several days earlier, vomited, and, as occasionally happens, inhaled the vomit into his lungs and sinuses. He died, in fact, from a respiratory infection that Sawatzky couldn't have known about. The cause of his death might have been planted when he was sick coming over King Solomon's Dome, but it was likely more recent than that.

Sawatzky felt paralyzed, casting his mind back over the race. "You just think of where you screwed up, you know," he said later. He thought maybe Jack had thrown up and breathed in the vomit while Sawatzky was in the infirmary at Dawson, with his broken ankle—one of the few times when his dogs weren't in his sight.

Coming toward Fortymile, he was worried, also, about what the media would think. Over the years, there has been intense pressure from animal rights groups to ban sled dog racing as an inhumane and ethically repugnant sport.

The positive result of this attention has been that today, mushers who are cruel to their dogs—and there are bad mushers, just as there are those who flout the rules in every sport—are weeded out and treated judiciously. The days of Jack London's hooded musher, inching down the trail in a forty-below blizzard, flicking a gangline-long whip against the tails of his whimpering team are long gone. Today's sled dogs are treated like champion athletes.

And, certainly, in a corner of the world where man and animal exist interdependently, a musher who trains and pushes his dogs through corporal punishment is not only hurting dogs and the image of the sport, he is hurting himself. It's very simple: dogs motivated by fear will try to escape, and succeed, when the going gets tough. Dogs motivated by love will remain loyal.

As David Sawatzky told me, several months after the race: "If you think you're going to stick-drive your dogs from Whitehorse to Fairbanks, it's not going to work. Dogs are not that stupid. They're going to do what they're doing because they like to do it, and they might be forced to do it for a short period of time, but you're not going to force them to do it for a thousand miles. They're going to lie down, and they're going to quit. And you can beat them to death, and they're not going to get up and do it. When the going gets tough and the dog is afraid of you, it's going to get worse. When the going gets tough and the dog loves you, it's going to pull through for you."

The only time most mushers will treat a dog harshly is when it attacks another dog, an action that, if allowed to continue, can jeopardize the survival of the entire team.

Arriving at Fortymile some two hours later, Sawatzky saw the halogen lights of a Japanese documentary film crew. They had set up a tent at the cabin and were filming mushers as they arrived.

They filmed Sawatzky as he pulled in, filmed as he opened his sled bag and gently removed Jack's stiffening body, the combined effects of forty-below temperatures and rigor mortis taking hold, and laid it on the snow next to the sled. He felt ill in the glare of the lights. As best he could, he arranged the open flap of the sled bag over Jack's body. The cameraman focused on the dog and kept it there for a good five minutes.

Then they asked Sawatzky if he would be willing to do an interview.

"No," he replied.

Sawatzky went into the cramped cabin of Sebastian Jones and Shelley Brown, where Tim Osmar and William Kleedehn were sitting, with dripping outdoor gear hanging around the barrel stove. Quietly, he related what had happened. Jones got on the radio and let the Quest checkpoint in Dawson City know that, in Quest terminology, a dog had "expired."

FROZEN AIR

SEBASTIAN JONES AND SHELLY BROWN have spent nine consecutive winters living alone together in a one-room cabin that is just over three metres wide and four metres long. They have a kitchen counter, a smallish double bed, shielded from the rest of the room by a crammed bookshelf, and a table. A barrel wood stove occupies one corner, over which sits an impressive lattice for drying coats, mitts, hats, dog booties, harnesses, and whatever other damp things end up in the cabin. The corner by the door has a coat rack, and on the floor sit the buckets Sebastian uses to feed his own dogs. There are two windows, one in the front and one on the side, next to the square table. The bed is in the third corner, and a homemade armoire is in the other. A trap door in the kitchen floor reveals the cold storage, and the stove is propane. Light is provided by candles and oil lamps.

There's not a shred of Ikea in sight, and no trace of a computer. The only technology in the place is a battery-operated radio and cassette player. It's awfully comfortable.

Sebastian and Shelley met a decade ago when Sebastian offered, on the bank of the Yukon River in Dawson, to take Shelley fishing. At first she demurred, then she changed her mind. They've been together—mostly in the same room—ever since.

He is forty-one, a bearded, long-haired English immigrant to Canada, but his accent has been softened and Canadianized by years of living with northern bush people. Sebastian has the sort of wit that has a gentle sarcasm to it, often directed at people who probably have no business being in such a remote place but are there anyway. Shelley, a decade younger than her partner, is blond, pretty, and has a pleasant, southern Ontario accent. She has a bubbly sense of fun that belies her intelligence. The two of them, it's obvious, get on like a house on fire.

The cabin has double doors, and, instead of handles, thick pieces of rope, knotted at each end, threaded through a snug hole.

Outside the cabin, which is marked "General Store" with a big sign on the front just below the moose antlers, are two rolls of rope, a propane barbecue, and a foam pad that Sebastian leans on to read when the weather is nice.

In the summer, the pair operates the Dawson City campground. Every fall, while the weather is good enough, they drive their pickup truck along a dirt trail off the Top of the World Highway to bring in supplies for the winter. They are paid a modest sum to act as caretakers for the season. In the summer, when Sebastian and Shelley are in Dawson City, Fortymile itself is open as a Yukon government campground. Staffed by heritage interpreters, it is a popular stop for canoeists.

Once they have their supplies in, and the snow starts to fall, Sebastian and Shelley must remain at the cabin until the river is sufficiently frozen to allow their dog team to travel on it between their cabin and Dawson City. Neither of them believes in using snow machines—they're not Amish, they just don't like the smell and the noise—so they don't own one. In February, their only way in and out to telephone service, running water, a grocery store, or another human being is an eight-hour dogsled run, if the weather is good. A small plane can land there in an emergency, as can a helicopter.

Needless to say, they don't have a door on their outhouse, which commands a sweeping vista of the confluence of the Yukon and Fortymile rivers. Standing on the bluff, overlooking mile upon mile of jumbled ice, scarred mountains, and a sky so blue it looks digitally enhanced, an intense feeling of solitude reigns. It feels truly like a throne.

Outhouses are a serious business in the North, and they can reveal a lot about a person. For instance, whether you have a one-holer or a two-holer speaks volumes about your eating habits, or how often the outhouse is used. It takes a little time in forty-below temperatures to realize why anyone would want two holes in a single outhouse, and the uninitiated might be forgiven for speculating that Alaskans and Yukoners are so very friendly that they prefer to defecate *à deux*. Although they are indeed very friendly, this is not the case.

After a while, in very cold weather, human waste, which freezes just about the time it begins to stick to whatever it lands on, will stack, stalagmite-like, sufficiently high to reach the level of the sitting area, meaning that unobservant users will be shown rather pointedly why a second hole is necessary: it more or less doubles the capacity of an outhouse in the winter. Single-holers run the risk of being forced, at some point during the winter, to address the so-called "shitsicle" with a carefully chosen stick.

A considerably less pleasant problem, however, stems from the challenge of installing an outhouse on permafrost. If one merely digs a hole, as might be done in southern latitudes, then heat from the air in the spring and summer can melt its sides, causing it, predictably, to well up with water. This, in turn, causes the unpleasant sensation of "splashback." The long-term remedy for this is to encase an outhouse pit in steel or some other impermeable membrane, thus preventing meltwater from filling it up. The short-term option is to keep a stack of newspapers nearby, and, as you venture into the W.C., you drop in the sports section before you drop your drawers. One day, perhaps, archaeologists will wonder why northern dwellers archived the record of their daily lives underneath little wooden huts, stacked among their waste.

Northerners are often intensely proud of their latrines. Where, in Italy or Portugal or the south of England, you might find posters or postcards depicting, say, "Doors of Sussex," in Alaska or the Yukon you are more likely to see images like "Portapotties of Pelly Crossing," and they are often far more interesting. Reading material, decor, posters, antlers, construction, design all go into the making of a great outhouse. They can be so elaborate that the path to them is illuminated by Christmas lights, and their interiors might be lit by aromatherapeutic candles, contain copies of *Anna Karenina* for literary edification, or have a Dutch-style double door, which allows the user to observe the view without being observed herself. (In Sebastian and Shelley's case, the view is a critical factor.) Or they can be there strictly to serve a functional need with no regard whatsoever to aesthetics. This was the case at one cabin on the Quest trail, whose facility ("facilities" would be an egregious overstatement) I was forced to use in 1998 when the temperature was thirty below. It was a rusty blue fuel drum with an appropriately jigsawed piece of plywood laid casually across the top. There, a single, spindly spruce tree tried in vain to protect me from the wind and the chuckles of other journalists, which became louder as the musher I had been waiting two hours to photograph breezed past, while I swore, snow pants around my ankles, looking helplessly for the toilet paper, which I had left just out of reach on my camera bag.

FORTYMILE IS WITHIN A DAY'S MUSHING of Dawson City. Before miners really even explored the confluence of the Klondike and Yukon rivers, when Dawson City was merely moose pasture and Whitehorse was a set of rapids, Fortymile was truly alone, more than a thousand kilometres from tidal water and civilization.

And it was a happening place.

Fortymile was the first major mining settlement in the Yukon, established in 1886. In its heyday, it boasted more than a thousand residents, six saloons, three restaurants, several doctors, a black-smith, a dressmaker, a watchmaker, a dance hall, a library, and a theatre. The first post office in the Yukon was established there, and the North West Mounted Police had a detachment in town.

Then, a decade later, when news of the Klondike strike came, Fortymile emptied out as fast as the river steamers could take passengers.

After the gold rush some people returned to the village, but it didn't last much longer.

Sebastian and Shelley get visitors only rarely, usually a musher passing by, snow-machine riders, or people who live in other cabins along the river.

The Yukon Quest hits them like a tornado.

Neither really gets much sleep during the five or so days it takes the race to pass through. There isn't any room, as their bed is usually given up to a pair of mushers, just regaining their trail stench after their shower the day before in Dawson. The floor of the cabin, where I slept, is often completely concealed by heaving, polypropylene-covered chests, the sounds and smells of snores and farts attacking the small volume of air space in the cabin.

THE YUKON QUEST TRAIL TURNS LEFT and heads up the Fortymile River, a scenic, narrow river that is popular with rafters in the summer. It is pretty, but most mushers remember it for one reason: it is, almost always, the coldest section of trail on the race.

In 1908, Jack London published "To Build a Fire," the most widely translated piece of short fiction in American literature. The story, about the dangers of travelling alone in the wilds of the Yukon bush, was a revised version of a prescriptive, shorter piece he'd written six years earlier for *The Youth's Companion,* a weekly sermon for teenaged boys.

In the kids' version, the man has a name, Tom Vincent, and, although he has a horrible fright with the cold, he survives to reveal his plight.

In the darker, colder, adult version, the man is an anonymous, arrogant fool, fatally underestimating the power of the cold that saps the river and creek valleys along the Yukon River. He has been walking along a trail south of Dawson City with his dog, heading to a claim where several of his friends are working. He's a *cheechako,* to use the aboriginal term, a tenderfoot spending his first winter in the North.

The temperature, he knows, is well below minus fifty; his spit freezes before it hits the snow. He has not heeded the advice of the old-timers, which is never to travel alone in cold weather.

He slips through a loose layer of snow into some river overflow and gets wet up to his calves. He loses most of the sensation in his fingertips and knows that he must build a fire to dry his moccasins and feet, which have gone numb. Though he manages to gather sticks, his cold fingers fumble and drop the matches and the piece of birchbark he carries to use as ignition for the fire.

After replacing his mitten and beating his hand against his chest for several minutes, he feels the excruciating pang of circulation, enough to grab the birchbark and the matches. He prepares to light a match.

> But the tremendous cold had already driven the life from his fingers. In his effort to separate one match from the others, the whole bunch fell in the snow. He tried to pick it out of the snow, but failed. The dead fingers could neither touch nor clutch. . . .
>
> After some manipulation, he managed to get the bunch between the heels of his mittened hands. In this fashion he carried it to his mouth. The ice [on his beard] crackled and snapped when by a violent effort he opened his mouth. He drew the lower jaw in, curled the upper lip out of the way, and scraped the bunch with his teeth in order to separate a match.

He ends up having to light a match with his teeth, holding the flame underneath his nostrils so that the sulphur makes him choke and the flames lick the tip of his nose.

He gets some kindling burning, but, before the fire can raise itself very high, the heat melts the snow on the cedar boughs above, which comes crashing down and extinguishes the fire. In his haste, he failed to ensure he was building his fire in a clear area.

The rest of the story details his slow death from hypothermia, as he panics but is forced to accept his fate:

> It struck him as curious that he could run at all on feet so frozen that he could not feel the weight of them when they struck the earth and took the weight of his body. He seemed to himself to skim along above the surface, and to have no connection with the earth. Somewhere he had once seen a winged Mercury, and wondered if Mercury felt as he felt skimming over the earth.

Running out of endurance, the tired man eventually decides to sit and rest.

As he sat and regained his breath, he noticed that he was feeling quite warm and comfortable. He was not shivering, and it seemed that a warm glow had come to his chest and trunk. And yet, when he touched his cheeks, there was no sensation. . . .

He was losing his battle with the frost. It was creeping into his body from all sides. The thought of it drove him on, but he ran no further than a hundred feet, when he staggered and pitched headlong. It was his last panic. When he had recovered his breath and control, he sat up and entertained in his mind the conception of meeting death with dignity. . . . With this newfound piece of mind came the first glimmerings of drowsiness. A good idea, he thought, to sleep off to death. It was like taking an anaesthetic. Freezing was not so bad as people thought. There were lots worse ways to die.

He pictured the boys finding his body the next day. Suddenly, he found himself with them, coming along the trail and looking for himself. And, still with them, he came around a turn in the trail and found himself lying in the snow. He did not belong with himself anymore, for even he was out of himself, standing with the boys and looking at himself in the snow. It certainly was cold, was his thought. When he got back in the States he could tell the folks what real cold was. He drifted on from this to a vision of the old-timer on Sulphur Creek. He could see him quite clearly, warm and comfortable, and smoking a pipe.

"You were right, old hoss, you were right," the man mumbled to the old-timer of Sulphur Creek.

Then the man dozed off into what seemed to him the most satisfying sleep he had ever known.

Freezing to death is a very real fear in the Yukon and Alaska. Every year, several people die from exposure, often in concert with alcohol, which impairs our judgment and ability to sense cold.

Depending on its severity, hypothermia can kill a freezing person in less than five hours, a time that jumps to less than half an hour in frigid water. The body's first reaction to being cooled down is vasoconstriction, which shrinks the surface area of the blood vessels to reduce the amount of heat that might escape from them. Hairs on arms and legs stand on end to create an insulated pocket of air around the skin.

If this doesn't work, the brain triggers minute muscular convulsions, otherwise known as shivering, to generate a quick source of heat from the movement.

As a person's body temperature begins to drop, he starts to lose sensation in his fingertips and feet as his body redirects blood supply to critical areas like the chest and brain.

When his core temperature drops two degrees Celsius from the normal reading of thirty-seven degrees, he is officially hypothermic, and unless he changes his environment he has started down the road to death.

After extremity numbness sets in, he feels a profound feeling of weakness take over his body. It becomes difficult to see properly, and even walking becomes an arduous task, as not enough oxygen-rich blood is getting to his brain to allow it to function properly. His muscles stiffen, and, if he had anyone to talk to, his speech would be so slurred that they would think he was drunk. The world stops making sense to him, and he becomes confused about where he is. Someone who came along would have a hard time finding his pulse; if it can be felt, it is weak and irregular. His breathing becomes shallow, and he seems unable to draw enough air into his lungs. He is fading away.

Then something sudden happens: he gets the feeling that he's not cold at all, that the weather outside is balmy. He feels as though he's sweating and overheating. In an effort to cool down, he removes whatever clothing he's wearing, tossing it aside to lie naked in the snow.

He falls asleep, feeling comfortable, as the vital organs shut down. Then, moments later, he is gone.

In urban centres, cold is treated with disrespect: we have gone to great lengths to avoid having to deal with it. In Toronto, you can navigate the entire downtown core underground, never leaving the heated and halogen-lighted comfort of a string of subterranean shopping malls. Even in Winnipeg, much of the city centre is accessible through a network of second-floor, heated pathways. It is possible to live in Canada and never really expose yourself to the winter for which it is justly famous.

This, however, is not true in the Yukon or Alaska, where cold wraps itself around your face and demands respect. In January 1996, in Whitehorse, the warmest it got was around minus forty-two, and the temperature hovered at fifty below for much of the month.

The air at forty or fifty below hurts to breathe; it's like sucking in a cupful of thumb tacks: it attacks your windpipe with tactile arrogance. You can feel exposed skin on your face turning rubbery, tightening and shrinking against your cheekbones. You become aware of the mucous that moistens your eyes, making you blink more often. Your eyes feel cold, and, if you close your eyelids to protect them, you feel your lashes begin to freeze together.

Participating in an event such as the Yukon Quest requires a different psychological approach to cold. New technology has made it relatively easy to stay physically warm. Psychologically, however, it's another story. "The mental part is dealing with the fear of the cold," says Frank Turner. "If you don't deal with that fear, you are going to get what you kind of expect. Just the nature of what we do means you're going to be cold. You know your toes are going to be cold. You're probably going to have frostbite on your cheeks. When it gets to be forty below, there's no way to stay warm on the back of a dogsled. We're not going to be warm, but we'll be comfortable."

Turner explains this while drumming his frostbite-scarred fingertips on his dining room table. "If you want to be warm, go to Florida."

Researchers have studied the ability of climbers to handle extreme cold at a "laboratory" 4,000 metres up the side of Mount Denali, the highest mountain in North America. They came up with a surprising discovery: people used to dealing with the cold can actually will themselves warmer. Using fingertip-mounted sensors, they were able to discern a measurable increase in circulation when chilled climbers were told to try to warm themselves up.

Despite this ability, though, cold tolerance has its limits. A decade ago, Turner himself was forced to pull out of a race because his fingers were so frostbitten that he, like the character in "To Build a Fire," lacked the dexterity to strike a match or join the bottom ends of the zipper on his parka.

Now, a little more savvy, he knows the tricks only years of experience—in the cold or dressing kindergarten children—can teach. He has the zipper on his parka stitched together at the bottom, so it can't come apart. When he puts his parka on he steps into it, pulling it up his legs like a dress, sliding his arms in at the end. It looks funny, but it saves him valuable time when the weather is cold.

More impressive, he, and other top mushers, use cold to their advantage while racing. Although it is mandatory, for obvious reasons, for mushers to carry a winter sleeping bag, Turner uses his only at checkpoints, when he's sleeping inside and there is a race official to wake him up. When he stops on the trail, even if the temperature is forty-five degrees below zero, he won't use it, choosing instead to lie on the top of his sled uncovered. His reason? He doesn't want to get too *warm*. Stories of mushers over-sleeping, like Andrew Lesh near Scroggie Creek, next to the embers of a warm campfire, are legion. "Cold," Turner says, "is a great motivator." He wants to avoid the snooze-button syndrome, where, cocooned in a warm sleeping bag, he looks out at the cold snow when he is supposed to get up and says, "Just five more minutes." This is, after all, a race.

Still, cold, in one manifestation or another, is behind most mushers' decisions to scratch. Jim Hendrick got such a bad case of frostbite in his feet one year that he couldn't walk. Others have lost parts of their noses, cheeks, and fingers. It's a fact of Quest life.

Nearly everyone who scratches does so by the end of the first half of the race. The attrition builds exponentially and then, suddenly, all but stops. One musher at Braeburn. One at Carmacks. Two at Pelly Crossing. Six at Dawson City. Heading into the second half of the race this year, one-third of the teams had dropped out.

Kirsten Bey, a rookie musher and lawyer from Nome, left Dawson and made it to Fortymile. Already one of the slowest in the race, her pace slowed to a crawl when her best leader, Red—a dog she had bought from Frank Turner after last year's Quest—was bitten in a fight. Dispirited, from Fortymile she contacted her handlers, one of whom was her husband, Bob Lewis, at times yelling into the radio. They had already left Dawson City for the long, twenty-hour drive around to Circle City. They had to turn around and come back to Dawson to pick her up.

FIFTY KILOMETRES UP THE FORTYMILE RIVER, there is a narrow swath cut in the undulating forest that stretches out as far as the eye can see on either side. Miles from anywhere, it's a vivid snapshot of the world's longest undefended border.

Welcome to the Last Frontier, the largest state in the Union. After another fifty kilometres, the river goes underneath the Taylor Highway bridge, on the road that connects tiny Eagle, Alaska, to the Top of the World Highway and the rest of the United States and Canada.

The highway is open only in the summer. In winter, the right-of-way makes a perfect mushing trail into the next checkpoint, which is still a long way off.

THE LAST FRONTIER

Joran Freeman left Dawson City just in front of John Schandelmeier, and the two, rookie and veteran, travelled together. One of the most experienced bush mushers around, Schandelmeier knows his animals exceedingly well. Vets marvel at his ability to notice even a very slight change in a dog's gait and make an accurate diagnosis of its condition, without any formal medical training. Unlike almost any other musher, he talks to his dogs as though they were adult humans, and they seem to respond.

Schandelmeier once issued a bold challenge while sitting in the old schoolhouse checkpoint in Eagle: allow him to pick fourteen dogs from the animal shelter in Fairbanks in September, and, by the time the Quest began in February, he would have trained a team capable of running and finishing the race. Interestingly, as he approached Eagle again, he was running with Freeman, whose team was made up almost entirely of castaways, giveaways, and dogs deemed unwanted by other people. And Freeman's team, which cost him less than $300, was far ahead of teams worth—on paper at least—more than a hundred times that amount.

Between Dawson and Eagle, with a little bit of John Schandelmeier's advice, Freeman's dogs achieved something nearly impossible when running 150 kilometres a day: they began to fill out and gain weight. And they were still running fast.

Eighty kilometres east of Eagle, where the Fortymile River crosses the Taylor Highway and the trail turns from river to road, Joran Freeman, Cim Smyth, Hugh Neff, John Schandelmeier, and Andrew Lesh stopped to camp. The discussion was sombre; news had passed back along the trail that David Sawatzky had lost a dog.

Although the word was that the death was an accident and couldn't have been prevented, mushers knew that when they arrived in Eagle the vets would be closely examining teams to make sure they didn't miss any other potentially sick dogs. Freeman was worried that, because of the condition of his dogs in Dawson, he would be forced to spend extra time in Eagle allowing his dogs more rest.

Worse, what he didn't know was that, behind him, a second dog had died on the way to Eagle.

EAGLE, WHICH SITS ON A SANDY DEPOSIT at a windy, sweeping bend in the Yukon River, is home to some fishermen, a tourist paddlewheel replica called the *Yukon Queen,* a motel, a bed-and-breakfast, and not much else.

Across the bend from the town is 300–metre-high Eagle Bluff, which sits as an almost perfectly triangular basalt sentry over the village. Its one of the most recognizable landmarks on the Yukon Quest trail.

Many of the old log cabins and other buildings look as though they are falling down, and more of them have already collapsed. The town boasts a pool hall, two landing strips, a laundromat, and a new school with two classrooms for its twenty-four students. The old school, a single-room, four-metre by four-metre hut with a gable-topped entrance at the north end of town (about a five-minute walk from the south end of town), springs to life for a week as the Yukon Quest's checkpoint.

Perhaps the most interesting artifact in the town is an unremarkable silver globe atop a small pedestal in a postage-stamp-sized park behind the motel. It recognizes Norwegian Arctic explorer Roald Amundsen, who came to Eagle in 1905 shortly after becoming the first person to successfully navigate the Northwest Passage. Then, Eagle was the northernmost settlement in North America to have a communications link to the rest of the world, and it was from Eagle that Amundsen broadcast the news of his new route connecting the Atlantic and Pacific oceans.

His granddaughter, Suzan, who was born in Calgary, Alberta, has run the Quest herself four times.

There are no traffic lights in Eagle, and there aren't even any stop signs (there are a couple of yield signs, however). There are no locks on the motel room doors, and only one grainy channel works on the television.

For much of the year, Eagle is cut off from the rest of the world by snow and ice; the Taylor Highway, the seasonal road connecting Eagle to the Alaska Highway, isn't maintained in the winter and is often buried under twenty or more metres of snow by the time the Quest comes to town in February. "Winter" in Eagle is determined by the number of months the road is closed, usually beginning in October and ending after highway maintenance crews have cleared the snow, opening several metres of road a day sometime in April. The town faces the river, where a wind funnel caused by Eagle Bluff results in a perpetual gale on the riverfront. Massive snowdrifts roll off the town's river frontage like frozen ocean breakers.

One hundred and forty-eight people live here year-round. Like most of the non-aboriginal villages along the upper Yukon River, the town's halcyon days were during the turn-of-the-century gold rushes. Han natives lived here long before any Europeans arrived, but they now reside in a village five kilometres upriver. Named after the eagles that nest on the bluff, Eagle City was founded in 1897 as a supply depot, and by the following year it had 1,700 residents. In 1901, it became the first non-coastal Alaskan town to be incorporated.

Eagle has no bank, although it has its own currency: every fall, people buy U.S. Postal Service money orders in various denominations and use them to pay for items at the general store. The recipient's name isn't filled in, however, and the blank orders get passed from person to person, just like paper money. Dennis Layman, who owns the Eagle Trading Post and the squat, cedar-stripped motel behind it, says it's just as convenient as cash, and in much greater supply.

Layman's store, about the same size as a single-car garage, is a wonder of merchandising: motor oil, baseballs, almond cookies, wallets, and bubble bath share a shelf next to the cash register; others nearby hold kerosene, rosehip tablets, and bottled Starbucks iced cappuccinos.

Because it is the first Quest stop in the United States, media and officials are occasionally greeted by a customs officer, who has flown in from the Yukon–Alaska border station at Beaver Creek. For several days, as the race passes through, he can be seen checking people's passports at the café over a cup of coffee.

Some people might climb a mountain to seek fresh air, wisdom, or skiing trails. In Eagle, you must somehow get to the top of American Summit, the mountain pass immediately behind the town, if you want a drink. Eagle is a dry town, officially, and it is kept so by a slim majority of evangelical Christians who prevent any sort of licensed establishment from opening up. Many people drink, but few have the motivation to change the law forbidding the sale of booze, which would require a community-polarizing referendum. "We don't bother bringing it up any more; they just vote it down," Dennis Layman says, resignedly, adding that he brings his beer in from Fairbanks every summer by truck.

In winter, however, unless you want the expense of having booze delivered by airmail, you take your snowmobile or skis or dog team and climb twenty kilometres to the top of a windswept mountain summit, where, ignobly plunked in a blindingly white landscape, is a prefab trailer that serves as both liquor store and bar. It's operated by a crusty, seventy-one-year-old man named Roy, who stays there with about ten Labrador retrievers.

Calling it a bar is stretching a point: it has one table and a chair, which are surrounded by stacked cases of dusty beer bottles from which you can make your selection.

There are no police officers based in Eagle, although the state troopers stop by four times a year. Amazingly, in a dry town inaccessible by car, the last time a police officer was here he managed to arrest a man for drunk driving. The man was apparently driving his car across front lawns while sipping from a vodka bottle.

It is said that those who don't fit into the lower forty-eight move to Alaska. Those who don't fit into Alaska, it would seem, live in Eagle. The stories are legion. There's the man who, apparently angry, emptied his revolver into a (mercifully unoccupied) single-engine plane parked on the tarmac. The largish woman who parades around town in the summer wearing the latest from the Victoria's Secret catalogue, and is always on hand to greet new, male arrivals coming by boat. The fellow who used to walk around town checking to see whether residents were locking their doors. (If they were locked, he'd pound on the door, demanding to know what the homeowner was hiding.)

At the Quest checkpoint in Eagle, there is usually a campfire outside the schoolhouse, tended by a bearded man with glasses wearing military fatigues. Reporters are warned not to make eye contact with him. He is, or was, before it closed, the owner, proprietor, and main diatribist of Republic Radio. His name is Mark Gilmore, and he lives in Eagle year-round with his wife, Helen, and eight children, under a tarpaulin.

MARK GILMORE AND I have descended, pushing our way along a rolled-out snow-machine track, into his 150-square-metre home through a dangling pile of black sleeping bags that shroud an ill-fitting wooden door. The roof—which, from the outside, sits about a metre off the snow—is an expanse of blue tarpaulins, held in place by ropes, bungee cords, discarded tires, and other community detritus. "In eight years, I've spent less than a thousand dollars on new materials," he says, with obvious pride, as we walk around the squat, bunker-like structure, which looks as if it could be covered up completely by a suitably large snowdrift. Rather than a house, it looks like something somebody might rig up to hide rusting car parts.

Inside, worn sheets of plywood and flattened-out cardboard boxes form an erratic floor over the bumpy, pitted dirt. None of it stays connected, thanks to the heaving of the permafrost, and the shelves, all made from scrap wood, tilt crazily, giving the warren of rooms an *Alice in Wonderland* quality. In the back are rows of bunks made from two-by-fours and old pallets. Along one corner sits a chicken coop with two chickens inside (there used to be another one, but "the dog ate it last fall," Gilmore explains). Rabbits run loose among the skids. The ceiling is made of more cardboard boxes salvaged from the grocery store, attached to erratically spaced logs. According to Gilmore's theory, the glue on the seams of the overlaid cardboard boxes melts from the heat of the house, which seals them together. (It's not clear whether there's a building code in Eagle, or whether there is anyone to enforce it if there is.) Sheltered by eight years' worth of crushed boxes that once held packages of Bounty paper towels, Swiss Miss hot chocolate, and Purina cat food, the Gilmore household presents a toasty homage to American consumer products.

As a real bonus, three months ago Gilmore hooked up to the town's electrical system, so now they have a colour television and VCR, and an oil monitor heater, which supplements the aging pot-bellied stove that had previously provided the heat.

On a piece of scrap wood nailed above what appears to be the kitchen counter, there is a jar filled with alcohol containing a white plastic clamp used to cut off circulation in the umbilicus. In hospitals, these are disposable, but Mark and Helen Gilmore have used this one for several of their nine children. Next to it, in a similar jar, is a scalpel. All their children save one have been born on their bed, which sits, raised, next to the kitchen. Michael, now six, "made a mess on the sofa," one of the children explains with a grin.

As I sit down, I'm mobbed by children under six, while the older girls smile politely. A toddler is climbing up my leg, asking me if I'm an M&M. "Hey, M&M-head!" Michael, the sofa-born boy, shouts at me across the room, causing me to notice that consumerism ekes its way into even the most resistant of households. The moniker sticks for my two-hour visit.

I am handed a cup of tea in which is floating a plant. Apparently it's good for my thyroid. Gilmore, a self-professed herbalist (*The Mushroom Handbook* sits nearby on a shelf, with other dog-eared volumes), then passes me a wet toothpick with a white powder on it. The powder, the name of which I cannot recall, is sweeter than sugar. I'm told to use the toothpick to stir my tea, which I do.

Rachel, their thirteen-year-old eldest daughter, screws up her face and whispers to me under her breath that she doesn't like it. I take a deep breath and imbibe the tea. It's unbelievably sweet and tastes vaguely of chamomile. After five minutes pass, and I haven't started to hallucinate (I hope, realizing that I am sitting on a dirt floor underneath a tarpaulin in Alaska in February), I conclude that the powder (which hasn't been approved by the U.S. Food and Drug Administration because of lobby efforts by the sugar producers, Gilmore alleges) is okay.

Gilmore wears plastic-rimmed glasses that seem to have a slight orange tint. They're the sort that automatically go dark when exposed to sunlight, and then take half an hour to return to normal once back inside. He is intense, so much so that at times it is difficult to look at him straight on when he is talking to you, for fear he will attack you for not listening. His thinning hair gives away his fifty-something age, although his beard—a goatee, more like—has a reddish-brown hue. He laughs a lot, in a nervous kind of way.

Mark Gilmore hands me a well-worn Bible and tells me to open it. On the first page, yellowed and dirty with age and use, are the details of his children in this order: Name. Date of birth. Weight. It's the sole record of their birth, he says. To weigh his newborns, he takes them to the Eagle post office, where they are put on the package scale. They don't have social security numbers or birth certificates, he says. In fact, he suggests, in the eyes of the state, they don't exist at all. Nor, apparently, does he. A last-generation hillbilly, he left his home in Tennessee to fight in the Vietnam War, and when it was done, he came to Alaska and fell off the map.

He somehow exists enough, however, to collect social security and a veteran's pension, which he used for a while, unbelievably, to fund a pirate radio station called Republic Radio, a keep-government-out-of-the-lives-of-the-people organ promoting God and guns and pledging to "take it to the new world order any way we can." Along with a general lack of interest in detail, he also seems blissfully innocent of the concept of irony.

I let him go on for several minutes, during which he castigates, in roughly this order, the social welfare state, communists, poor treatment of veterans, Santa Claus, and the Tooth Fairy. (They have never told their children any lies, Helen interjects, and both explain that they think it is immoral for parents to perpetuate these myths. It makes children believe it is all right to fib, they say.) I didn't ask him what he thought of Timothy McVeigh. I didn't want to know.

For all this, however, it doesn't appear that his children are suffering, or that the department of social services is knocking on his sleeping-bag door. One boy, their eldest, ran away from home at seventeen, Gilmore says, and he now works in a mine in southern Alaska. The others all seem articulate, friendly, and well adjusted. A copy of *Charlotte's Web* lies on the ground, suggesting that their learning goes beyond polemics.

On the second page of the Bible is stapled the only family portrait they've ever had taken, a standard, Sears-style photograph that looks ridiculously out of place amid the jury-rigged cardboard, scrap wood, and blue plastic that defines their home. He plans to tear the tarp down next summer, anyway, he admits, and reconstruct the home farther back from the road, where trees will provide a little more privacy. He has other plans for this spot, he says, without a trace of a smile. He is going to build a tarp hotel.

I KNEW NONE OF THIS, however, when Mark and his brother-in-law, "Crazy" Roy Loughmiller, offered to take me and three other journalists out on the trail to take photographs. For $50 each—modern highway robbery—we would be taken to O'Brien Creek Lodge, about 100 kilometres back down the trail over American Summit, where Tim Osmar and William Kleedehn were reportedly camped.

The military fatigues they were wearing didn't faze me, nor did the snow machines that looked as though they had seen better days in the 1970s. Even the metal dogsled attached to the back of

Roy's machine seemed stable enough. We set out. Nick Wrathall, in independent videographer from England, was on the back of Mark's snow machine. Gillian Rogers, the *Yukon News* photographer, sat behind Roy on his. *Fairbanks Daily News-Miner* shooter Sam Harrel was in the basket of the sled. This left me to stand on the runners of the metal sled that was hooked to Roy's aged machine by a cotter pin.

Only as we climbed the hill on the unploughed Taylor Highway out of Eagle towards the summit did I realize that I had forgotten to purchase emergency medical insurance in Dawson City before I left. My right knee had been surgically rebuilt the previous July and hadn't really worked very well since. I offered a silent prayer that it would still be in one piece when we returned.

Every minute or so on the way up, Sam waved his arms behind him, hitting my legs to make sure I was still there. If I fell off, there would be no way of knowing over the growl of the engine.

It was only after we'd stopped for a rest that I noticed something: the handlebar of the sled that I had been holding onto for the last twenty kilometres or so actually wasn't, in fact, properly attached. With a good tug, I could have pulled it right off. It appeared that sheer good luck alone was all that had kept me from tumbling down the side of the mountain, trying to self-arrest with a useless piece of metal tubing. No matter; for Roy, it was nothing that couldn't be fixed with a handy piece of baling wire.

American Summit is perhaps the least heralded summit on the entire Quest trail, which isn't really fair. It is probably the most beautiful. Stunted spruce trees buckle with the weight of powdery snow stacked impossibly high on the boughs. A giant valley spreads out beneath it, with nary a sign of civilization glinting in the extravagant sunlight. The whiteness is nearly blinding.

Behind us, the Eagle bar and liquor store sat unpatronized. Roy, the proprietor, has it open twenty-four hours during the Quest when the mushers are coming through, hoping to attract a thirsty dog-driver or two. None are likely to stop, however, with the prospect of hot water and straw for the dogs an hour's run away. If they do stop for a beer—and some do—it's more likely to be at O'Brien Creek Lodge, our destination this sunny, cool afternoon.

American Summit has neither the height of King Solomon's Dome nor the pitch of Eagle or Rosebud summits, but it has one aspect that make it perhaps the most technically challenging of them all for dogsleds: a three-kilometre stretch of trail that slopes, sideways, very steeply. Travelling on a slanted trail like this is called sidehilling, a delicate balancing act that requires both strength and finesse. The reason for the extreme sidehill is that the Taylor Highway, some four metres below the trail under a wind-hardened crust of snow, doesn't actually traverse the top of the summit. It terraces around it, which is fine when the road has been built with bulldozers and massive earth-moving machines that can carve out a nice flat space. However, the Quest trail, cut out of snow, doesn't stay flat and more resembles the natural pitch of the mountainside. As a result, when crossing American Summit, you can touch the snow with your right hand, and with your left reach over a considerable drop. Sidehilling on a dogsled means standing on the uphill runner, leaning uphill, pulling both hands over to one side of the handlebar, and fighting against the weight of the sled, which gravity wants to yank down the hill. The lower runner stays suspended about half a metre off the snow. In the case of American Summit, particularly late in the year, there might be nothing to stop that downward motion for hundreds of steep metres. Looking down into the valley beneath the summit, it would be difficult to imagine how a team could escape without mechanical assistance.

The sidehill was now so steep that there was no chance we could follow the trail on a snow machine. We tried, and, suddenly, the hitherto silent Gillian let out a little yelp as the machine tipped over on its side. We tried again: same result. Sam got out of the sled, and he and Gillian started to walk. Roy drove on, leaning hard over, both feet on the uphill side of the snow machine, with me on the sled practically dragging my elbow in the uphill snow. It still didn't work. The machine rolled again, and I jumped clear of the sliding sled, which weighed nearly a hundred kilograms. We stood there, dumbfounded, while Sam and Gillian walked to catch up.

We'd assumed, when we'd agreed to pay him fifty bucks, that he'd actually done this before.

Eventually, Roy hit on the idea of abandoning the trail, and, rather than try to terrace around the top of the mountain, he decided to head straight up and over the top, bushwhacking as the sled bounced and burrowed through the deep powder, hitting only a few small shrubs. On skis, this would have been great fun.

After getting across the summit, we carried on, with little event, down the other side. Roy and Mark were driving quickly, but not so fast that I couldn't hang on. At one point, we crossed some overflow—on which the sled went sideways and dragged the sliding snow machine with it—but soon the spiked, tightly knitted spruce-trunk fencing of O'Brien Creek Lodge came into view, with two dog teams parked in front.

As we disembarked and untied the photography gear, Tim Osmar and William Kleedehn came out. We warned them of the overflow just ahead on the trail. "Maybe we should go in and have another beer," Osmar said, chuckling.

As they readied their sleds and pulled out, David Sawatzky came into sight along the trail, and he soon passed the lodge, following close behind them. We didn't realize it at the time, but in his sled bag was Jack's body. Fortymile isn't a dog drop, and Sawatzky had to carry the dog's body 160 kilometres to Eagle. Andrew Lesh followed shortly thereafter, also bypassing the warmth and free food.

Frank Turner came next, pulling in after a straight-through, 130-kilometre run from Fortymile. He had just had a rather strange experience.

He had been on the Fortymile River, trying to keep his hands warm in the forty-below temperatures, when he came around a bend in the river and nearly ran into a cyclist.

Klaus Pusl, a garage manager from a small town in Germany near its border with Austria, had travelled over to Dawson City to ride his specially made bicycle along the Quest trail to Fairbanks. It looked like a mountain bike, with tires about ten centimetres wide. They were actually tires from a small plane, and the bike had been designed to ride over sand dunes in California.

He had planned to cover half the Quest trail in two weeks, but high winds and cold temperatures had forced him to hole out in his tent for two days at Fortymile.

Lest one be tempted to think he was an apparition, the product of a hallucination-prone mind, several other mushers reported seeing him as well. Bill Pinkham saw his tent at the top of American Summit, his bicycle lying close by, and tossed a candy bar at its door as he passed by. Later, I met Pusl as he rode into Eagle.

A veteran of the Iditasport, a winter bike/ski/snowshoe race that follows the Iditarod trail, he had heard of the Quest and thought it would be an interesting way to spend his vacation. He had lost time, however, and had to fly on to Circle, where he rode the last 400 kilometres into Fairbanks along the highway.

BACK AT O'BRIEN CREEK LODGE, even the sight of a cyclist on the Quest trail hadn't prepared us, Frank Turner included, for what was going on inside.

O'Brien Creek Lodge was officially closed for the season but had been opened up by several Eagle residents—friends of Mark's and Roy's, evidently—for the mushers on the race. Few of the mushers even knew it would be open, as the word from Dawson City had been that none of the Taylor Highway stops would be available to teams.

The wood stove was sizzling, and seated at the bar were several men. In a space about the same size as half a tennis court, there were sixteen racks on the walls—moose, caribou, deer—as well as a skull-and-crossbones poster advertising the Special Forces ("Live Free or Die," it pronouced) and a copy of the front page of the *Honolulu Star-Bulletin* from the day the Japanese bombed Pearl Harbor. There was a pool table in the middle of the room, which served as a counter for mittens, parkas, and hats.

In the kitchen, where someone was cooking delicious-smelling salmon, was an AK-47 assault rifle, just lying on the floor. The men in the bar were drunk. Cases of Budweiser and Coors were ripped open, and we were invited to partake, which we did.

The conversation was electrifying, the men all talking past each other, nobody really listening, most talking at the same time. From across the room, I made out only snippets:

". . . you know there are three billion Chinese out there just waiting to eat your children for lunch . . ."

". . . You know Greenpeace? It's like watermelon. Green on the outside and PINK on the inside."

Frank said he was planning to rest there for six hours. He cleared a spot on the pool table and, stripped down to his blue polypropylene long underwear, crawled on top to lie face down, his head and still-dripping beard cradled in his arms. He looked up, found me, and motioned me over.

"Do you think you could stay here with me? I don't think I want to be here by myself," he said, only half joking.

"I can't," I replied, because we were getting ready to leave. "Crazy" Roy and Mark Gilmore had already gone outside to start up the snow machines. "But don't worry. I won't tell them you voted NDP."

"And I won't tell them you worked for Greenpeace," he said, laughing, if a little nervously.

MARK AND ROY, perhaps enervated by their discussion, set a rather different pace on the snow machines on the return trip to

Eagle as afternoon darkness set in. I could just make out the lighted speedometer of the snow machine as it hit eighty kilometres an hour. Sam, I think, was yelling at Roy to slow down, but neither he nor Gillian, who was hunched forward into his back, could hear him over the scream of the motor. I just tried to hang on, as the sled fishtailed around corners, the dropping temperature biting at my face.

Forty minutes or so later, we were back at American Summit, this time in the dark, trying once again to follow the reflective markers along the Quest trail. Ahead we could see the headlights of at least three mushers, but they were moving faster than we were, because we had to stop and right the rolled snow machines every few metres. Nearly through the summit traverse, the snow machine Mark was driving 100 metres behind us quit. We had already reached the liquor store, so while Roy went back to help Mark get his machine going, we had a beer with the other Roy.

About half an hour later, machines running again, we were on our way back down the mountain into Eagle, again at eighty kilometres an hour, swishing around the "S" turns that switched back and forth, each time, it seemed, the sled coming a little closer to the ditch. Sam was still yelling, to no reply.

First, at far too high a speed, we passed Andrew Lesh, who wore a dumfounded expression on his face as he saw us swerve by. He would later tell me he couldn't believe how fast we were going. Then we picked off David Sawatzky, followed by William Kleedehn and Tim Osmar, travelling almost in tandem.

Nearly back in Eagle, the highway was actually ploughed for the last three or so kilometres, revealing a stiff sheen of hard-packed snow on which snow-machine (and sled) runners would have a harder time keeping a grip. Instead of slowing down, however, to compensate for this, Roy sped up. As the machine lurched forward, its rear end kicked a little, a movement that was exaggerated by the weight of the three people in the sled. Within several seconds, moving in what seemed like slow motion, I was passing Gillian and Roy on their right. Gillian noticed, but Roy didn't. We were on the left side of the road and there was lots of room for us to swing out. However, physics being what it is, the sled soon yanked back with extreme prejudice.

It was as it slammed into the metre-high snowbank that I let go, tunnelling some six metres through the snow in the ditch. I lay there, on the side of the road, for some time before I summoned the courage to see whether all of my parts were intact. Miraculously, they were. Thankfully the ditch was clear of trees, and Eagle residents don't seem to put mailboxes at the ends of their driveways. I could walk, although my back was mighty stiff the next day.

At least I'd managed to get Roy's attention. And, after picking me up (as well as Sam and Nick, who also flew into the snowbank), he drove much more slowly.

As we arrived at the checkpoint, we were rushed by the remaining media and race officials, who had been apprised of where we had been taken, and, more important, by whom. Our near-death experience at the hands of Mark and Roy made the evening news in Whitehorse.

LEAVING O'BRIEN CREEK LODGE, the three leaders, Tim Osmar, William Kleedehn, and David Sawatzky, travelled together, as they had since the top of King Solomon's Dome before Dawson City.

On the run into Eagle, however, a newcomer had joined them. With a very fast run out of Fortymile, Andrew Lesh had come along, as the sun came down on O'Brien Creek Lodge, several minutes after Kleedehn and Osmar had left. He'd waved, his purple parka almost glowing in the setting sun as he went by.

Now there were four in the front pack.

As they approached American Summit in the darkness, Lesh, who was behind Kleedehn, watched him negotiate the treacherous sidehill. All the way across, the sled kept trying to wash out, downhill, following gravity.

Lesh figured that Kleedehn, with his prosthetic leg, would lose time across the summit, because balancing is a key element of traversing sidehill. They both used the same type of sled, so, all things being equal, Lesh, a fit, athletic man, should have passed Kleedehn quite easily.

Not so.

Ahead of him, Lesh watched Kleedehn smoothly control the sled, perched on one runner with his other leg sticking straight out to the uphill side. For his part, Lesh fell numerous times trying to do the same thing. By the time he reached the liquor store on the far side of the summit, he had lost fifteen minutes to Kleedehn.

The four teams came down the hill into Eagle: Osmar, Kleedehn, Sawatzky, and Lesh. Osmar and Kleedehn arrived two minutes apart, exactly as they had in Dawson City, 200 kilometres back. Sawatzky and Lesh arrived within twenty minutes. It was a tightly packed group.

Kleedehn and Osmar had travelled virtually the entire distance together and were chatting like old friends. So much for Kleedehn's promise to avoid the convenience of travelling with other teams in the interests of pure racing. The Quest trail doesn't really allow that.

At Eagle, Lesh, still amazed at Kleedehn's performance at the top of the summit, asked him how he did it. "Pure desperation measures," Kleedehn replied, grinning.

As Sawatzky made the final descent from American Summit into Eagle, the point where the road was ploughed, he noticed a pickup truck was parked there. It carried Mark Lindstrom, a race official, and Allan Hallman, a veterinarian. They had been told about Jack by the Dawson checkpoint and had come to take the dog from Sawatzky, so he wouldn't have to unload it in front of the full media entourage. Unlike Fortymile, which few photographers or reporters can get to, most of the media following the race come to Eagle.

Doug Harris, the race marshal, and Margy Terhar, the head veterinarian, briefed reporters on Sawatzky's circumstance shortly after he arrived.

"Unfortunately, we have some kind of sad news," Margy began, tears welling up in her eyes. "Dave Sawatzky lost a dog, Jack, a three-year-old. The rest of his team looks good. There's no indication that it was driver error, or negligence, or anything like that, so we'll proceed as we usually do, which is to send the remains to a pathologist to get a definitive diagnosis."

"Dave's upset about this," Harris added. "He wants to look after his dogs, and then he wants to phone his wife."

The Japanese film crew came over to Sawatzky again, before any of the reporters, asking him if they could film the plane carrying Jack's body as it took off for Fairbanks. "I don't care," he said, gruffly. "If that makes you happy then you go right ahead and do it."

Then other members of the media trickled over, mostly politely and deferentially, and he answered their questions as best he could. "The only thing I wanted to do was go to some place I could call my wife and tell her so she wouldn't have to read about it in the newspaper," he later said.

He didn't learn that Carrie Farr had lost a dog until he got home.

Farr, a forty-four-year-old fisherwoman and hunting guide from Nenana, Alaska, had been having trouble even before the race started. While she was at the pre-race banquet, two of her dogs got into a fight back at her billet's house just outside Whitehorse.

When dogs fight for real, it's not at all like the jostling and wrestling, or even nipping, one sees in the off-leash section of a public park. Dogs don't fight for fun. And they don't fight half-heartedly, to beat each other up to prove a point. They fight to kill.

I once, at a race, came across a dog fight that had started when a musher fell off her sled. The team had carried on alone, left the trail, and were running along the side of the highway. The team got tangled up, and two of the dogs, twisted together, got into a fight. One dog bit down on another's thigh, cutting clean through the muscle, locking its jaw on the bone. Its mouth had to be pried off the other dog's leg. The bitten dog ultimately died from its injuries.

Farr came back from the banquet to find one of her dogs lying dead in a pool of its own blood, its neck broken.

As mushers often do, she had brought more than fourteen dogs, so she was still able to start with a fresh team.

Then, as she left Fortymile, on her way to Eagle, Igor, a two-and-a-half-year-old male, started to wobble as he ran. She picked him up and carried him in the sled until, when he seemed fine and in good spirits and eager to run, she tried him back in the team.

In less than five minutes, he collapsed and died.

Margy Terhar said there was no evidence it was Farr's fault. Although Igor had been treated for mild tracheo-bronchitis in Dawson City, he seemed fine. His death seemed to feature hall-mark symptoms of sled-dog myopathy.

The owner of a fishing camp in rural, mostly aboriginal Alaska, Farr's attitude to the loss of the dog was philosophical. She hadn't had him terribly long, she said, and wasn't terribly attached to him, although, she added, like any death, it was disconcerting.

"I'm just trying to stay focused and positive for the rest of the race," she said.

As he'd expected, Joran Freeman turned the corner off the Taylor Highway into the Eagle checkpoint to a crowd of officials and veterinarians.

Freeman parked his team and six veterinarians walked over to examine his eight dogs. He had arrived in fifth place, maintaining his position, just ahead of John Schandelmeier. If he had to stay in Eagle any longer than he'd planned, he would start losing positions quickly.

After several minutes of foot examinations, prodding of hips, and taking of pulses, the vets nodded to each other and stood up.

They were smiling and offering him congratulations. His dogs were healthy, had fine, raspberry-free feet, and their weight was ideal. Their pulses had rapidly dropped to normal, indicating that they were exerting themselves in a sustainable way.

It was one of the most satisfying moments of his dog-mushing career, Freeman would later say.

The same, unfortunately, could not be said for Hugh Neff.

Between Dawson City and Eagle, Neff dropped seven places, and he arrived in Eagle the morning after the leaders. Unlike Joran Freeman's, his dogs did not look any better. They looked worse.

As they had with Freeman's, several veterinarians examined Neff's team, and, although the dogs' weights were acceptable, the condition of a number of his dogs' feet was not. This time, the vets got up frowning, not smiling.

Harris and Terhar told him he should rest his team for at least a full twenty-four hours, and that they would re-evaluate the team later.

Neff was carrying the bare minimum number of booties, so he had no choice but to reuse them, drying them out where possible and picking up other mushers' lost booties on the trail. Most mushers carry a sufficient supply of new booties to replace those that get so torn or damaged that they can't do their job. Neff had few spares, and his booties were in terrible shape.

Frank Turner recalled seeing him at Fortymile, getting ready to leave. Seeing the condition of his booties, he thought he had just arrived.

Hugh Neff, in his wish to race frugally, hadn't packed enough booties to protect his dogs' feet, and, apparently, he wasn't carrying any foot ointment to help abraded feet heal.

Grumbling, Neff acquiesced to the vets' suggestion—he had little choice; if he disregarded their rules, he would be disqualified—but he believed the standards of the race were too high.

When I talked to him later about the rules, he expressed a startling view of dog mushing, one that is not the norm among modern dog drivers. "We're harder on dogs, and I believe in it, to tell you the truth," he said.

He never made it clear exactly who the "we" was he was claiming membership in, but he went on to explain that his dogs come from a line of small, tough sled dogs called Aurora huskies, which are still bred in the Alaskan native villages. Native people, he argued, breed tougher dogs because their animals are not given the velvet treatment offered by Europeans, who lack the historical, working relationship with sled dogs.

A dog will manage without booties, and they did for hundreds of years. It can run with raspberries on its feet. They are bred to overcome physical pain. However, in races like the Quest and the Iditarod, where dogs are racing hundreds of kilometres a day, a musher has a practical and a moral responsibility to give them the best possible care. They perform better, and there's no reason not to protect their feet. Most mushers see their dogs as their friends, and to make them suffer would contradict the reason they enter the race in the first place, which is to travel together as a happy team through the wilderness.

Hugh Neff, however, seemed somehow to leave his dogs out of the equation.

"I see nothing wrong with pushing dogs as hard as I push myself. That's the big dichotomy with what's going on with PETA," he said, referring to the radical animal rights group People for the Ethical Treatment of Animals. "Are you going to please them, or are you going to let us live the lives that we live every day? I mean, I've run these dogs down a river that had a foot of overflow for close to twenty miles, man, and it was below zero [Fahrenheit] then. And they did well."

He believes the race has become prejudiced against the smaller kennels it was originally conceived to serve, that only big kennels could afford to meet the standards of the race.

Doug Harris, explaining that they wanted him to wait a day, took him over to Frank Turner's dogs, resting in straw in the late-morning sunlight, showing him what a team with well-protected, well-treated feet should look like.

Neff said Turner's big, hairy dogs are a different breed, and that it isn't fair to compare them. "It's like comparing a coyote with a wolf," he complained later.

According to Neff, Harris said they had gone through Neff's drop bags and determined that he didn't have enough food or booties to make it to Circle.

Neff was upset by what he saw as an invasion of privacy.

That evening, I had dinner with Margy Terhar, who said Neff's dogs' feet were in such bad shape there was little chance he would be allowed to leave the following morning, either.

Mild abrasions on a dog's paw can turn into raspberries, where a raw hole in the pad begins to develop. The hole is ripe for bacterial infections, which can cause afflictions like pneumonia. If the dog isn't treated with antibiotics, it can literally die from sore feet.

There's another, simpler reason for not allowing dogs to run with raspberry feet: it is cruel. The sores are excruciatingly painful.

The following morning, Harris went back to Neff, and told him he should stay longer to wait for his dogs' feet to heal.

This time, Neff refused. "I'm going to Fairbanks," he said. "I'm going to do what I'm going to do."

He was officially disqualified from the race.

Harris dismissed the claim that the race was biased against Neff's poverty. "I'm here to look after people's dogs, to ensure dog care and that people follow the rules. I don't care if you're a millionaire. If you don't look after your dogs, you'll be disqualified. And if you come in here, and you have absolutely nothing, and you look after your dogs properly, then I'll wish the best for you. I'll do everything possible to get people to the finish line, because that's the whole purpose. It's the same with the vets," he said. "Having said that, I'm not going to neglect the other responsibilities of a race official and allow dogs to continue when they shouldn't."

Neff packed up his gear, took some of the leftover food offered him by race officials, and readied to leave.

Recognizing that he lacked the resources to fly himself or his team out of Eagle, race officials provided him with booties, ointment, and antibiotics to mitigate possible infections, using extras left behind by other teams. He was given enough to get to Circle, the next checkpoint and the closest road access to the trail.

When a musher is disqualified, he cannot be banned from the trail, which runs over public property, and the race has no control over him. Neff would be allowed to access his food drop bags at checkpoints and, if he liked, could carry on as usual. But, officially, at least, his Quest was over.

THE CODE OF THE TRAIL

ONCE TEAMS PASS UNDERNEATH the protective stare of Eagle
Bluff, they head out into the teeth of the windy Yukon River,
navigating the ice for the next 250 kilometres. Some years, it is like
a smooth highway. This year, as it was around McCabe Creek, it is
a jumbled mess.

Sixty kilometres along the trail, there is a cabin where the Trout
Creek flows into the Yukon River. Ever year, an Eagle resident
named Mike Sager, a fisherman, trapper, and carver, travels there
from the town to open his cabin to provide hot coffee, some floor
space, and food for the teams passing by. For veterans, stopping
there is a ritual, like Stepping Stone and Fortymile. His outhouse

is famous for being perched precariously on the edge of a cliff, about five metres above the spot where mushers park their teams; David Sawatzky unceremoniously fell one year, landing among the sleeping dogs.

As he does every year, Sager went out to the cabin to heat it up a couple of days before the first teams were likely to arrive. But this year, none showed up.

The original Quest trail had been blazed on the left side of the river, near the cabin. But several days before the race, when the trail markers were put in, the trail-breakers evidently missed that part of the trail and routed mushers to the far side of the river, a kilometre away. Among the massive jumbles and slabs of ice, there was no way to guide a team safely across the river to Sager's cabin, so that teams planning to stop there were forced to camp on the exposed river itself.

"That was a big screw-up on the part of the Quest. I knew damn well where the cabin was. I could see it. But you couldn't get there. The ice was so bad, you couldn't get there," David Sawatzky later said.

It was more serious than that, though. When planning his race, Sawatzky, like Osmar and Kleedehn and Lesh, had made up his running and resting schedule to include a stop at Trout Creek. Now, he could see the smoke coming from the cabin. He could almost smell the coffee, and he had to pass by. The trail's routing, he thought, was inexplicable. Even when it came to a flat open spot on the river, the trail ignored it and continued on through the jagged, painful jumble ice.

Sawatzky, leading the race, kept going for about an hour past Trout Creek, hoping to find a sheltered bend in the river, or even an ice chunk big enough to provide some respite from the wind. The wind kept pummelling, however, and no shelter seemed likely.

The dogs were going along fine, he thought, but he was exhausted and fighting to stay awake. Finally, he just stopped.

"That's enough," he said. "I've picked the windiest damn spot on the river."

Soon, Tim Osmar came along, and William Kleedehn, and, similarly annoyed with the trail-breakers, they stopped and camped with Sawatzky. An hour or so later, Andrew Lesh showed up, and the four leaders crouched together, trying to get out of the wind while the dogs burrowed in the snow to sleep.

Kleedehn, after one of the roughest sections of jumble ice, could feel the stump of his leg, where the prosthesis attached with the bungee cords, starting to rub raw. Coming towards Trout Creek, he'd fallen off the sled numerous times as it careened off the ice. At one point, he'd hit a piece of ice so hard it knocked his artificial leg off off completely, and it made a long bruise banging up against his thigh. In the wind and thirty-below temperatures, he'd had to stop, strip down, and reattach the leg.

As he'd done so, Andrew Lesh had caught up to him, only to find Kleedehn bent over with his snowpants and long underwear around his ankles. Lesh gave Kleedehn an understanding, if surprised, look. "I'm sure he wondered what the fuck I was doing," Kleedehn said later. "I was just black and blue all over from banging over the ice." Every time he hit a piece of ice, a searing pain shot through his legs and back. "It starts bleeding, and I'm raw meat," he said, referring to the rubbing where his prosthesis attached to the stump of his leg.

Kleedehn can get angry at his disability, especially when he's around the other mushers. "It takes everything you have just to do the chores, while those other guys, sure they are tired, but they do the chores, they don't have to deal with that," he says.

"I know I get myself through, because if it really comes down to hardball I can ignore any damn thing." For Kleedehn, to give up the Quest is to give in to his disability. "I just have to ignore it. If I can't, then I'm done. Then I might as well sit at home and be at my desk. Then this damn old bitch out of the hospital was right. But so far I've beaten her."

When he caught up to Sawatzky, he asked the other musher why he had stopped in such a windy, cold spot.

"I'm physically exhausted," Sawatzky replied. "I've had it. I can no longer stay on this sled. I need a break. I don't care if the dogs need a break, but I need a break."

Osmar and Lesh conceded they were fairly tired, too.

Kleedehn, although banged up—he was so sore he could barely walk up and down the length of his dog team—felt he could have continued on for several more hours. Although he decided to stay with the others, it brightened his mood. "I was thinking, 'Hey man, that's not so bad. This guy says that he needs a break, and he's tired, but I'm still feeling fairly strong.'"

In theory, as he left eagle, Joran Freeman's eight-dog team gave him a significant advantage. The ice on the Yukon River was said to be the worst on the trail, with apartment-sized chunks forcing a weaving, winding path that would have the dogs in long, strung-out teams running in several different directions at the same time. The wheel dogs, in particular, who can be yanked from one side of the trail to the other—and into the icy boulders—as the team in front of them changes direction, can take a beating.

With eight dogs, although the team is still nearly as long as a tractor-trailer, it is more manageable, the sled is lighter, and thus everything is more manoeuvrable.

Freeman, however, still found the going very rough, and he had to slow the team down frequently to allow dogs to choose their steps more carefully through the jagged, cracked ice. The first warm place to rest was Trout Creek. However, like the leaders before them, Freeman and Schandelmeier found it impossible to cross the jumble ice and had to carry on.

They soon caught up to Tim Osmar, William Kleedehn, and David Sawatzky, camped on a horrible, exposed section of glare ice. The wind was whipping up, and although it wasn't an ideal place to camp, they decided to stop. It was Freeman's first glimpse of the leaders on the trail since he had seen them camped just before Scroggie Creek.

Within half an hour, the leaders had gone, travelling together again, vanishing into the gale.

DAVID SAWATZKY HAD AN UNUSUAL STRATEGY that he was hoping would crack the four-way race wide open. Using the network of cabins along the trail for the next several hundred kilometres, he would avoid stopping at the next two checkpoints, Circle and Central.

The Yukon Quest depends on the cabins along the trail for support. The race couldn't happen without the people like Jerry Kruse, the Tredgers, Sebastian Jones and Shelley Brown, and Mike Sager, who open their homes for the mushers and any other travellers who might be coming along the river. It's a tradition that has existed as long as people have travelled in remote, inhospitable places.

All along the river, people with otherwise busy lives spend several days playing host to the mushers on the Yukon Quest, sharing coffee, stew, and stories in front of a toasty wood stove. It makes the race what it is. "The code of the trail" it's called, and it's a creed that is closely followed by those who live in a place where, as Robert Service put it, "deaths hang by a hair."

The courtesy extended by people who live in their cabins is also extended by those who don't; uninhabited cabins are there to be used, and they don't have a lock on the door. If you stop to use a cabin, there's one simple rule: leave it as you found it, ready for the next person who may be in need of shelter. Whatever wood you burn, you replace by gathering more and chopping it up. You always share what you have, because you never know when you will need someone else to share with you.

This spirit of community and sharing is at the heart of the Yukon Quest. It was there when Bill Steyer gave Andrew Lesh his spare runners, when Frank Turner lent Hugh Neff his dog truck. It can be as simple as offering a cigarette to a fellow musher who has run out, or some dog food to a competitor who is running low. In the 1999 race, Petra Noelle, a musher from Germany, was running the race with a team leased from Frank Turner. A sprint-mushing champion in Europe, she admitted before the race that she had little experience camping in winter, and that she'd never really experienced temperatures below minus ten degrees. A Fairbanks musher, Andy Polleczek, an experienced bushman, had lost his leaders to injury and was having a hard time motivating his team to run. So the pair of them struck a deal: Noelle, with her good leaders, would lead the teams; Polleczek, with his outdoor skills, would look after the camping arrangements.

We usually think of a community as a group of people who live close together, or share a set of values. In the North, however, neither is true. The political spectrum here is more polarized than anywhere else on the continent, and many people don't want contact with the rest of the world at all. The population density in northern Canada and Alaska is among the lowest in the world.

Yet, despite all this, there is a definite "northern" community, one that exists across time and a vast space, a close-linked network that was in place long before modern telecommunications shrank the universe. It is less a collection of shared political values than a set of moral imperatives imposed upon dwellers by a difficult landscape, a kind of secular humanism that tells us to respect and protect each other from the power of our environment. It exists in more southern regions, too, but is concealed by the insulation of modernity, where we, as individuals, have the power to control our immediate surroundings with awnings, umbrellas, and underground malls.

It's more than simply a fight for survival that binds northerners together. Most bush people are perfectly capable of surviving alone. Nor is it a smug collegiality that comes from belonging to a select group of people who have eschewed civilization and thrive on their own merits. Indeed, the Yukon's infrastructure would cease to exist should the federal Canadian government decide to stop artificially propping up its economy with millions of dollars in annual subsidies.

The community of the North stands on a realization that, whatever one's creed, religion, ethics, or circumstance, there will come a time when you'll need someone else's help. Not a friend, not a firefighter, police officer, therapist, or taxi driver, but the help, immediately, of whoever happens to be nearest to you. And that knowledge demands a civic-mindedness that, sadly, is gone in areas where we have come to rely on a professional corps to address our survival needs.

Moreover, with civic-mindedness also comes a sort of civic cheerfulness; it's not just a sense of duty to be helpful, a sort of backwoods noblesse oblige. People draw meaning from being in the position, and take pride in being a link in a chain of survival. The chain is the community.

However, there are always going to be those who don't follow the code. In 1986, Frank Turner and another musher, Ron Rosser, stopped at a cabin on the Yukon River not far from Eagle. It was a blizzard, and the two tired, cold men were pleased to see the light and a welcoming smile at the door. The man's name was Darryl— Turner can't remember his last name—and he was a very large fellow. He made hot chocolate for the mushers and chatted while they warmed up. A few hours later, the pair decided it was time to go, even though the weather outside was still nasty. Darryl suggested they stay, pointing at the howling wind and driving snow.

Turner demurred, politely, and the pair readied to leave. Once on their sleds, they travelled a few hundred metres, but they could barely see the trail in front of them. They decided to go back to Darryl's cabin, turning the teams around. This time, however, their host's demeanour had changed. He refused to let them in and swore repeatedly at them, as if he'd been insulted by their decision to disregard his advice and leave. The mushers were forced to continue on to Eagle.

And many northerners harbour a deep mistrust of rules. Indeed, the very thought that anyone may be able to tell them what to do is often met with downright hostility.

This was made clear to me one morning on the Yukon River, west of Eagle. I was waiting out on the river for a team to come by, near a beautifully gruesome, three-metre-high chunk of jumble ice. Two hours had gone by. My feet were freezing, and the sun was slowly drooping below the jagged horizon. Finally, I could make out a team in the distance. It was Cim Smyth. As he approached, I got into position for the photograph, just as a snow machine appeared, coming from the other direction. At his pace, I could see he would pass Smyth's team right where I was standing, ruining the possibility of a photograph. Smiling, I waved at him to stop. He accelerated and got to me sooner, as Smyth was about fifty metres away.

"Could you just wait," I asked, "while I get a picture of this team as it goes by here? If you carry on, you'll be in the shot."

The man, who hadn't lifted up the visor on his helmet, suddenly flipped it up and snarled at me. "This is the United States of America," he growled. "I can go anywhere I want." Then he sped off, just as Smyth went by.

I missed the shot, more out of incredulity than anything.

Biederman's cabin, the next cabin down from Trout Creek, is one of the most storied on the river, and it is still a popular rest stop for teams. It is operated by people from Central, Alaska, farther down the trail, and by other area cabin-dwellers.

One year a man who had been opening up Biederman's cabin offering hospitality to mushers, for a couple of years, hit upon the idea of charging teams for his help. He set up a sort of bed-and-breakfast for Quest mushers: $40 for a room, $5 for a bowl of soup, and $3.50 for a bun. Cash only.

Predictably, mushers don't carry much money with them on the trail, particularly if they've already been to Diamond Tooth

Gertie's casino in Dawson City, and nobody had ever tried to profit from the mushers—few of whom are wealthy—before. Every team passed him by, and he hasn't returned.

Those who open the cabin these days don't charge mushers a dime. Listening to stories from the trail is payment enough.

CHARLIE BIEDERMAN WAS ONE of the last people to deliver the mail in Alaska by dogsled, at the end of a long era of northern postal service that began before the turn of the century and ended, in 1940, when he and his brother, Adolphe, lost the contract to an airline.

The last dogsled mail-carrier route was cancelled in 1963.

Biederman delivered mail from Eagle, Alaska, to Circle City, the next checkpoint on the Quest trail.

It was an eight-day trip, and the massive sleds were pulled by up to ten large dogs—most more than twice the size of today's racing dogs—hitched in single file with leather traces. They went whatever the weather, and Biederman's reputation was that he delivered the mail on time, all the time. It was a perilous trip; once, another musher came across the fur hat of an overdue mail-carrier lying next to a big hole in the river ice.

The mail-carriers kept the river trails open, and Biederman's route formed a link with the mail route of Percy DeWolfe, who carried mail between Dawson City and Eagle. The mail route was the only highway, in those days, open as soon as the ice was stable enough in fall and there until it began to break up in spring. On it, the dogsled mailmen were the sole link between Dawson City, Fortymile, Eagle, and the Alaskan interior.

When Biederman retired, his hickory sled was donated to the Smithsonian Museum, where it remains on display in Washington, D.C.

Most years, mushers in the Quest still carry envelopes that are date-stamped in Whitehorse and Fairbanks as a way to recognize the long relationship between mushers, dog teams, the Yukon River, and the mail. The 1996 Quest was dedicated to Charlie Biederman, who died in 1995.

Many of the items at Biederman's cabin have remained as they were when he spent his summers there. There are still Kennedy-era tins of soup lining the wooden kitchen shelves.

I GOT TO BIEDERMAN'S CABIN from Eagle with Gary Nance, one of half a dozen volunteer pilots who ferry race officials, veterinarians, and the media to the checkpoints inaccessible by road.

Nance owns one of the smallest bush planes around, a Super Cub, one of the most versatile workhorses in Alaska. It has two seats, one behind the other, and getting into the back seat requires some gymnastic skill. Heat comes from a flexible pipe that runs back from the engine, and you simply point it at where you want to warm up, taking turns in the front and back.

Gary Nance, sometimes called "Scary Nance," has a meat-freezing business back in Fairbanks and volunteers as a pilot for the Quest. He laughs a lot from under his mop of blond hair and moustache, and he wears camouflage pants.

As we were getting on the plane, he asked me if I got sick flying. "Not yet," I replied.

Coming over to Biederman's cabin, from Eagle, I asked him how many metres he needed to land the plane. "About three," he replied, "if I fly into the side of a mountain."

Since we were flying a couple of hundred metres above the river, certainly lower than the surrounding peaks, I wasn't sure whether to laugh, scream, or pray.

Across the river from Biederman's cabin, someone had gone to great lengths to plough out a runway, marked with sticks and little flags.

Nance looked at that, and then at the cabin, which was a good 400 metres from the landing strip. "Fuck that," he said, and looped around, heading right at the cabin. It looked as if we were going to crash into the arching bank of the Yukon River, but at the last second he turned again and set the skis of the plane down on a narrow stretch of relatively flat snow, about thirty metres' worth, which was surrounded by jumble ice and the riverbank. The plane bounced once, and then came to a stop about thirty metres after landing on the soft snow, and about a hundred metres from Frank Turner's dog team, which was passing the cabin but not stopping. I got out of the plane and dumped my camera gear on the snow just as somebody whose name I didn't catch pulled up in a snow machine to run me up the bank to the cabin.

There's a saying in Alaska, home of the world's best bush pilots, some of whom even have flying licences (a reported fifth of them don't and fly unregistered planes): There are bad pilots, and there are old pilots, but there are no bad old pilots.

As I tied my camera bag to the back of the snow machine, Nance took off again, using the ten metres of flat ground he didn't use while landing.

When it was time for me to go, Gary Nance came back to take me on to the next cabin, Slaven's, thirty kilometres downstream.

We flew on down the trail, the plume of smoke rising from Biederman's slowly fading. The river widens out, flattens, and finally, the jumble ice starts to calm down.

After about twenty minutes, another, bigger cabin came into sight, and we did a loop around it before flying back about 500 metres and landing on a shovelled runway. Biederman's cabin is opened by Nance's friends. Slaven's cabin, on the other hand, is operated by the U.S. National Parks Service, because it's in the

Yukon-Charley National Wildlife Preserve and is not very popular with the cabin dwellers on the river.

In Eagle, where residents make a year-round sport of bashing the U.S. federal government on a variety of issues, one of their biggest fights is against the U.S. Parks Service, which has apparently been burning down unused cabins located on the Yukon-Charley Preserve, which sits to the west of the town. The cabin burnings, residents say, risk the lives of trappers and other people who live off the land, who may need the cabins for shelter if they get into trouble during bad weather.

That hostility might be why Nance landed on the proper runway this time.

Slaven's Roadhouse is known for the best chili on the trail, and a sign to that effect is staked on the trailside where it turns to go up Coal Creek.

The roadhouse was built in 1932, by, not surprisingly, a fellow named Frank Slaven. Most accounts describe Slaven as a former heavyweight boxing champion from Australia, whose brief clash with fame came after losing a bid for the World Heavyweight Championship in London, England, in 1891. In June 1897, after losing a fight in San Francisco, Slaven reportedly began competing in exhibition fights in the U.S. Pacific Northwest.

Learning of the Klondike gold strike, he, along with his manager and sparring partner, arrived in Dawson City later that year.

The popular version of the story credits him with eventually building the roadhouse, which was a popular stop for mail-carriers and travellers between Circle City and Eagle. However, as it turns out, there seem to have been two Frank Slavens in the Klondike and Upper Yukon area around that time, and, in fact, the boxer's name was spelled with an "i," not an "e."

Or maybe there weren't. Many old-timers, according to a study written by historian Doug Beckstead, swear the two were the same man. Others describe the Slaven with an "e" as "small and bald," hardly the physique of a heavyweight champion. The boxer reportedly died in 1920.

A census of the era reveals that a Frank Slaven living near Coal Creek was born in Ohio, not Australia, and died in 1942, aged seventy-two, in Seattle.

Roadhouses, the Motel 6s of the gold rush era and beyond, were generally spaced along the river about a day's dog trip apart. They provided hot meals, a bed—or at least a place on the floor— and sometimes a barn for dog teams.

According to Beckstead, Slaven, whoever he was, built his roadhouse only six kilometres away from the nearest one, at Woodchopper Creek, apparently after an argument with the owner.

Slaven's Roadhouse, which has two storeys—there is a sleeping room up a ladder staircase—was restored by the Parks Service in 1993. As part of the park, it's open to the public in summer, and during the Quest it is a dog drop staffed by park rangers and one Quest veterinarian.

OF THE FOUR MUSHERS LEADING THE RACE, three—Tim Osmar, David Sawatzky, and William Kleedehn—were travelling more or less together. Over the course of an eight-hour run, they might get separated by a couple of minutes, and they would take turns breaking the trail. Andrew Lesh was with them, too, usually a bit behind. As the trio passed Slaven's Roadhouse, they noted that they hadn't seen Lesh since they'd left Biederman's cabin earlier that day.

David Sawatzky felt relief in his ankles: the trail out of Biederman's cabin was good and smooth, at least compared to what they had been travelling over for the last couple of hundred kilometres.

The trio of leaders stopped at another cabin, past Slaven's but before Doug Dill's cabin, also called Fortymile for its distance from Circle.

Generally, if a musher has stopped at Biederman's cabin, he will not stop at Slaven's except to drop a dog, if necessary. From there, as at Scroggie Creek and Eagle, the dogs are flown on to Circle for fifty dollars each. Then it's 100 kilometres to Circle City, where the trail rejoins the road system and leaves the Yukon River for good.

The river widens here and has long, flat stretches and channels separated by small islands. It was a week into the race, and the weather was clear, sunny, and pleasant. Osmar, Sawatzky, and Kleedehn—the latter's plan to race alone shattered by his bruised legs and back—had been running together for so long they seemed like a family. Kleedehn was chatty, making jokes in his German-inflected English, and Sawatzky was his companion in pain, joking along with him. Tim Osmar, who both could see was having a nearly perfect race (although he had dropped a couple of dogs, his run so far had been virtually injury-free for both dogs and musher), offered his wry humour and sarcasm, and listened to his Nirvana tapes on a Walkman as he drove his well-disciplined dogs along the trail.

When they were all stopped at the Fortymile cabin, David Sawatzky took a close look at his team. It didn't look good. More than a thousand kilometres of stress and heightened testosterone was taking its toll. The dogs looked thin, and, with one female still in heat, they still weren't entirely concentrating on the race.

To follow his strategy of cabin-hopping, Sawatzky's team would have to be in optimum shape. It wasn't. He could feed them as much as they could eat, but it probably wouldn't help. What they needed was a few days' rest.

He looked at the team again, and then at Osmar's dogs, parked in front of his, with their perfect feet and litres to spare in the gas tank. Sawatzky was running on fumes. He would be lucky, he thought, to finish in the top five, and he began to worry for the first time about Joran Freeman, with his eight-dog team, only a few hours behind him. "They might just suck me up yet," he thought.

He abandoned his radical strategy and just hoped his dogs would follow Osmar's for the rest of the race and not get too far behind. He would give it the best that he could, but, he concluded, he was not going to win the race.

Then Andrew Lesh appeared from behind them and blew by with just a smile and a wave. His dogs were chugging along at a good trot.

Sawatzky walked over to Osmar.

"Timmy," he said, almost in a whisper, "you know, he's going to do exactly what I was going to do."

"Which was?" Osmar asked.

And Sawatzky told Osmar exactly how he'd been planning to run the race the rest of the way. "If you're smart, Timmy, that's what you'll do. You've got the dog team to do it with. You go all the way to Doug Dill's cabin, and you don't stop in Circle, you go all the way to Cochrane's cabin, and then from Cochrane's cabin, you go right into Central, and you don't stop at Central. You go to Mile 101, and that's where you take your break. From there, you go into Angel Creek. There'll be nobody that will even try to stick or compete with you. There isn't anybody in this race that would try to do it. They'll all stop at Central."

This unorthodox strategy could pay off in several ways. First, the checkpoints at Circle and Central are noisy, busy, and not ideal places for dogs to sleep. They would get better rest stopping at the cabins along the way. Second, that plan makes for slightly longer runs, which saves time spent preparing to camp. Third, it offers a significant competitive advantage: the musher becomes virtually invisible on the trail, keeping everybody else guessing his intentions, and maybe forcing other teams off their own schedules in an effort to keep up.

Central is the stop just before the tortuous climb up Eagle Summit, a formidable physical—and psychological—barrier late in the race. To skip a rest in Central and try to climb Eagle Summit at the end of a long run was a gutsy and risky proposition. If the dogs were too tired, they might balk at the climb, and a musher might be forced to camp on the mountainside, waiting for the dogs to rest up and watching other teams go by.

Osmar looked at Sawatzky. Mushers have a race plan for a reason, and the top advice given to rookies is always to stick to that plan. Don't follow the lead of another team, because then you lose control of your race; you begin running on someone else's schedule, and not your own.

Osmar decided he would continue to run the race according to his own schedule.

VISIONS

Circle city got its name by mistake. It was founded in 1893 by an entrepreneur named Joe McQuesten, who erroneously thought he was on the Arctic Circle—which, in fact, is about 100 kilometres north.

The mountains around Circle City look tired, old, and worn. At this point the Yukon River is wide and muddy. Compared with the narrow, swiftly moving current at Whitehorse, the river here ambles along, barely moving. It looks tired, too. Swampy taiga lines its banks on both sides, with stunted, short spruce trees punctuating a nearly featureless landscape.

There is a small, winding tributary called Birch Creek that flows into the Yukon at Circle City, a meandering river that, in summer, is home to millions of mosquitoes and, in winter, is notoriously cold and rife with overflow. However, just over a century ago, the creek and its surrounding area produced some four million dollars' worth of gold.

Circle was the site of the first major gold rush on Alaskan soil. And, like Fortymile before it, and Dawson and Eagle after it, the city boasted a population of more than 1,000. It also had a two-storey opera house, eight saloons, a library that housed the complete works of Charles Darwin, a hospital, a school, and a church. Log cabins stretched for two kilometres along the riverbank, earning it the title of the biggest log-cabin city in the world. It even had its own newspaper, the *Yukon Press*. By summer 1897, there were 1,700 people living there, and acts from across the United States were performing at the opera house.

That winter, however, there were rumours of another, huge strike about 500 kilometres upriver, east of Fortymile, near the confluence of the Yukon and Klondike rivers.

By the following summer, in a familiar pattern, Circle City was deserted.

Today, about eighty people live there, and it is still a dismal place. To add historical insult to injury, the Yukon River washed away most of the remains of the old town in a series of floods during the 1930s and 1940s. Much of what was left was used, ignominiously, for firewood. Most of the people who live there are Gwich'in, the same northern aboriginal group that lives in the northern Yukon Territory in Old Crow, and further to the west in Alaska at Fort Yukon.

In one building, there is a restaurant (which serves excellent diner-type food), two general stores, and a bar. The only other real commercial building in the town is a laundromat.

When the Quest comes to Circle City, mushers sleep in the basement of the restaurant, and when that is closed, they lay cots above the cement floor of the fire department's garage (the truck is moved outside for the duration of the Quest). Everybody else sleeps on the floor itself. Seating for race officials, media, and spectators is on several large picnic tables that are brought inside.

However, what Circle lacks in aesthetics, it makes up for in community spirit. The walls of the fire hall are decorated with huge, hand-painted banners the children create as a school project. Every musher in the race has his or her name painted on a banner, decorated gaily with bright magic markers. The same enterprising class bakes its own pizzas and sells them, at ten dollars each, to the media and spectators who come to watch the race pass through.

Circle was one of the first rural communities in Alaska to have telephone service. (It also claims that Roald Amundsen called home from its telegraph office, although there is no statue.) Today, the service, which operates by a radio-satellite relay system, is terrible. It takes about two seconds for the person on the other end of the line to hear what you say, and vice versa. Filing a photograph or a story digitally over the phone lines is virtually impossible, which is why it's good to know Dick Hutchinson. A lanky, angular man with a smoke-rasped voice and a pair of reading glasses persistently perched halfway down his nose, he owns the telephone utility, and, for want of a better term, might as well be called the mayor.

From his house opposite the yard where the dogs are parked, Hutchinson can see pretty much everything that is going on, if he squints past a couple of single-engine planes and a huge satellite dish parked in the way. In the basement of his modern, wood-panelled home, he operates one of the town's two stores, where he sells marked-up calling cards that appear to have come from Wal-Mart.

A tall man with a sharp goatee, he is a wizard with technology. His house is also about the only one where you can access the Internet reliably to send information, if, say, you're a newspaper reporter or photographer. And he is almost certainly the only Circle resident with a website, which he uses as a vehicle for his real passion: photographs of the northern lights. Perhaps it is because the landscape around Circle is so drab, and the sky is the only thing worth admiring, that Hutchinson has an array of beautiful images of the aurora borealis, including one, which he sells in his shop, of the Hale-Bopp comet passing through a magenta plume.

It wasn't as though Andrew Lesh planned to make a big break on the leaders. It just kind of happened that way. When Tim Osmar, William Kleedehn, and David Sawatzky left Biederman's cabin, Lesh didn't feel that his dogs were ready to go, so he gave them an extra hour's rest. It was early morning, and his dogs just didn't seem too motivated. So he went back into the cabin and sketched out a plan for the next few hundred kilometres.

He decided, initially, to go to the Fortymile cabin, where the others would stop, expecting the trail out of Biederman's to be as rough as the trail coming in. When he got out on the trail, however, he saw that he had made it through the worst of the jumble ice, and the dogs seemed to appreciate it. They were running well along the smooth trail. The sky was clear, and the temperature, about twenty below, was nearly perfect mushing weather. He saw the smoke of the Fortymile cabin after just over four hours. If he pushed his run to six or seven hours, he would reach Doug Dill's cabin, only thirty kilometres from Circle. Moreover, he would arrive there in early afternoon, rest his team through the heat of the warming day, and then leave in the evening when it was cooler and easier on the dogs. So that's what he did, waving to a suprised-looking David Sawatzky as he went past.

Lesh was resting at Dill's cabin when Kleedehn, Sawatzky, and Osmar passed him on the way to Circle, where they would stop for a good rest. Lesh, however, would bypass Circle, which he knew was traditionally a terrible place for dogs to rest, and carry on to Carl Cochrane's cabin, about a four-hour run past Circle, where the dogs—and Lesh—would get better rest in a quiet environment.

When Lesh pulled in to Circle to grab some food and supplies from his drop bags, Tim Osmar saw him repacking his sled and approached him. "They have really nice hamburgers here, Andrew. You sure I can't buy you one?"

Lesh demurred. "I don't think so," he replied, smiling. With a whistle, he pulled out of the checkpoint minutes after arriving. He was officially the race leader.

Sawatzky looked at Osmar. "Timmy," he said, "that guy could suck you in. He could beat you yet."

He said it partly to goad Osmar. He doubted that Lesh, with only a fraction of Osmar's racing experience, could pull off an upset. Lesh, he thought, would underestimate his own team's strength. He would err on the conservative side, never having been exposed, like Osmar had, to the stiffer competition of the Iditarod, where drivers tend to push their dogs harder as they approach the finish line.

"Lesh could win it," Sawatzky added, smiling, "Except for the fact that he doesn't know what he's doing."

Sawatzky's assertion, however, didn't seem to stop them from cutting their rest short and leaving as soon as possible.

ONE HUNDRED KILOMETRES BEFORE CIRCLE, Joran Freeman hatched a plan to catch the leaders again, and this time he wasn't going to let them out of his sight. His team was moving well, they'd had plenty of rest since leaving Dawson, and he had managed to climb to within an hour of the frontrunners. His eight dogs had, in his mind, turned into champions.

At Circle, Freeman decided he would trade an hour of rest for the chance to leave, and run, with the lead group of three. Andrew Lesh, who was camped at Doug Dill's cabin, would be behind them, and stay there thirty kilometres out, he hoped.

Three-quarters of the way into the race, with the challenge of Eagle Summit looming ever closer, Freeman thought he might not get another chance to make a move.

It didn't happen.

When Andrew Lesh blasted through Circle, it roused Osmar, Kleedehn, and Sawatzky, who decided to cut two hours' rest to give chase.

Freeman couldn't justify cutting three hours—effectively snipping his rest time in half—and so he stayed back, resting the full six hours. He hoped he'd get another chance to challenge for the lead, but, for the time being, he'd remain in fifth place.

FROM CIRCLE, THE TRAIL ONCE AGAIN FOLLOWS THE GOLD and crosses the end of the Steese Highway, which connects it to Fairbanks, before dropping onto Birch Creek, wending its way through the swamp and soggy, stumpy-treed area towards Central, the second-last checkpoint on the Yukon Quest and the staging area for the climb up Eagle Summit.

Coming off the Yukon River, with 400 kilometres to go, the race, so to speak, really begins. The travelling pacts made in the thick of the jumble ice start to fall apart, and mushers begin to assess how much their team has left in the gas tank.

There is a sign at Crabb's Corner, the best restaurant and motel in Central, Alaska, heart of the Circle Mining District. It hangs next to a Yukon Territory flag.

NOTICE WE RESERVE THE RIGHT TO REFUSE SERVICE TO ANYONE—
INCLUDING SPECIAL INTEREST GROUPS AND GOVERNMENTAL
AGENCIES—WITH GOALS THREATENING TO THE LIFESTYLE OF
THE CIRCLE MINING DISTRICT AND OUR MEANS OF MAKING AN
HONEST LIVING.

It's signed by Jim and Sandy Crabb, the owners of the grocery store-bar-restaurant-motel, which is the heart of the town of

Central, population 120. Mushers and miners are welcome. Sierra Club members are not.

Calling it a motel is pushing it somewhat. It's a separate, prefab, Atco trailer, where the rooms have saggy single beds and there is no washroom or shower at all. But that's a minor complaint. At this stage in the race, when you've been wearing the same pair of long underwear for a week, soap and hot water would just complicate things.

Really, Crabb's Corner is one of the most hospitable stops on the Yukon Quest trail. There is even a cheeseburger on the menu named after the race.

On one wall is a big, permanent, plywood scoreboard with a square for each of the checkpoints in the Yukon Quest and a space for each of about forty-five mushers. Covered with clear plastic, it allows Jim Crabb and the residents of Central to follow the race as it approaches their town, and it allows race spectators to see where other teams are on the trail, information that isn't always readily available.

Hanging outside on the front wall of the restaurant are flags bearing the logo of the Yukon Quest and a couple of crabs. Don't let the iconography fool you. The Crabbs are anything but cantankerous. First of all, food and drink are on the house. Jon Rudolf, a musher from Whitehorse competing in the 1986 Quest, decided to stay an extra day there to get more rest. He went into the bar to buy a beer, got his money out, but the bartender refused to allow him to pay. "I don't care if you stay a week," he was told. "You don't pay for anything here."

At the end of the nineteenth century, Central was nothing more than a roadhouse called Windy Jim's, on the trail from Circle to Fairbanks. Like Slaven's, it offered beds, food, and a sheltered place for dog and horse teams. It was the hub of a network of trails that went to various nearby creeks that were mined. Eventually, it became known as Central House, and when the Steese Highway was built, connecting Circle to Fairbanks, it passed right by.

Central is now home to a highway maintenance camp and has a school, a library, a post office, and other facilities used by area miners.

AT CIRCLE, DAVID SAWATZKY DROPPED another dog, because it had sore feet.

He prepared to leave, but his leaders didn't want to go. By switching some dogs around in the team, he eventually came up with a combination that seemed to work.

Jeanne, watching him get frustrated as he tried to pull out of the dog lot, suggested that he scratch. He wasn't having a lot of fun, with his ankles still sore, and the dogs seemed to have lost a lot of their interest, too.

But Sawatzky could see that William Kleedehn was having a hard time with his dogs. He was beginning to pay the price for having run the first half of the race so quickly. Sawatzky still figured he could pull off a top-five finish, maybe top-three. Moreover, it was obvious that the trials of running through the jumble ice with only one leg had sapped Kleedehn's spirit, and his strength. The indications were subtle. His teeth didn't flash so often when he smiled; it was more like he was stretching his lips, grimly, in a tired facsimile. His limp was more pronounced when he worked up and down his gangline, and routine tasks were taking him longer to do than they had several hundred kilometres earlier.

Still, in order to beat Kleedehn, Sawatzky knew he was going to have hell to pay to cover the last 400 kilometres to the finish line.

Osmar and Kleedehn got a half-hour jump on him getting out of the checkpoint, so Sawatzky ran for four and a half hours on his own before taking a two-hour rest, ran again, and caught up to Osmar and Kleedehn.

The trail along Birch Creek was awful. It was obvious that it was newly laid, about a week before the race, and hadn't been travelled over enough to be firmly packed down. The snow machines used for grooming had flattened out some of the snow, but underneath that crust it was soft and hollow, with the consistency of sand. Walking on it, every few steps the snow would crack around his boot, and his foot would sink in a dozen centimetres. It annoyed the dogs, too, breaking through the crust every fifteen or twenty paces. It made for tough, and slow, sledding.

William Kleedehn appeared at his wits' end. He told Osmar and Sawatzky that he was just too sore, that he was going to take a ten-hour break at Central.

Sawatzky and Osmar planned to take eight hours.

They weren't sure about Andrew Lesh, who had stopped at Carl Cochrane's cabin to rest, about halfway to Central. They saw his sleeping dog team parked outside the cabin as they went by, but saw no sign of Lesh himself.

Lesh didn't see them, but he could tell, from the footprints and the sled-runner marks on the trail, that they were ahead of him again. He had no idea how far ahead, however. Travelling along the trail, he saw a discarded bootie. Like a detective examining a crime scene, he picked it up and squeezed it to see whether it was frozen.

The bootie was still soft, which meant, in the twenty-five-below weather, that they couldn't be that far, maybe an hour ahead. It was only when he came off the trail and onto a side road that led to Central that he realized how close he was.

"You're only five minutes behind," a spectator told him.

"Cool!" Lesh shouted back.

Once again, the four mushers arrived together. Only thirteen minutes separated Osmar, Kleedehn, Sawatzky, and Lesh.

After Central, there was one checkpoint between them and the finish line. One checkpoint, and, more important, one mountain.

LEAVING CIRCLE, WITH 400 KILOMETRES TO GO, Joran Freeman was tired. Taking advantage of the flat, slow trail with few distractions for the dogs, he crawled into the basket of his sled, lay down, and ordered the dogs to carry on.

Every fifteen or twenty minutes the sled, with no driver to steer it around corners, careened off the trail and into the bushes, spilling its sleepy contents onto the snow. However, Freeman somehow managed to get a couple of hours' sleep over the next 120 kilometres.

Riding in the sled is an uncommon way of travelling, unless there is someone on the runners behind you. But it illustrates one of the biggest challenges in long-distance sled dog racing: the simple difficulty of remaining awake.

Freeman had, for several days, felt a pride welling up in his chest at the progress of his dogs. At the same time, he was worried about his own performance, knowing that to finish in his current position he would have to stay sharp and focused. He had had about ten hours' sleep in the last five days. Fatigue would come in flashes: one minute he would be awake, and then, an instant later, he would feel a desperate need for sleep. Over the past few days, every time he'd stopped for a nap, he knew it was a matter of chance whether he would wake up to the alarm on his watch or fall into a blissful, deep slumber and sleep right through it.

Forcing yourself to stay awake longer than you should leads to hallucinations.

Coming along the trail, Freeman suddenly saw a teepee off to one side. Standing beside it was a native woman in her traditional clothing. As he went by, she didn't say anything; she just stared, her hands folded across her chest, over the simple leather robe she was wearing.

Visions like those are common on the Quest. Two years earlier, Peter Ledwidge, a musher from Dawson City, was on this same stretch of trail when he saw the bright lights of a UFO hovering in front of him. After several seconds, he looked down, and his dogs had all turned into what he would later modestly refer to as "female body parts."

Usually, the illusions are temporary, and most mushers can shake their heads and move on. But occasionally they are dangerous, and even life-threatening.

Bill Stewart, a Whitehorse psychologist, was running in third place near the end of the 1996 Quest. After going without food for twenty-four hours, and without sleep for almost twice that long, he ran into an imaginary musher who told him he was going the wrong way. So he duly turned his team around and started retracing his tracks, even though he had been merely sixty kilometres from the finish.

Four hours later, he ran into a real musher, who corrected his course. Stewart turned his team around again.

Several hours later, he bumped into yet another imaginary musher, who told him there was a hotel just off the trail. So Stewart pulled his sled into a meadow and lay down to sleep on what he believed was a bed.

The temperature was minus twenty-five.

Luckily, the same, real, musher who had corrected him the first time found Stewart lying asleep in the snow and roused him. As a result, Stewart managed to end the race rather than his life.

After he crossed the finish line, he retired from long-distance sled dog racing.

After getting out of the basket and back on the runners, Freeman craned his neck on every straight section of trail, trying to catch a glimpse of the teams running ahead. He never did, however. He arrived in Central with an hour and a half still separating him and the four leaders.

In Central, with roughly 300 kilometres left to race, Tim Osmar held a five-minute lead over David Sawatzky. William Kleedehn was third, three minutes behind Sawatzky, with Andrew Lesh five minutes behind him.

Joran Freeman arrived in fifth place. He had pulled ahead of John Schandelmeier, who was sixth, just over four hours behind the leaders.

Frank Turner, meanwhile, had become a solitary traveller. Four hours behind Schandelmeier, and more than four hours ahead of Cim Smyth, he was running in his own cushion of comfort, likely too far ahead of the team behind him to be caught, and too far behind the team in front to catch up.

It was pleasant. He had no need to push the team at all, and, in the thick of the race, he was enjoying the chance to commune, quietly, with his dogs.

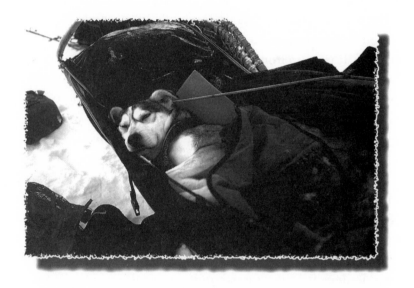

MOUNTAINEERING
IN MUKLUKS

ABOVE THE SCOREBOARD in the restaurant at Crabb's Corner is an aerial photograph of a snow-white mountain with a stark, wind-blown summit. Tracing the side of the mountain, someone has drawn a line in permanent marker. Without any sense of scale, it looks like a climbing route, the sort you see superimposed over photographs of Mount Everest. But this is not a climbing route, per se, and Eagle Summit is not 8,000 metres high. It's the trail of the 2001 Yukon Quest International Sled Dog Race, which, with more than 1,400 kilometres already under its belt, is about to get nasty.

Eagle Summit is the Heartbreak Hill of the Yukon Quest. It's where mushers find out whether they have run the race intelligently or whether they have been running out of their league. It is a thirty-degree climb up the side of a mountain, and it is reputed to be the hardest section of trail on a dogsled race anywhere.

From a distance, or from the air, Eagle Summit is a wondrous spectacle. It rises up from the tentacles of several small creeks to an almost perfectly symmetrical saddle, 100 metres wide. That saddle, however, grabs hold of the frigid north wind, tosses it, twists it, and slams it back onto the ground. Nothing survives on Eagle Summit, unless it is made of rock or can live while growing no more than several centimetres off the ground.

The wind picks up the snow dumped by the low-pressure air masses that can't quite make it over the White Mountains, and if it's in the mood, scours it away, sculpting it into swirling cornices that loom like parapets while leaving the frozen rocks and tussocks bare. It freezes exposed flesh in seconds.

Sometimes it leaves the summit alone, allowing the snow to pile deep, waist high, on its sides, daring anyone to try to get across the top.

Eagle Summit screams or howls or whispers, or makes no noise at all, depending on its whim.

And from Central it was forty-five kilometres away, looming in the night.

VERN STARKS, ONE OF THE RACE VETERINARIANS in Central, looked at David Sawatzky's team and frowned. "You know, you've got some really skinny dogs," he said.

"I know," Sawatzky replied. "Don't pull any punches, Vern. If you think they need to be out of here you tell me right now, and I will drop them."

Starks told Sawatzky he'd like to see his eleven dogs eat one more time, so Sawatzky fed them. Blackie was still in heat, and was still distracting the other dogs (she would remain in heat for the rest of the race), but most of the dogs ate relatively well.

Starks looked at them a second time and announced that he was happier. Sawatzky was happy with them too.

As usual, Tim Osmar, who was still having a near-perfect race, pulled effortlessly out of Central first. "Okay," he said, and the dogs trotted away.

David Sawatzky was ready to go as Osmar pulled his snow hook, but it took him twenty minutes to get out of the campground. His leaders, as usual, were too busy barking and growling at each other, turning around, trying to get at Blackie.

He put Banjo, an old—and, more important, neutered—dog in lead. Banjo was his slowest leader, but at least he would be thinking with his head, unlike most of the other dogs on the team.

Sawatzky was furious. "It was frustrating to be in the position. Everything was just going to hell in a handbasket right in front of me and there wasn't a damn thing I could do about it."

His ankle was still swollen, and the pain was excruciating. "Whenever it bumps against anything, it makes me piss my pants," he said, not making it clear whether he was speaking literally or metaphorically.

Andrew Lesh left Central a few minutes after Sawatzky, and William Kleedehn, who could barely walk, waited an extra hour before taking off.

Once he did get going, Sawatzky found he was moving along fine. He covered the first thirty-odd kilometres in just under two hours, travelling, he figured, at about sixteen kilometres an hour.

He reached the foothills that form the base of Eagle Summit. There he stopped, gave the dogs a fish snack each, and removed their booties, so they could use their claws more efficiently when scrabbling up the steep pitch. He had just started moving again when Andrew Lesh caught him and passed him, leading the way towards the summit.

Sawatzky's dogs couldn't keep up with Lesh's team, and he was steadily dropping behind. His dogs had lost their concentration. A big dog named Kodiak was running beside Blackie in the team and decided, rather than pull 180 kilograms of man and sled up the steep pitch, that he would rather have sex instead. He stopped pulling and leaned over the gangline, putting his head on Blackie's shoulder in an attempt to brace himself while he mounted her.

The two dogs in front of Blackie and Kodiak then turned around to watch the ruckus behind them. Another dog, in front, also found the display behind him more interesting than the trail before him.

Out of the eleven dogs Sawatzky had in harness, only six were actually pulling the sled. Lesh, in front of him with nine dogs—all of whom were focused on the job at hand—was pulling farther and farther away.

Sawatzky yelled up the slope to Lesh: "I might not make it! When you get to the top can you wait five minutes and holler so I can drive them up over the top of the hill?"

"Yeah, sure," Lesh replied, and continued on.

As the trail up Eagle Summit curls above the treeline, the slope begins to get suddenly steeper, switching back and forth until it reaches a several-hundred-metre pitch that is too steep even to walk down without slipping and pitching forward.

Andrew Lesh was already past it, waiting in the saddle, when Sawatzky and his dogs, moving slowly, reached the base of the steep pitch, the "Hillary Step" of the summit.

Sawatzky looked up at the pitch and whistled at the dogs to go. Slowly, they began to inch forward. As they started to gain momentum, Wino, a thirty-kilogram male and one of the biggest on the team, suddenly collapsed in the snow.

With the ghost of Jack before him, Sawatzky hopped forward to the dog. There was no need to set the hook this time. His team wasn't about to take off up the hill.

Wino, while exhausted, was breathing fine. He was worn out from doing the work of the dogs that weren't pulling. Sawatzky picked him up and carried him back to the sled basket.

As he put Wino in the basket, his nightmare was fully realized.

Banjo decided that he had had enough of the Yukon Quest, and, in particular, he had had enough of pulling a dogsled up the side of some ridiculous mountain. He wanted to go home, and he had decided that home was not in the direction he was going.

He turned around.

Then Blackie and Kodiak turned around.

Like dominoes, the other seven dogs in harness turned as well, and Sawatzky had just enough time to jump on the sled's runners as it spun around and started heading back down the mountain.

He screamed in pain as the two chipped pieces of bone in his ankle rattled against his nerves, and, through it all, he stomped down on the brake as hard as he could.

Driving a dog team down a steep, extended pitch is one of the most dangerous aspects of mushing. If Sawatzky hadn't managed to jump on the runners, the sled, with ninety kilograms of gear inside, would, within seconds, have overrun the team, quite possibly killing the wheel dogs and several others as it bore down on them, dragging the team into a hopeless and life-threatening tangle. When the race goes in the other direction, and teams head down the steep side of Eagle Summit, most mushers tie chains around the bottoms of the runners to increase resistance, and remove the tuglines from the dogs' harnesses to reduce their pulling power.

Sawatzky, of course, had, in the two seconds it took the team to turn around, no time to prepare. He just jumped on, dug in, and held tight.

Fortunately, the team had yet to reach the steepest part of the climb when it turned back, and he was able to control the speed of the sled with the brake, standing on it with both feet and pulling the handlebar up, so the rear half of the runners was off the snow.

When they reached the bottom of the mountain, Sawatzky stopped the team. He tried to get them to turn back and head up again. This time, they refused.

The dogs had nothing left.

Racing a high-performance dog team, Frank Turner explains, is like taking your thumb and forefinger and seeing how close you can get them without actually letting them touch. The musher's job is to get the best out of the dogs, with one condition: he must never ask them to do something they're not capable of doing. The dogs work for him because they love him, and, just as important, they trust that he will not make them do anything that is beyond their ability. Asking them to do something they can't destroys that careful trust the dogs have in the musher, a trust that takes a long time to earn, and even longer to get back.

That night on Eagle Summit, the weight of ten days and 1,250 kilometres of heightened hormones, bad eating habits, and distracted rest and recovery had caught up to David Sawatzky's dogs.

His fingers touched.

David Sawatzky stood at the bottom of the mountain, dejected, his shoulders sagging with defeat. He left the team facing the wrong way and let them run back along the trail to a spot where it crossed the Steese Highway. There, he would wait for Jeanne, load the dogs onto the truck, return to Central, and scratch.

Then he was going home.

As he came off the bottom of the summit pass, William Kleedehn, who had left two hours after Sawatzky, passed him as he stood there with his dogs. He asked what had happened.

"I'm heading back. They're turning around on me and I can't get them to go back up the hill. I've had a dog go down on me," he replied, asking Kleedehn to tell Jeanne to drive back up the highway when he saw her waiting at Mile 101.

Andrew Lesh waited twenty-two minutes for David Sawatzky to make it to the top of Eagle Summit, which is a long time when you are only ten minutes behind the race leader. Then he left, feeling guilty, but figuring that was the most he could give up of the race to Tim Osmar. He cruised, uneventfully, down the other side into Mile 101, the abandoned gas station that serves as a post–Eagle Summit dog drop.

Even though he'd lost more than half an hour to Osmar, he was so thrilled to be over Eagle Summit in one piece that he started to dance among his dogs, waving his arms and jumping up and down. It made for a strange sight, this man jumping around to an imaginary tune, perhaps not unlike the spectacle George Carmack presented when he discovered gold at Bonanza Creek.

There was good reason for Lesh to celebrate. The last time he had attempted Eagle Summit in that direction, it had been what he describes as the worst experience of his life.

In 1997 he'd been wearing bunny boots, which in deep snow provide terrible traction. He'd had two new leaders he didn't know terribly well, and the wind had been blowing around fifty-five kilometres an hour. Thirty metres from the summit, he'd seen that his dogs were moving off to the right of the trail.

He made a critical mistake. To get them back on the trail, he called out a "haw," sled dog–speak for "turn left." The leaders turned left, to go back onto the trail, but didn't stop there. They started to turn 180 degrees to head back down the hill.

Lesh put his hook in as quickly as he could and tried to run forward to cut them off, to stop them from turning the entire sled around. He could barely stand, but he managed to get them straightened out, facing the right way. He had a pair of cleats to put on, which attached with a rubber strap. He put one on, and the strap immediately broke. He managed to get the other one on, stumbled to the front of the team, and tried to pull them up.

He couldn't grip the snow well enough, however, and the dogs refused to move. He sat there for several minutes, thinking, and then went back to the sled for his axe. His cleated left foot and the axe gave him two points with which to grip the snow. He managed to chop his way up, carving steps for the dogs in the snow. It took him more than an hour to cover a few metres.

This year, with dogs he knew better and in much less nasty conditions, he'd crossed over with relative ease. For a moment, he couldn't care less what position he was in. He was just proud of his dogs.

JORAN FREEMAN LEFT CENTRAL some six hours after Osmar. He had thought about hurrying off, but since he had done the run from Circle to Central in one go, he gave his dogs a good, long rest, which proved a smart idea. Although it was difficult, his small team of dogs pulled consistently up the climb.

Stopping just before the last pitch, Freeman looked up. An experienced mountaineer, he was amazed how a dog team could manage to climb such a steep section of trail. Kicking in steps on the side of the hill, he worked his way forward several metres at a time, pushing the sled, stopping, encouraging the team, pushing the sled, stopping, and encouraging. After several minutes, he and his dogs had cleared the steepest section and were on to the saddle at the top of the summit, a mountainous panorama surrounding him.

Freeman wasn't admiring the view, however, he was wondering about a pair of gouge marks he had seen in the hard-packed snow. A sled had come down Eagle Summit the wrong way, moving at a pretty good clip, which, given the slope, would be the only option. The driver had almost certainly been struggling to stop the sled from sliding over the wheel dogs, a metre in front of the brush bow.

Freeman arrived at Mile 101 ten minutes ahead of John Schandelmeier, who had made up time. At Mile 101, Freeman cut half an hour of rest. With only one checkpoint to go, this was his last chance to try to catch the leaders before the long, flat, fast run into Fairbanks from Angel Creek.

FRANK TURNER LEFT CENTRAL in a good mood, despite being nervous about Eagle Summit. The nervousness vanished, however, as his young team charged along the creek and into the foothills.

For the previous year's Quest, he had trained at a gym, improving his fitness for climbing hills—particularly this one—by running on a treadmill. While training, he'd held on to a mental image of the climb up Eagle Summit to motivate him. But when he finally got to run up the mountain behind his sled, all he could think about was running on the treadmill.

This year, however, with the new house, he hadn't had time to train at a gym, and he was probably in worse shape for it.

As he started up the final pitch, he was struggling and exhausted, trying to push the sled. He kept slipping and falling onto his knees, landing between the runners. He was making slow progress when he had an idea. Quickly, he let go of the sled and walked forward, along the gangline, until he reached the front of his team.

Then, he kept going, walking ahead thirty metres or so, at which point he turned around and sat down in the snow.

Tank and Birch, his two lead dogs, were watching him intently, just standing there. They hadn't taken their eyes off him as he'd walked ahead. Turner felt as though a laser connected him to his dogs, they were concentrating so hard.

He gave two short whistles, the second higher in pitch than the first, and the dogs lurched forward in their harnesses and quickly closed the distance between them. As they reached him, both dogs leaned forward and put their heads in his lap, expecting—and receiving—a hearty rub.

He got up and repeated his march forward. Again, without ever taking their eyes off him, Tank and Birch led the team forward.

A third time, and they had made it over the summit.

If Birch and Tank had doubted him, not trusted him, or just plain been too tired, they could have turned around and headed back down the hill like David Sawatzky's dogs. From thirty metres away, there would have been nothing Turner could have done except watch, horrified, as the sled ran over his dogs like a bull-dozer.

But that was the trick. He didn't think about it. He didn't rationalize it. If he had, he never would have left the sled. He walked in front of his dogs because, at the time, it felt like the right thing to do.

After the race, and after having thought about it, he admitted that he might not be able to do it again, for fear of losing the team. But for those few moments at Eagle Summit, he and his dogs, from hours and days and, indeed, years of working together as a team, didn't need to communicate verbally at all. It was under-stood, intuitively.

Those are the moments that mushers like Turner live for.

MILE 101, WHICH REFERS TO ITS DISTANCE from Fairbanks on the Steese Highway, used to be a gas station and a motel. Now it's just a tiny cabin, two rooms separated by a mangy curtain, the rear area reserved for mushers to catch a few hours' kip.

It is usually run by people who frequent Ivory Jack's, a bar and restaurant in the Goldstream Valley north of Fairbanks, in the heart of dog-mushing country. Peter Kamper, a German-Alsakan who was running the show this year, was grilling fresh halibut for the mushers. He also had around two hundred hamburgers, donated by the Fairbanks Burger King. (It's the same restaurant that once gave Frank Turner enough hamburgers to feed his entire dog team, when all he'd asked for was one for himself.)

When the race ends in Fairbanks, Mile 101 has traditionally been the place where mushers will sit and watch each other, playing head games, trying to get a final jump on their competi-tion. The Quest has been won—and lost—over the strategic deci-sions and gamesmanship that goes on in this tiny cabin.

In 1998, Bruce Lee, a musher from Denali Park, and André Nadeau, from Ste. Melanie, Quebec, had been duelling for the lead since Dawson City. Well ahead of the third-place team, the pair had been exchanging the lead between them for most of the second half of the race. It was a classic tortoise-and-hare spectacle: Nadeau, with his big Siberian huskies, marched along the trail, slowly, but for hours on end. Lee, with his faster, smaller dogs, would dash ahead, resting more often.

Lee had a terrible time coming over Eagle Summit in a blizzard, coming within minutes of suffering hypothermia while ferrying his dogs, inch by inch, to the summit. He arrived first at Mile 101, exhausted and frostbitten.

Nadeau arrived an hour or so later, and, apparently, had simply marched over the summit in much the same manner that he had covered the previous 1,400 kilometres of trail.

Lee was resting in the back when Nadeau came into the cabin, carrying a pot for hot water to cook his food. Lee watched him put the pot down and go back outside. Since he'd left the pot there, Lee figured he was coming back in and dozed off again.

Nadeau never came back, deciding that the loss of a cooking pot was a small price to pay for a jump on his competitor. He went outside, got on his sled, and took off, leaving Lee snoring.

In the end, Lee's team proved too fast. He reeled Nadeau in shortly before Angel Creek, and never looked back. But the enigmatic rookie Quebecer—who spoke very little English, kept to himself, and apparently fed his dogs whole chickens, feathers and all—nearly won the race.

This year, the atmosphere in the Mile 101 cabin was warm and cordial. When Lesh came in, Osmar's face was still red from the effort of getting over the summit. The pair sat eating and chatting with Peter Kamper and Bruce Lee, who had driven out to watch the conclusion of the race. After Osmar had been there two hours, he stood up and put on his parka.

"You leaving already?" Lesh asked him as he reached for the door handle.

"I'm just going to put some goo on my dogs' feet," he replied.

"Yeah, right," Lesh thought.

Osmar walked out of the cabin, and was on his way to Angel Creek within five minutes.

Lesh could have chased him, but he knew he had a handicap coming up: he had to serve a half-hour time penalty in Angel Creek, the penance for borrowing the sled runner more than a week and a thousand kilometres ago. At Carmacks. At the time, of course, he'd had no idea it would factor into whether or not he might win the race. It would also deprive the people at Fairbanks of the thrill of watching a photo finish.

When Lesh had first pulled into Mile 101, it had occurred to him that he could go straight through and perhaps make up time. But he saw that Osmar's sled was packed, and his team was lined out. If he'd gone through, Osmar would have been on the trail behind him within five minutes.

Shortly after Osmar left, Kleedehn arrived with news of Sawatzky's reversal of fortune. He told Lesh he was going to stay only half an hour. Not sure whether Kleedehn was telling the truth, or whether he knew about the time penalty, Lesh decided not to take any chances.

He left.

THE QUEST TRAIL HOLDS ONE MORE SURPRISE before the last checkpoint at Angel Creek. Although it is not as high, or as spectacular, as Eagle Summit, Rosebud Summit, about thirty kilometres from Angel Creek, is an exposed ridge, above the treeline, that has seen its share of mushers bail out into the valley below while trying to negotiate a sled-splintering descent. Ironically, before the race, David Sawatzky said he was far less concerned with getting over Eagle Summit than he was with making his way down Rosebud Ridge.

After Rosebud, the trail is firmly in the grip of the Chena River valley. After travelling down through a big spruce forest, teams will pull into the yard behind the Angel Creek Lodge, at Angel Creek, Alaska, population two.

That would be Steve and Ann Vernabec, the owners of the lodge.

The lodge, which is more like a restaurant with some cabins around it, is made of thick spruce logs, which tonight, the busiest night of the year, are sweating with the heat of the assembled spectators, officials, media, and mushers. Only an hour's drive from Fairbanks along the Chena Hot Springs Road, it's easily accessible to mushing enthusiasts, of which there are more in Fairbanks than anywhere else in the world.

There are often crowds of people around each team, and mushers find it hard to get peace. When the race starts in Fairbanks, and there are thirty teams here at once, the place is an absolute zoo. There is never enough space for all the mushers to sleep.

There is a strange law in Alaska that prohibits sleeping in bars, which, when there aren't any cabins left, is exactly what some mushers try to do. Curled up in a corner, they get woken up by the staff. (There was also once a law in Alaska making it illegal to provide alcoholic beverages to moose.) The sleeping-in-bars law isn't always enforced, however. Frank Turner can recall sleeping under the pool table at the Angel Creek Lodge and being woken up periodically by wayward boots and spilled Budweiser. Now he, like most veteran mushers, doesn't even bother to try to rest inside. He just sleeps on his sled.

The trail used to be routed another twenty kilometres east to Chena Hot Springs, which had better accommodations for the mushers, but after a couple of years it was moved to its present location. Because of the geothermal heat, there was hardly any snow at the hot springs, and what snow there was tended to be a gooey slush that stuck and froze to dogs' coats.

Since the race was coming from Whitehorse this time, the lodge was less crowded, as the teams were now spread out over at least four days. As Tim Osmar pulled into Angel Creek, Bruce Milne, the last musher in the race, had yet to reach Circle, 250 kilometres back down the trail.

All teams coming into Angel Creek are required to stop for at least eight hours, a rule designed to stop mushers from driving their dogs too hard as they approach the finish line.

Although the cases are rare, there have been incidents in which teams crossed the line with dogs so badly parched that they required intravenous hydration. A musher once finished with a dead dog, counting it among the bare minimum he required in harness to finish. The rule was changed the following year to clarify that dogs in harness need to actually be breathing.

TIM OSMAR PULLED INTO ANGEL CREEK to a cheer from the hundred or so people who had driven out from Fairbanks to watch mushers arrive at the last checkpoint.

He arrived at 9:06 a.m., Wednesday, February 21.

He'd had a calm trip over Eagle Summit, but a bit of a hairy ride down Rosebud Ridge. His sled tipped over, the bag inside it came loose, and he'd found himself careening downhill, one foot on the brake, his knee on the snow-machine track, and the snow hook in his hand. "I was holding on for dear life," he later explained, calmly. Otherwise, he was running a virtually flawless race, and, heading onto the last bit of trail to Fairbanks, he had an hour-and-a-half cushion, thanks to Andrew Lesh's penalty and the time Lesh spent waiting for David Sawatzky, as well as his decision not to chase Osmar out of Mile 101.

"A lot of things can happen," Osmar said. "My main concern is staying awake and not getting lost. There are a million trails between here and there, and there's only one you're supposed to be on." Asked by a reporter, he told his side of what happened at Mile 101: "We ate food, joked a little bit, and then I snuck out. I just said, 'I'm going to go out and do some work on my dogs' feet,' and then I left. He knew."

Lesh, for his part, was still thrilled when he pulled into Angel Creek. "I don't think Tim's all that catchable. Number two, though, that will be *swee-eet,*" he said as he emptied unnecessary gear from his sled.

William Kleedehn arrived two hours behind Andrew Lesh, after having rested longer than he said he was going to at Mile 101. He looked terrible. He could barely walk from one side of his sled to the other as he cleaned it out. He was asked how he felt, and he paused before answering. "I feel like I went through a gruelling race," he said, cracking a weak smile. He turned back to work, and then stood up again. "I'm going to Mexico this spring. I have said that for a long time, but this time I'm going. But first, I'm going to be sitting in a bathtub for a few hours with a bunch of Aspirin, that's the first thing I'm going to do."

Joran Freeman came in three hours after Kleedehn in fourth place. He was happy, if a little nervous about the last leg. The Yukon Quest trail went right past his dog yard, and his tired, hungry dogs would be forced to trot right past their beds and food bowls. If they had a choice, they would gladly stop for a nap. He had practised driving his team past the entrance to the dog yard, and had one leader, Muskrat, whom he hoped would listen to him and not his own instincts.

John Schandelmeier arrived nearly an hour after Freeman, conceding that he wasn't likely to catch up. "If he stalls out by his house, I'll take him. If he doesn't stall out, then I won't take him," he said, smiling.

DAVID SAWATZKY'S PROBLEMS DID NOT END with his return to Central and withdrawal from the race. William Kleedehn, when he'd heard Sawatzky say that he'd had "a dog go down," assumed he meant another dog had died.

The fact that his dogs were loaded into the truck before he scratched and not examined (race rules don't require it) did nothing to alleviate the suspicions. A rumour passed down the trail from musher to musher, but none would discuss it with the media.

Schandelmeier had evidently spoken to Kleedehn, and obviously believed Sawatzky had lost another dog. "I can't imagine something happening like that, it would just destroy you. Knowing how Dave feels about his dogs. To have that sort of bad luck twice in the same race . . ." he said at Angel Creek, his voice trailing off. He stopped talking when he saw the incredulous looks on reporters' faces.

Kleedehn was more circumspect: "That's an issue for Dave and Dave alone to talk about."

Eventually, it was sorted out, through several telephone calls and a discussion between Doug Harris and Sawatzky. "You guys are more than welcome to come down here and look at the dog," he told Harris. "They're all accounted for and present here in the dog yard."

BEFORE DRIVING INTO FAIRBANKS to get a bit of sleep and be there for the finish, which would likely be some time in the pre-dawn hours, I sat quietly by myself for a moment on a bench outside the Angel Creek Lodge.

Suddenly, for me, the magic of the race was diminished, with a parking lot full of cars and trucks and dozens of unfamiliar faces. The Quest, for the race officials, handlers, veterinarians, and the media, is like a travelling circus. Moving from checkpoint to checkpoint, cramming into some small plane or crouching on the back of a snow machine, the same faces and personalities had been with me nearly twenty-four hours a day for nearly two weeks. The group seemed like an extended family by the end of the race. Or a cult.

Following the Quest, on those remote parts of the trail, is like belonging to some exclusive club in which only lack of sleep, eating dozens of overcooked hamburgers and fries, and a predilection for standing around at thirty or forty below for hours waiting for some ice-encrusted musher to show up at a checkpoint earns you membership.

People who previously didn't know each other's names can, by Angel Creek, identify each other by the colour and condition of their long underwear. The co-operation on the trail extends, generally, to the media, who share information liberally, even with their competitors. Like the race, it's an ethos that says survive first, get the exclusive story later.

And now it was over, the group was being broken up, as other, unfamiliar faces joined the entourage and got between us. People who didn't get the inside jokes, the nods or the winks that had come to bind us together. As we climbed into the truck to head to the finish line in Fairbanks, I had a knot growing in my stomach. For the past ten days, this event had consumed my every waking and sleeping hour. I didn't want it to end.

THE 160-KILOMETRE-RUN FROM ANGEL CREEK to Fairbanks is probably the easiest leg of the race. There are no hills to speak of and the trail is fast and well-groomed. That, however, is as much a curse as a blessing. The trail passes through Two Rivers, which has the highest concentration of dog teams in the world and thousands of barking distractions for a tired bunch of sled dogs.

There are myriad trails criss-crossing the correct path, all used frequently, and, if the musher isn't sufficiently vigilant, he can end up well off the trail, or in someone's dog yard. The Quest trail runs for a stretch along the Chena River, which is prone to overflow and glare ice, and for a time alongside the Chena Hot Springs Road, where teams must contend with the glare of oncoming headlights, snow machines, and noise.

There are also lots of moose along this stretch of trail, which have a tendency to charge dogsled teams.

In 1993, Jeff Mann, a musher in the Quest, was near Angel Creek when a moose—which had already charged at, but missed, several other teams—came right up the trail towards him and his dogs. It ran straight up the gangline, miraculously not hitting any dogs, but it hit the sled, knocking Mann off it.

Getting up, Mann saw the moose getting ready to charge again. This time, as it reached the sled, it met the blunt end of Mann's axe. The moose fell to its knees and, after another blow, was dead.

Yukon Quest rule number sixteen dictates that any musher who is forced to kill a game animal in self-defence must gut it to salvage any edible meat before continuing down the trail. Mann complied.

Shortly before entering Fairbanks, the trail passes through North Pole, a suburb whose claim to fame is, not surprisingly, Santa Claus's home, a gaudy roadside attraction that draws tourists year-round.

Twenty kilometres from the finish line, the river turns under the Nordale Bridge in Fairbanks, and then wends and winds its way through town, ending, finally, in the shadow of the Cushman Street bridge next to the Church of the Immaculate Conception, whose parking lot becomes a combination television studio and dog truck repository. Even if the winner crosses the finish line at four o'clock in the morning, there will be a healthy crowd out to cheer.

THE END

GOLD WAS NOT DISCOVERED IN FAIRBANKS until 1902, and—
like Dawson City and Fortymile and Circle City and just about
every other checkpoint on the Yukon Quest trail—the area was
until then sparsely occupied by native North Americans.

The discovery was credited to an Italian prospector named
Felice Pedroni, who truncated his name to Felix Pedro. Fairbanks
was born when Pedro told a shady trader named E. T. Barnette that
he thought he had some good prospects in the area. Barnette was
looking to establish a trading post on the Tanana River, of which the
Chena is a tributary. Although Barnette had wanted to move farther
up the river, low water conditions had kept him on the Chena.

Pedro made his strike on July 22, 1902, and, Barnette, who wanted a rush in Fairbanks to create a market for his goods, dispatched Juriya Wada, a Japanese immigrant, to spread the news in Dawson City that gold had been found in Fairbanks.

Wada travelled by dog team up the Chena and along Birch Creek until he reached the Yukon River. Then he followed the established trail up the Yukon to Dawson City, making him the first person to travel in one go what would later become the Yukon Quest trail.

Those miners in Dawson who hadn't already departed for Nome, where another stampede was underway, came to Fairbanks at Wada's urging, where they found they had no choice but to work as Barnette's employees, prospecting gold on his behalf.

Wada's life was chronicled in a fictionalized story by Tooru J. Kanazawa, in a book called *Sushi and Sourdough*. According to Kanazawa, the miners from Dawson were so angry with Wada that they held a meeting to determine whether he should be lynched or hanged. Wada pleaded for his life, arguing that he had been sent by Barnette. He escaped unharmed but was told he could never show his face in Fairbanks again. In Kanazawa's account he moved to Nome and worked on behalf of the Inuit, who eventually made him a chief.

Felix Pedro died in Fairbanks, ten years to the day after his gold strike.

Fairbanks did well, and, as it prospered, so did Barnette, who became mayor and the owner of a bank. When gold production in the Fairbanks area fell off, Barnette's bank failed, and he was run out of town in 1911. Nobody knows what became of him, but there is a Barnette Street in Fairbanks today, which people refer to as the crookedest street in the city.

On a clear day, looking south from Fairbanks, you can see the Alaska Range, the ridge of mountains that includes Mount McKinley, the highest mountain in North America. Like Whitehorse, Fairbanks is a city that people choose to live in, rather than merely ending up in by accident of birth or happenstance. Perhaps as a result, it, too, has a disproportionate number of talented people for a place its size. There is a thriving arts community, vibrant sports leagues, wonderfully groomed ski trails, and a healthy outdoor spirit, which contrasts the sterile, grey collection of 1950s- and '60s-era buildings that make up its deserted downtown core and an industrial wasteland that lines much of the Chena River as it meanders through the 60,000-strong town.

Fairbanks has an army base and an air force base, and the military presence is felt throughout the town.

Foremost, however, it is the dog-mushing capital of the world. There are reputed to be more than 10,000 sled dogs in the Fairbanks area, in recreational, sprint, middle-distance, and long-distance racing kennels. In winter, you can't drive more than a few blocks without seeing a dog truck.

Almost every bar bears a collection of signed Yukon Quest posters or a bunch of starting bibs hung among the standard posters of Michael Jordan or Bud Light basketballs. Which is hardly surprising in a town whose Girl Scouts, which billing themselves as the northernmost troop in the world, offers a dog-mushing badge. To earn the badge, the Girl Scouts must interview a musher, learn how dogs are trained, visit a kennel, make a model of a dog sled, and do a service project for the Yukon Quest. They start them young here.

The variety store in Goldstream Valley, a suburb (the term is loosely applied) north of Fairbanks, seems like any of the other thousands across North America, until you notice that it stocks Eukanuba performance dog food among the bags of Cheetos and cans of Coke and Sprite and Whoop-Ass. There is a bulletin board outside where people try to sell trucks, boats, sofas, and, of course, dogs. Consider this ad, handwritten on a torn-off piece of foolscap: "For sale, three-year-old, pulls well, ideal for skijoring." Perhaps anywhere else, such an ad might have the Children's Aid Society in a fit. In Fairbanks, however, everyone knows it's an ad for a husky.

ONE BY ONE, the leading mushers packed their sleds for the last time, sealing the Velcro straps on their sled bags easily: with one long, non-stop run to go, through a well-inhabited area, they jettisoned things like their stoves, extra outerwear, and other, unnecessary gear that filled their sleds to a bulge.

The last leg of the Yukon Quest is pure, all-out racing. It's flat, on a well-groomed trail. The dogs know, from the excitement of the people around—and the excitement of their musher—that the end is nigh.

They are allowed to go, to run, to lope, unencumbered by the drag brake or the exhortations of the musher to slow down. For the dogs, this is what they dream about, and you can see the pleasure in their eyes as, whistled up one last time, they lunge forward, pull the sled free of its parking spot, clear their flattened out straw beds and turn into the forest. One hundred and sixty kilometres to go, a drop in the Quest bucket.

TIM OSMAR WENT FIRST, pulling the hook at 5:08 p.m., waving to loud cheers as the television camera lights lit the reflective triangles on the back of his snowsuit.

One and a half hours later, his time penalty served, Andrew Lesh roared out of the dog yard, vanishing into the dark. William Kleedehn, visions of Mexico dancing in his head, followed Lesh after another hour and a half. Joran Freeman left at 11:24 p.m., officially in fourth place now that David Sawatzky had scratched.

Only disaster would alter that order at the finish line, which, for most, was a relief. There was no point in trying to push the dogs; the time difference was too great.

As the orange haze of the streetlights of Fairbanks gradually filled the overcast sky, Joran Freeman smiled. He had made it past his dog yard. Although the dogs had paused, looked back and barked, he had convinced them to keep running past their home and down the trail.

Now, he allowed himself to think about what he had accomplished on this race, after losing six dogs to injury less than a quarter of the way through, how his eight dogs had silenced the critics, gained weight, and performed at a level beyond anyone's expectations.

He had expected more problems with his sled and gear. After running the Iditarod, he hadn't expected the kind of hospitality he'd encountered along the trail. He didn't feel as though finishing was going to be some glorious, stupendous moment, although he felt that his life had changed. He felt connected to the land, connected to all the travellers who had plied this path before. Most important, he felt connected to his dogs in a way that he hadn't conceived.

Rather than feeling relief, he felt as though he'd walked up one step in a flight of stairs. Now, it was on to the next journey, the next trail.

Rather than remembering specific events along the trail, he recalled emotional intensities. Fear, dread, joy, and finally pride welled up around him in a moment. He had achieved. He had made it, and he would be back.

AT 3:48 A.M., THURSDAY, FEBRUARY 22, in front of a small but boisterous crowd that clearly includes the dregs of the previous night's area bar patrons, Tim Osmar and his ten dogs dash across the finish line to win the 2001 Yukon Quest International Sled Dog Race in eleven days, fourteen hours and thirty-eight minutes. It is snowing, slightly, but relatively warm.

Hoisted up on a raised platform for television cameras, he smiles as he fields questions from the crowd. "Everything was perfect, I can't explain. Nothing could go wrong, for me, anyway. A lot of people have problems, but for me, everything went right. So here we are," he says to a massive cheer. "They just ate everything they were supposed to eat, and their feet were all perfect, and they kept their weight on. I had eight leaders to start with, and four at the end. Way more than usual."

He takes his team over, behind the bridge, to where his dog truck and family are waiting: his wife, Tawny, and their four children, Nicole, David, Daniel, and Merissa.

He hears good news: his friend Sig Stormo, after a week in intensive care in Fairbanks, is to be released from hospital. He has been lucky to survive.

Somebody hands him a can of Budweiser, which he downs in a couple of swigs. "What's for breakfast?" he asks, before getting in his truck and driving away, to eat and catch up on some sleep before setting off to finish preparing for the Iditarod, which starts in just a week's time.

Andrew Lesh comes across at 5:14 a.m., and as he steps off his sled, he tilts his head back, stretches his arms out and lets out a loud war whoop. "This is awesome," he shouts, as somebody hands him a bouquet of flowers.

Despite peals of protest, he reiterates his contention that this was his last dog race. "I can't top this," he says.

He is asked, just before heading off, what he is going to do with the rest of his life. "I'm going to take a shower, with a wire brush and kerosene," he replies. "I'm going to look for a job. I'm a schoolteacher, but I want to try something else, too. I don't know. I'm going to look around. Got any ideas?"

As dawn breaks, just after eight in the morning, William Kleedehn comes in, smiling, as the snow crackles down with increasing intensity. "What you need is a tough dog team," he says, trying to get out of the finish line area as quickly as possible. "There's no such thing as a tough dog musher. Everything you have and a little bit more is the minimum, otherwise you won't make it."

Joran Freeman is going underneath bridges now, where he can see from the vapour wafting above the railings that people have stopped their cars and climbed out to cheer him on. It's the first time he has seen real people on the side of the trail in nearly two weeks.

Then he recognizes the Nordale Bridge, which connects downtown Fairbanks to the southeast section of town. He can see Christmas lights ahead. He can see the finish line. "All right," he says to himself. "We're in the money."

After crossing the finish line, he jams in the snow hook (not that the dogs have anywhere to go, anyway) and dives on Muskrat and Sam, the dogs in lead.

"We've done it. We've done it," he says to the bewildered-looking dogs.

After a brief nap and getting the dogs home, Freeman comes back to Fairbanks for dinner at a Mexican restaurant (he might remember the name, he later quips, if it offered him a sponsorship) and a few beers.

Besides picking up $17,000, Freeman also earns Rookie of the Year honours, for being the highest-placing rookie. He is also given the Challenge of the North Award, handed to the musher who best exemplifies the spirit of the Yukon Quest by overcoming obstacles and showing true grit and determination.

Later that day, Frank Turner flies across the finish line, setting a record for the leg from Angel Creek to Fairbanks, surprising Anne and his handlers, who barely make it to the finish line in time to greet him.

There, the nine dogs sit patiently while Anne hands them each a filet mignon, their annual prize for completing the race. The steaks last for just a couple of minutes. "We're already kind of looking forward to next year," Turner says. "I'm enjoying the race more, in many ways, than I ever have. I just enjoy being out there with my dogs. We pretty much travelled the whole trail by ourselves, it was just a wonderful experience. I'm so proud of my dogs."

WHEN I SEE DAVID SAWATZKY, some time later, he is philosophical about scratching. "I could have probably sat there for twelve hours, along the highway. I could have even gone all the way back to Central, and still ended up in the top ten. But that wasn't really what I was there for," he tells me, excusing himself if he sounds arrogant, which he doesn't. "I went to Nome six times. I've been down the Quest trail now nine times. I don't need to go down the trail any more, just to go down the trail. I want to go down the trail to come home with a championship dog team. That's what I want to do."

A couple of months after the race, Blackie and Maimie, two of his Quest females, will each gave birth to healthy litters. He will name each puppy after a Quest checkpoint.

EPILOGUE

A PERFECT WORLD

WHILE THE CELEBRATIONS WERE GOING ON at the finish line, Bill Pinkham was frantically searching for his dog team on Eagle Summit. Travelling near the back of the pack, he had spent much of time over the last few days travelling with Hugh Neff, who, although disqualified, was still running his team along the Quest trail, and Kyla Boivin. The pair of them seemed enamoured of each other, and he would later learn that they became boyfriend and girlfriend before the race was over.

Before Circle, he had left them behind, and he had been travelling on his own for the last 150 kilometres or so. He left Central early in the evening, and, as he came to the lower reaches of Eagle

Summit, he lost the trail. His team had had enough, and he left them resting while he went wading through the sometimes waist-deep snow looking for a trail marker.

Now he was lost, sitting near the top of the summit, cold, tired, a blanket of freshly fallen snow collecting on the hood and shoulders of his parka. He was furious for having left his team, and frightened for his and their survival. He wondered whether he would ever see his dogs again. He had a lot to think about, like foolishness, while he was waiting for the sun to come up.

When it finally did rise, he could see that the trail markers had been knocked down and the lights in them no longer worked.

For more than an hour, he walked and stumbled around, looking for some glimpse of his team. Finally, he saw something far off that looked as though it might be his sled, half submerged in the snow. As he got closer, he could see the dogs, most of whom were staring at him as he approached, looking irritated. All except Jake, the blind dog, who was thrilled to hear his owner's footfalls and voice.

Pushing the sled, he tracked the team over the hundred metres to the trail, and, as the dogs had had such a long rest, he easily made it over the summit and down into Mile 101. They were just about to send out a search party.

A day later, coming into Fairbanks, just in time for the finishing banquet, he felt dread.

The Quest had consumed his life since he'd begun training for it the previous August, the same month he was divorced. The Quest had kept him focused.

Now, with the race nearly over, he couldn't bear the thought of having to face the real world again. He considered stopping, or just mushing straight past the finish line, like French sailor Bernard Moitessier, who, after spending several months at sea during a round-the-world race in 1963, decided not to return to France and the finish line but continue on another lap around the world. "It is kind of a high, and then you're done," Pinkham explained.

"I don't equate the Yukon Quest to a war, but it's similar in the fact that it might be the biggest challenge that you've built up to do. And then what do you do, coming back from that kind of environment where life and death and all kinds of tragic things can happen? You're back into the so-called world walking around like a zombie."

Pinkham did cross the finish line, happy enough, and he made it to the finishing banquet. Months later, I asked him to sum up his experience of the Quest and of being a musher in the North in general.

"We're kind of like those kids who want to stay kids. We want to shirk responsibility and stay out there with our dogs. You just want to keep going to the next checkpoint and not have to deal with civilization and reality and all that other stuff.

"It's neat out there, because it's one of the few places where you can really just be yourself, in front of the dogs, and there's nobody looking at you and judging you.

"It's a perfect world, really."

SELECTED BIBLIOGRAPHY

Berton, Pierre. *Klondike: The Last Great Gold Rush 1896–1899.* Toronto: Doubleday, 2001

Firth, John. *Yukon Quest: The 1,000-mile Dog Sled Race Through the Yukon and Alaska.* Whitehorse: Lost Moose, 1998.

Kershaw, Alex. *Jack London: A Life.* New York: St. Martin's Press, 1997.

Labor, Earle, ed. *The Portable Jack London.* London: Penguin, 1994.

London, Jack. *The Best Short Stories of Jack London.* Garden City, New York: Garden City Books, 1953

Lopez, Barry. *Arctic Dreams: Imagination and Desire in a Northern Landscape.* New York: Bantam, 1996.

Service, Robert W. *The Best of Robert Service.* Philadelphia: Running Press, 1996.

Spotswood, Ken, *The History of Carmacks, Yukon Territory.* Published on www.yukonalaska.com, 1998.

Walker, Franklin. *Jack London and The Klondike.* San Marino: Huntington, 1994.

WEB SITES OF INTEREST:

www.yukonquest.org (official site of the Yukon Quest)

www.yukonweb.com (general Yukon information)

www.yukonalaska.com (general Yukon and Alaska information)

www.sleddogcentral.com (general sled dog information)

www.muktuk.com (Frank Turner's kennel)

www.alaskan.com (general Alaskan information)

http://members.aol.com/pooh0302/circle_body (official site of Circle City, Alaska)

www.city.whitehorse.yk.ca (general Whitehorse information)

www.co.fairbanks.ak.us (general Fairbanks information)

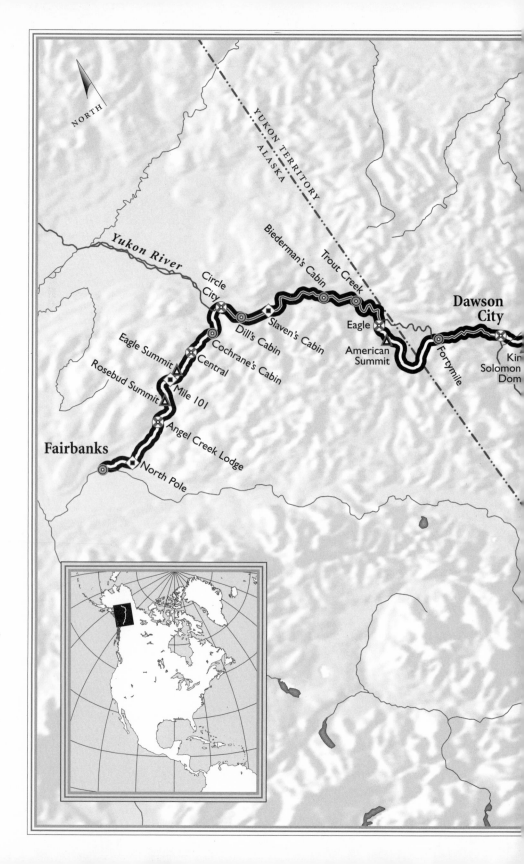